BERLITZ®

LATIN-AMERICAN
SPANISH
for travellers

By the staff of Berlitz Guides

How best to use this phrase book

● We suggest that you start with the **Guide to pronunciation** (pp. 6–9), then go on to **Some basic expressions** (pp. 10–15). This gives you not only a minimum vocabulary, but also helps you get used to pronouncing the language.

● Consult the **Contents** pages (3–5) for the section you need. In each chapter you'll find travel facts, hints and useful information. Simple phrases are followed by a list of words applicable to the situation.

● Separate, detailed contents lists are included at the beginning of the extensive **Eating out** and **Shopping guide** sections (Menus, p. 39, Shops and services, p. 97).

● If you want to find out how to say something in Spanish, your fastest look-up is via the **Dictionary** section (pp. 164–189). This not only gives you the word, but is also cross-referenced to its use in a phrase on a specific page.

● If you wish to learn more about constructing sentences, check the **Basic grammar** (pp. 159–163).

● Note the **colour margins** are indexed in Spanish and English to help both listener and speaker. And, in addition, there is also an **index in Spanish** for the use of your listener.

● Throughout the book, this symbol ☞ suggests phrases your listener can use to answer you. If you still can't understand, hand this phrase book to the Spanish-speaker to encourage pointing to an appropriate answer.

● Sometimes you will find alternatives for words given in brackets [ ]. Try these if your listener doesn't understand the first expression (usually Mexican).

Library of Congress Catalog Card No. 86-70986.

Second revised edition - 2nd printing 1987   Printed in Hungary

Contents

Acknowledgments
We are particularly grateful to José Carasa for his help in the preparation of this book, and to Dr. T.J.A. Bennett who devised the phonetic transcription.

Guide to pronunciation

This and the following chapter are intended to make you familiar with the phonetic transcription we've devised, and to help you get used to the sound of Spanish.

As a minimum vocabulary for your trip, we've selected a number of basic words and phrases under the title "Some Basic Expressions" (pages 10–15).

An outline of the spelling and sounds of Latin-American Spanish

You'll find the pronunciation of the Spanish letters and sounds explained below, as well as the symbols we use for them in the transcription. Note that Spanish has some diacritical signs—special markings placed over letters—which we don't use in English.

The imitated pronunciation should be read as if it were English except for any special rules set out below. It is based on Standard British pronunciation, though we have tried to take account of General American pronunciation also. Of course, the sounds of any two languages are never exactly the same, but if you follow carefully the indications supplied here, you'll have no difficulty in reading our transcriptions in such a way as to make yourself understood.

Letters written in **bold** type should be stressed (pronounced louder).

Consonants

Letter	Approximate pronunciation	Symbol	Example
ch, f, k, l, m, n, p, t, y	as in English		

b	generally as in English but between vowels a sound between **b** and **v**	b	**bueno**	**bway**noa
c	1) before **e** and **i** like **s** in **s**it (except a small area in Columbia, where it is pronounced like **th** in **th**in)	s/ss	**centro** **ración**	**sayn**troa rah**ss**yoan
	2) otherwise, like **k** in **k**it	k	**como**	**ko**amoa
d	generally as in **d**og, although less decisive; between vowels and at the end of a word, more like **th** in **th**is	d	**donde**	**doan**day
g	1) before **e** and **i** like **ch** in Scottish lo**ch**, except in the Caribbean and Central America, where it is pronounced like **h** in **h**at	kh	**urgente**	oor**khayn**tay
	2) otherwise, like **g** in **g**o	g	**ninguno**	neen**goo**noa
h	always silent		**hombre**	**oam**bray
j	like **ch** in Scottish lo**ch**, except in the Caribbean and Central America, where it is pronounced like **h** in **h**at	kh	**bajo**	**bah**khoa
ll	usually like **y** in **y**et; in Argentina, generally like **s** in plea**s**ure	y	**lleno**	**yay**noa
ñ	like **ni** in o**ni**on	ñ	**señor**	say**ñoar**
qu	like **k** in **k**it	k	**quince**	**keen**say
r	quite strongly trilled (like a Scottish **r**), especially at the beginning of a word	r	**río**	**ree**oa
rr	very strongly trilled	rr	**arriba**	ah**rree**bah
s	generally like **s** in **s**it, often with a slight lisp;	s/ss	**vista** **cuantos**	**bees**tah **kwahn**toass

PRONUNCIATION

	in certain regions, like in the Caribbean, the final **s** is often omitted in conversation			
v	generally like **b** in **bad**, but less decisive; between vowels, a sound between **b** and **v**	b	**viejo**	byaykhoa
x	1) usually, like **x** in **taxi**	ks	**examen**	ayksahmayn
	2) before a consonant, like **s** in **sit**	s	**extraño**	aystrahñoa
	3) in several Indian words of Mexico, Central and South America, like **ch** in Scottish lo**ch**	kh	**México**	maykheekoa
z	like **s** in **sit**	s/ss	**zumo** **brazo**	soomoa brahssoa

Vowels

a	like **a** in **cart**, but fairly short	ah	**gracias**	grahssyahss
e	like **a** in **late**, or like **e** in **get**, but fairly short; can always be pronounced like **a** in **late** (N.B. It is a "pure" vowel, not a diphthong, so the tongue does not move while you are pronouncing it)	ay	**de**	day
i	like **ee** in **feet**, but fairly short	ee	**sí**	see
o	similar to **o** in **rope**, or like **o** in **hot**, but fairly short; can always be pronounced like **o** in **rope** (cf. **e**)	oa	**sopa**	soapah
u	like **oo** in **loot**, but fairly short	oo	**una**	oonah
y	also a vowel (when alone or at the end of a word); like **ee** in **feet**, but fairly short	ee	**y**	ee

Pronunciación

Diphthongs

In forming diphthongs, **a**, **e** and **o** are strong vowels, and **i**, **u** and **y** are weak vowels. This means that in diphthongs the strong vowels are pronounced more strongly than the weak ones. If two weak vowels form a diphthong, the second one is pronounced more strongly. In our transcriptions of diphthongs before a strong vowel, we use **w** for the weak **u**, e.g. *bueno* = **bway**noa and **y** for the weak **i** and **y**, e.g. *abierto* = ah**byayr**toa. Furthermore, in our transcriptions, **igh** should be pronounced as in **sigh**, e.g. *hay* = igh, and **ou** as in l**ou**d, e.g. *autobús* = outoa**booss**. Lastly, **eu** (transcribed **ayoo**) should be pronounced quite simply as a strong Spanish **e** followed by a weak Spanish **u**.

Stress

1) In words ending with a vowel, or **n** or **s**, the next-to-last syllable is stressed. 2) In words ending with a consonant, except **n** or **s**, the last syllable is stressed. 3) In words which depart from these two rules, an acute accent is used to mark the stressed syllable, e.g. *último, árbol, Bogotá*.

Note: Some Spanish words have more than one meaning; the accent mark is employed to distinguish between them, e.g.:

él = he   *el* = the   *sí* = yes   *si* = if   *tú* = you   *tu* = your

Pronunciation of the alphabet							
A	ah	H	ahchay	Ñ	aynyay	V	bay
B	bay	I	ee	O	oa	W	bay doablay
C	say	J	khoatah	P	pay	X	aykeess
CH	chay	K	kah	Q	koo	Y	ee graygah
D	day	L	aylay	R	ayrray	Z	saytah
E	ay	LL	ayyay	S	ayssay		
F	ayfay	M	aymay	T	tay		
G	khay	N	aynay	U	oo		

Some basic expressions

Yes.	**Sí.**	see
No.	**No.**	noa
Please.	**Por favor.**	poar fahboar
Thank you.	**Gracias.**	grahssyahss
Thank you very much.	**Muchas gracias.**	moochahss grahssyahss
You're welcome.	**De nada.**	day nahdah
That's all right/ Don't mention it.	**No hay de qué.**	noa igh day kay

Greetings   *Saludos*

Good morning.	**Buenos días.**	bwaynoass deeahss
Good afternoon.	**Buenas tardes.**	bwaynahss tahrdayss
Good evening.	**Buenas tardes.**	bwaynahss tahrdayss
Good night.	**Buenas noches.**	bwaynahss noachayss
Good-bye.	**Adiós.**	ahdyoass
See you later.	**Hasta luego.**	ahstah lwaygoa
This is Mr. ...	**Este es el Señor ...**	aystay ayss ayl sayñoar
This is Mrs./Miss ...	**Esta es la Señora/ la Señorita ...**	aystah ayss lah sayñoarah lah sayñoareetah
How do you do? (Pleased to meet you.)	**Encantado(a)* de conocerle.**	aynkahntahdoa(ah) day koanoassayrlay
How are you?	**¿Cómo está usted?**	koamoa aystah oostayd
Very well, thanks. And you?	**Muy bien, gracias. ¿Y usted?**	mwee byayn grahssyahss ee oostayd

---

* In the case where there are masculine and feminine forms of a word, we give the masculine first, with the feminine in parentheses afterwards; in this example, a woman would say **Encantada.**

How's life?	**¿Cómo le va?**	koamoa lay bah
Fine.	**Muy bien.**	mwee byayn
I beg your pardon?	**¿Perdóneme?**	payrdoanaymay
Excuse me. (May I get past?)	**Perdóneme.**	payrdoanaymay
Sorry!	**Lo siento.**	loa syayntoa

Questions *Preguntas*

Where?	**¿Dónde?**	doanday
How?	**¿Cómo?**	koamoa
When?	**¿Cuándo?**	kwahndoa
What?	**¿Qué?**	kay
Why?	**¿Por qué?**	poar kay
Who?	**¿Quién?**	kyayn
Which?	**¿Cuál** (sing.)	kwahl
	¿Cuáles? (plur.)	kwahlayss
Where is ...?	**¿Dónde está ...?**	doanday aystah
Where are ...?	**¿Dónde están ...?**	doanday aystahn
Where can I find/ get ...?	**¿Dónde puedo encon- trar/conseguir ...?**	doanday pwaydoa aynkoan- trahr/koansaygeer
How far?	**¿A qué distancia?**	ah kay deestahnssyah
How long?	**¿Cuánto tiempo?**	kwahntoa tyaympoa
How much?	**¿Cuánto?**	kwahntoa
How many?	**¿Cuántos?**	kwahntoass
How much does this cost?	**¿Cuánto cuesta?**	kwahntoa kwaystah
When does ... open/ close?	**¿Cuándo abre/ cierra ...?**	kwahndoa ahbray/ syayrrah
What do you call this/that in Spanish?	**¿Cómo se llama esto/ eso en español?**	koamoa say yahmah aystoa/ ayssoa ayn ayspahñoal
What does this/that mean?	**¿Qué quiere decir esto/eso?**	kay kyayray daysseer aystoa/ayssoa

Do you speak ...? ¿Habla usted ...?

Do you speak English?	**¿Habla usted inglés?**	ahblah oostayd eenglayss
Does anyone here speak English?	**¿Hay alguien aquí que hable inglés?**	igh ahlgwayn ahkee kay ahblay eenglayss
I don't speak (much) Spanish.	**No hablo (mucho) español.**	noa ahbloa (moochoa) ayspahñoal
Could you speak more slowly?	**¿Puede hablar más despacio?**	pwayday ahblahr mahss dayspahssyoa
Could you repeat that?	**¿Podría usted repetir eso?**	poadreeah oostayd raypayteer ayssoa
Could you spell it?	**¿Podría usted deletrearlo?**	poadreeah oostayd daylaytrayahrloa
Please write it down.	**Por favor, escríbalo.**	poar fahboar ayskreebahloa
Can you translate this for me?	**¿Puede usted traducírmelo?**	pwayday oostayd trahdoosseermayloa
Can you translate this for us?	**¿Puede usted traducírnoslo?**	pwayday oostayd trahdoosseernoasloa
Please point to the word/phrase/sentence in the book.	**Por favor, señale la palabra/la expresión/la frase en el libro.**	poar fahboar sayñahlay lah pahlahbrah/lah aysprayssyoan/lah frahssay ayn ayl leebroa
Just a moment. I'll see if I can find it in this book.	**Un momento. Veré si lo puedo encontrar en este libro.**	oon moamayntoa. bayray see loa pwaydoa aynkoantrahr ayn aystay leebroa
I understand.	**Comprendo/Entiendo.**	koamprayndoa/ayntyayndoa
I don't understand.	**No comprendo.**	noa koamprayndoa
Do you understand?	**¿Comprende usted?**	koampraynday oostayd

Can/May ...? ¿Puede ...?

Can I have ...?	**¿Puede darme ...?**	pwayday dahrmay
Can we have ...?	**¿Puede darnos ...?**	pwayday dahrnoass
Can you show me ...?	**¿Puede usted enseñarme ...?**	pwayday oostayd aynsayñahrmay

I can't.	**No puedo.**	noa **pwaydoa**
Can you tell me ...?	**¿Puede usted decirme ...?**	**pwayday oostayd daysseer**may
Can you help me?	**¿Puede usted ayudarme?**	**pwayday oostayd** ah**yoodahr**may
Can I help you?	**¿Puedo ayudarle?**	**pwaydoa** ah**yoodahr**lay
Can you direct me to ...?	**¿Puede usted indicarme la dirección a ...?**	**pwayday oostayd** een**deekahr**may lah **deerayk**syoan ah

Wanting ... *Deseos*

I'd like ...	**Quisiera ...**	kees**syay**rah
We'd like ...	**Quisiéramos ...**	kees**syay**rah**moass**
What do you want?	**¿Qué desea usted?**	kay day**ssay**ah **oostayd**
Give me ...	**Déme ...**	**day**may
Give it to me.	**Démelo.**	**day**mayloa
Bring me ...	**Tráigame ...**	**trigh**gahmay
Bring it to me.	**Tráigamelo.**	**trigh**gahmayloa
Show me ...	**Enséñeme ...**	ayn**say**ñaymay
Show it to me.	**Enséñemelo.**	ayn**say**ñaymayloa
I'm looking for ...	**Estoy buscando ...**	ays**toy** boos**kahn**doa
I'm hungry.	**Tengo hambre.**	**tayn**goa **ahm**bray
I'm thirsty.	**Tengo sed.**	**tayn**goa sayd
I'm tired.	**Estoy cansado(a).**	ays**toy** kahn**sah**doa(ah)
I'm lost.	**Me he perdido.**	may ay payr**dee**doa
It's important.	**Es importante.**	ayss eempoar**tahn**tay
It's urgent.	**Es urgente.**	ayss oor**khayn**tay
Hurry up!	**¡Dése prisa!**	**day**ssay **pree**ssah

It is/There is ... *Es/Está/Hay ...*

It is ...	**Es ...**	ayss
Is it ...?	**¿Es ...?**	ayss
It isn't ...	**No es ...**	noa ayss

Here it is.	Aquí está.	ahkee aystah
Here they are.	Aquí están.	ahkee aystahn
There it is.	Ahí está.	ahee aystah
There they are.	Ahí están.	ahee aystahn
There is/There are ...	Hay ...	igh
Is there/Are there ...?	¿Hay ...?	igh
There isn't/aren't ...	No hay ...	noa igh
There isn't/aren't any.	No hay ninguno(a)/ningunos(as).	noa igh neengoonoa(ah)/neengoonoass(ahss)

It's ... *Es/Está ...*

big/small	grande/pequeño*	grahnday/paykayñoa
quick/slow	rápido/lento	rahpeedoa/layntoa
hot/cold	caliente/frío	kahlyayntay/freeoa
full/empty	lleno/vacío	yaynoa/bahsseeoa
easy/difficult	fácil/difícil	fahsseel/deefeesseel
heavy/light	pesado/ligero	payssahdoa/leekhayroa
open/shut	abierto/cerrado	ahbyayrtoa/sayrrahdoa
right/wrong	correcto/incorrecto	koarrayktoa/eenkoarrayktoa
old/new	viejo/nuevo	byaykhoa/nwayboa
old/young	viejo/joven	byaykhoa/khoabayn
next/last	próximo/último	proakseemoa/oolteemoa
beautiful/ugly	hermoso/feo	ayrmoassoa/fayoa
free (vacant)/occupied	libre/ocupado	leebray/oakoopahdoa
good/bad	bueno/malo	bwaynoa/mahloa
better/worse	mejor/peor	maykhoar/payoar
early/late	temprano/tarde	taymprahnoa/tahrday
cheap/expensive	barato/caro	bahrahtoa/kahroa
near/far	cerca/lejos	sayrkah/laykhoass
here/there	aquí/allí	ahkee/ahyee

Quantities *Cantidades*

a little/a lot	un poco/mucho	oon poakoa/moochoa
few/a few	pocos/(alg)unos	poakoass/(ahlg)oonoass
much	mucho	moochoa
many	muchos	moochoass

*For feminine and plural forms, see grammar section page 159 (adjectives).

more (than)/	más (que)/	mahss (kay)/
less (than)	menos (que)	maynoass (kay)
enough/too	bastante/demasiado	bahstahntay/
		daymahssyahdoa
some	unos(as)	oonoass(ahss)
any	alguno(a)	ahlgoonoa(ah)

A few more useful words   *Algunas palabras útiles*

at	a, en	ah, ayn
on	sobre, en	soabray, ayn
in	en	ayn
to	a, para	ah, pahrah
after	después	dayspwayss
before(time)	antes	ahntayss
before(place)	delante(de)	daylahntay(day)
for	por, para	poar, pahrah
from	de, desde	day, daysday
with/without	con/sin	koan/seen
through	por, a través de	poar, ah trahbayss day
towards	hacia	ahssyah
until	hasta	ahstah
during	durante	doorahntay
next to	junto a	khoontoa ah
near	cerca	sayrkah
behind	detrás	daytrahss
between	entre	ayntray
since	desde	daysday
above	encima	aynseemah
below/under	debajo	daybahkhoa
inside/outside	dentro/fuera	dayntroa/fwayrah
up/upstairs	arriba	ahrreebah
down/downstairs	abajo	ahbahkhoa
and/or	y/o	ee/oa
not	no	noa
never	nunca	noonkah
nothing	nada	nahdah
none	ninguno(a)	neengoonoa(ah)
very	muy	mwee
too(also)	también	tahmbyayn
yet	todavía	toadahbeeah
only	sólo	soaloa
soon	pronto	proantoa
now	ahora	ahoarah
then	entonces	ayntoansayss
perhaps	quizá, tal vez	keessah, tahl bayss

Arrival

Most Latin-American countries require a tourist card or visa in addition to a valid passport. Tourist cards are usually issued by the airline when you obtain your ticket. Otherwise, inquire at the local consulate.

CONTROL DE PASAPORTES PASSPORT CONTROL		
Here's my passport/tourist card.	**Aquí está mi pasaporte/tarjeta de turista.**	ahkee aystah mee pah-ssahpoartay/tahrkhaytah day tooreestah
I'll be staying ...	**Pienso quedarme ...**	pyaynsoa kaydahrmay
a few days	**unos días**	oonoass deeahss
a week	**una semana**	oonah saymahnah
a month	**un mes**	oon mayss
I don't know yet.	**No lo sé todavía.**	noa loa say toadahbeeah
I'm here on holiday.	**He venido de vacaciones.**	ay bayneedoa day bahkahssyoanayss
I'm here on business.	**Estoy aquí de negocios.**	aystoy ahkee day naygoassyoass
I'm just passing through.	**Estoy sólo de paso.**	aystoy soaloa day pahssoa

If things become difficult:

| I'm sorry, I don't understand. | **Lo siento, no comprendo.** | loa syayntoa noa koamprayndoa |
| Does anyone here speak English? | **¿Hay alguien aquí que hable inglés?** | igh ahlgyayn ahkee kay ahblay eenglayss |

Customs   *Aduana*

As at almost all major airports in Latin America, an honour system for clearing customs has been adopted: follow the green arrow if you have nothing to declare. Or leave via the doorway marked with a red arrow if you have items to declare.

nada que declarar	artículos para declarar
nothing to declare	goods to declare

I've nothing to declare.	**No tengo nada que declarar.**	noa **tayng**oa **nah**dah kay dayklah**rahr**
I've ...	**Tengo ...**	**tayng**oa
a bottle of whisky	**una botella de whisky**	**oo**nah boa**tay**yah day ''whisky''
a bottle of wine	**una botella de vino**	**oo**nah boa**tay**yah day **bee**noa
a carton of cigarettes	**un cartón de cigarrillos**	oon kahr**toan** day seegahr**ree**yoass
It's for my personal use.	**Es de uso personal.**	ayss day **oo**ssoa payrsoa-**nahl**
It's a present.	**Es un regalo.**	ayss oon ray**gah**loa

Su pasaporte, por favor.	Your passport, please.
¿Tiene usted algo que declarar?	Do you have anything to declare?
Abra esta bolsa, por favor.	Please open this bag.
Tiene que pagar impuestos por esto.	You'll have to pay duty on this.
¿Tiene usted más equipaje?	Do you have any more luggage?

Baggage – Porters *Equipaje – Maleteros*

The porter may take your luggage to the customs for you. Where no porters are available, you'll find luggage trolleys for the use of passengers.

Porter!	**¡Cargador!** [**¡Maletero!**]	kahrgah**doar** [mahlay**tayroa**]
Please take this luggage.	**Por favor, lleve este equipaje.**	poar fah**boar** yay**bay** ays**tay** aykee**pah**khay
That's my bag/suitcase.	**Esa es mi bolsa/maleta.**	**ays**sah ayss mee **boal**sah/mah**lay**tah
Take this luggage ...	**Lleve este equipaje ...**	yay**bay** ays**tay** aykee-**pah**khay
to the bus	**al autobús**	ahl outoa**booss**
to the luggage lockers	**a la consigna automática**	ah lah koan**seeg**nah outoamah**tee**kah
How much is that?	**¿Cuánto es?**	**kwahn**toa ayss
There's one piece missing.	**Falta un bulto.**	**fahl**tah oon **bool**toa
Where are the luggage trolleys (carts)?	**¿Dónde están los carritos de equipaje?**	**doan**day ays**tahn** loass kah**rree**toass day aykee-**pah**khay

Changing money *Cambio de moneda*

Where's the currency exchange office?	**¿Dónde está la oficina de cambio?**	**doan**day ays**tah** lah oafee-**ssee**nah day **kahm**byoa
Can you change these traveller's cheques (checks)?	**¿Puede cambiarme estos cheques de viajero?**	**pway**day kahm**byahr**may **ays**toass **chay**kayss day byah**khay**roa
I want to change some dollars/pounds.	**Quisiera cambiar dólares/libras esterlinas.**	kee**ssyay**rah kahm**byahr** **doa**lahrayss/**lee**brahss aystayr**lee**nahss
Can you change this into ...?	**¿Puede cambiarme esto en ...?**	**pway**day kahm**byahr**may **ays**toa ayn
pesos	**pesos**	**pay**ssoass
bolívares	**bolívares**	boa**lee**bahrayss
What's the exchange rate?	**¿A cuánto está el cambio?**	ah **kwahn**toa ays**tah** ayl **kahm**byoa

BANK—CURRENCY, see page 129

Where is ...? *¿Dónde está ...?*

Where is the ...?	**¿Dónde está ...?**	doanday aystah
booking office	**la oficina de reservaciones**	lah oafeesseenah day rayssayrbahssyoanayss
car hire	**la agencia de alquiler de automóviles [carros]**	lah ahkhaynsyah day ahlkeelayr day outoamoabee-layss [kahrroass]
duty-free shop	**la tienda libre de impuestos**	lah tyayndah leebray day eempwaystoass
newsstand	**el puesto de periódicos**	ayl pwaystoa day payryoadeekoass
restaurant	**el restaurante**	ayl raystourahntay
How do I get to ...?	**¿Cómo podría ir a ...?**	koamoa poadreeah eer ah
Is there a bus into town?	**¿Hay un autobús que va al centro?**	igh oon outoabooss kay bah ahl sayntroa
Where can I get a taxi?	**¿Dónde puedo conseguir un taxi?**	doanday pwaydoa koansaygeer oon tahksee
Where can I hire a car?	**¿Dónde puedo alquilar un automóvil [carro]?**	doanday pwaydoa ahlkeelahr oon outoamoabeel [kahrroa]

Hotel reservation *Reservación de hotel*

Do you have a hotel guide?	**¿Tiene una guía de hoteles?**	tyaynay oonah geeah day oataylayss
Could you reserve a room for me at a hotel/boarding house?	**¿Podría reservarme una habitación en un hotel/una pensión?**	poadreeah rayssayrbahrmay oonah ahbeetahssyoan ayn oon oatayl/oonah paynsyoan
in the centre	**en el centro**	ayn ayl sayntroa
near the railway station	**cerca de la estación de ferrocarril**	sayrkah day lah aystahssyoan day fayrroakahrreel
a single room	**una habitación sencilla**	oonah ahbeetahssyoan saynseeyah
a double room	**una habitación doble**	oonah ahbeetahssyoan doablay
not too expensive	**no muy cara**	noa mwee kahrah
Where is the hotel/boarding house?	**¿Dónde está el hotel/la pensión?**	doanday aystah ayl oatayl/lah paynsyoan
Do you have a street map?	**¿Tiene un plano de la ciudad?**	tyaynay oon plahnoa day lah syoodahd

HOTEL/ACCOMMODATION, see page 22

Car hire (rental)   *Alquiler de automóviles*

There are car hire firms at most airports and terminals.
There will most probably be someone who speaks English.

I'd like to hire (rent) a ... car.	**Quisiera alquilar un automóvil [carro]** ...	keessyayrah ahlkeelahr oon outoamoabeel [kahrroa]
small	**pequeño**	paykayñoa
medium-sized	**no de lujo**	noa day lookhoa
large	**grande**	grahnday
automatic	**automático**	outoamahteekoa
I'd like it for a day/ a week.	**Lo quisiera para un día/una semana.**	loa keessyayrah pahrah oon deeah/oonah saymahnah
Are there any week-end arrangements?	**¿Hay condiciones especiales para los fines de semana?**	igh koandeessyoanayss ayspayssyahlayss pahrah loass feenayss day saymahnah
Do you have any special rates?	**¿Tienen tarifas especiales?**	tyaynayn tahreefahss ayspayssyahlayss
What's the charge per day/week?	**¿Cuánto cobran por día/semana?**	kwahntoa koabrahn poar deeah/saymahnah
Is mileage included?	**¿Está incluido el kilometraje?**	aystah eenklweedoa ayl keeloamaytrahkhay
What's the charge per kilometre?	**¿Cuánto cobran por kilómetro?**	kwahntoa koabrahn poar keeloamaytroa
I want to leave the car in ...	**Quiero entregar el automóvil en ...**	kyayroa ayntraygahr ayl outoamoabeel ayn
I want full insurance.	**Quiero un seguro contra todo riesgo.**	kyayroa oon saygooroa koantrah toadoa ryaysgoa
What's the deposit?	**¿Cuánto hay que dejar como depósito?**	kwahntoa igh kay daykhahr koamoa daypoasseetoa
I've a credit card.	**Tengo una tarjeta [carta] de crédito.**	tayngoa oonah tahrkhaytah [kahrtah] day kraydeetoa
Here's my driving licence.	**Aquí está mi licencia de manejar.**	ahkee aystah mee leessaynsyah day mahnaykhahr

CAR, see page 75

Taxi *Taxi*

Virtually all taxis have meters, but they are not always used. It would, in any case, be wise to ask the approximate fare beforehand. Extra charges are added for night work and often for baggage.

Where can I get a taxi?	¿Dónde puedo conseguir un taxi?	doanday pwaydoa koansaygeer oon tahksee
Please get me a taxi.	Búsqueme un taxi, por favor.	booskaymay oon tahksee poar fahboar
What's the fare to ...?	¿Cuál es la tarifa hasta ...?	kwahl ayss lah tahreefah ahstah
How far is it to ...?	¿Qué distancia hay hasta ...?	kay deestahnssyah igh ahstah
Take me to ...	Lléveme ...	yaybaymay
this address	a esta dirección	ah aystah deerekssyoan
the airport	al aeropuerto	ahl ahayroapwayrtoa
the town centre	al centro	ahl sayntroa
the ... Hotel	al Hotel ...	ahl oatayl
the railway station	a la estación de ferrocarril	ah lah aystahssyoan day fayrroakahrreel
Turn ... at the next corner.	Gire ... en la próxima esquina.	kheeray ayn lah proaksseemah ayskeenah
left	a la izquierda	ah lah eeskyayrdah
right	a la derecha	ah lah dayraychah
Go straight ahead.	Siga derecho.	seegah dayraychoa
Please stop here.	Pare aquí, por favor.	pahray ahkee poar fahboar
I'm in a hurry.	Tengo prisa.	tayngoa preessah
Could you drive more slowly?	¿Podría conducir más despacio?	poadreeah koandoosseer mahss dayspahssyoa
Could you help me carry my luggage?	¿Podría ayudarme a llevar mi equipaje?	poadreeah ahyoodahrmay ah yaybahr mee aykeepahkhay
Could you wait for me?	¿Puede esperarme, por favor?	pwayday ayspayrahrmay poar fahboar
I'll be back in 10 minutes.	Vuelvo dentro de 10 minutos.	bwaylboa dayntroa day 10 meenootoass

TIPPING, see inside back-cover

Hotel—Other accommodation

Early reservation (and confirmation) is essential in major tourist centres during the high season. Most ports of entry and other larger towns in Mexico, Venezuela and Puerto Rico have a tourist information office—and that's the place to go if you're stuck without a room.

Hotel (oatayl)	Prices and facilities according to the five categories (Luxury, A, B, C, D).
Motel (moatayl)	Local automobile associations (e.g. AMA in Mexico) have lists of recommended motels.
Apartamento amueblado/sin amueblar (ahpahrtah**maynt**oa ahm**way**blah**doa**/seen ahm**way**blahr)	Furnished/unfurnished flat (apartment); consult an estate agent.
Casa de huéspedes (kahssah day **way**spaydayss)	Guest house, usually for stays of several weeks or even months. The choice is between *pensión completa* (payn**syoan** koam**play**tah—full board) or *media pensión* (**may**dyah payn**syoan**—bed and breakfast plus one other meal).
Pensión (payn**syoan**)	The equivalent of a boarding house, often offering *pensión completa* or *media pensión*.
Albergue de juventud (ahl**bayr**gay day khoobayn**tood**)	Youth hostel, in most major towns in South America.

Can you recommend a hotel/a boarding house?	**¿Puede recomendarme un hotel/ una pensión?**	pwayday raykoamayndahrmay oon oatayl/ oonah paynsyoan
Are there any flats (apartments) vacant?	**¿Hay apartamentos libres?**	igh ahpahrtah**maynt**oass leebrayss

CAMPING, see page 32

Checking in—Reception   *Recepción*

My name is ...	**Me llamo ...**	may yahmoa
I've a reservation.	**He hecho una reservación.**	ay aychoa oonah raysayrbahssyoan
We've reserved two rooms.	**Hemos reservado dos habitaciones.**	aymoass rayssayrbahdoa doass ahbeetahssyoanayss
Here's the confirmation.	**Esta es la confirmación.**	aystah ayss lah koanfeermahssyoan
Do you have any vacancies?	**¿Tiene habitaciones libres?**	tyaynay ahbeetahssyoanayss leebrayss
I'd like a ... room ...	**Quisiera una habitación ...**	keessyayrah oonah ahbeetahssyoan
single	**sencilla**	saynseeyah
double	**doble**	doablay
with twin beds	**con dos camas**	koan doass kahmahss
with a double bed	**con cama matrimonial**	koan kahmah mahtreemoanyahl
with a bath	**con baño**	koan bahñoa
with a shower	**con ducha**	koan doochah
with a balcony	**con balcón**	koan bahlkoan
with a view	**con vista**	koan beestah
We'd like a room ...	**Quisiéramos una habitación ...**	keessyayrahmoass oonah ahbeetahssyoan
in the front	**que da al frente**	kay dah ahl frayntay
facing the sea	**con vista al mar**	koan beestah ahl mahr
It must be quiet.	**Que haya tranquilidad.**	kay ahyah trahnkeeleedahd
Is there ...?	**¿Hay ...?**	igh
air conditioning	**aire acondicionado**	ighray ahkoandeessyoanahdoa
heating	**calefacción**	kahlayfahksyoan
a radio/television in the room	**radio/televisor en la habitación**	rahdyoa/taylaybeessoar ayn lah ahbeetahssyoan
a laundry service	**servicio de lavandería**	sayrbeessyoa day lahbahndayreeah
room service	**servicio de habitación**	sayrbeessyoa day ahbeetahssyoan
hot water	**agua caliente**	ahgwah kahlyayntay
running water	**agua corriente**	ahgwah koarryayntay
a private toilet	**servicios particulares**	sayrbeessyoass pahrteekoolahrayss

CHECKING OUT, see page 31

| Could you put a cot/
an extra bed
in the room? | ¿Podría poner un
catre/otra cama en
la habitación? | poadreeah poanayr oon
kahtray/oatrah kahmah ayn
lah ahbeetahssyoan |

How much? ¿Cuánto cuesta?

What's the price ...?	¿Cuál es el precio ...?	kwahl ayss ayl prayssyoa
per night	por noche	poar noachay
per week	por semana	poar saymahnah
for bed and breakfast	por dormir y desayunar	poar doarmeer ee dayssahyoonahr
excluding meals	sin las comidas	seen lahss koameedahss
for full board (A.P.)	por pensión completa	poar paynsyoan koamplaytah
for half board (M.A.P.)	por media pensión	poar maydyah paynsyoan

Does that include ...?	¿Está incluido ...?	aystah eenklweedoa
breakfast	el desayuno	ayl dayssahyoonoa
service	el servicio	ayl sayrbeessyoa
tax	el impuesto (IVA)	ayl eempwaystoa (eebah)

Is there any reduction for children?	¿Hacen reducción a los niños?	ahssayn raydooksyoan ah loass neeñoass
Do you charge for the baby?	¿Hay que pagar por el bebé?	igh kay pahgahr poar ayl baybay
That's too expensive.	Es demasiado caro.	ayss daymahssyahdoa kahroa
Haven't you any- thing cheaper?	¿No tiene algo más barato?	noa tyaynay ahlgoa mahss bahrahtoa

How long? ¿Cuánto tiempo?

We'll be staying ...	Nos quedaremos ...	noass kaydahraymoass
overnight only	sólo una noche	soaloa oonah noachay
a few days	unos días	oonoass deeahss
a week (at least)	una semana (por lo menos)	oonah saymahnah (poar loa maynoass)
I don't know yet.	No lo sé todavía.	noa loa say toadahbeeah

NUMBERS, see page 147

Decision *Decisión*

May I see the room?	**¿Puedo ver la habitación?**	pwaydoa bayr lah ahbeetahssyoan
That's fine. I'll take it.	**Está bien. La tomo.**	aystah byayn. lah toamoa
No, I don't like it.	**No, no me gusta.**	noa noa may goostah
It's too ...	**Es demasiado ...**	ayss daymahssyahdoa
cold/hot	**fría/caliente**	freeah/kahlyayntay
dark/small	**oscura/pequeña**	oaskoorah/paykayñah
noisy	**ruidosa**	rweedoassah
I asked for a room with a bath.	**Pedí una habitación con baño.**	paydee oonah ahbeetah-ssyoan koan bahñoa
Do you have any-thing ...?	**¿Tiene algo ...?**	tyaynay ahlgoa
better	**mejor**	maykhoar
bigger	**más grande**	mahss grahnday
quieter	**más tranquilo**	mahss trahnkeeloa
higher up/lower down	**más arriba/más abajo**	mahss ahrreebah/mahss ahbahkhoa
Do you have a room with a better view?	**¿Tiene una habitación con mejor vista?**	tyaynay oonah ahbeetah-ssyoan koan maykhoar beestah

Registration *Inscripción*

Upon arrival at a hotel or a boarding house you'll be asked to fill in a registration form (*una forma de registro*—**oo**nah **foar**mah day ray**khees**troa).

Apellido/Nombre	Name/First name
Domicilio/Calle/Número	Home address/Street/Number
Nacionalidad/Profesión	Nationality/Profession
Fecha/Lugar de nacimiento	Date/Place of birth
Procedencia .../Destino ...	Coming from .../Going to ...
Número de pasaporte	Passport number
Lugar/Fecha	Place/Date
Firma	Signature

What does this mean?	**¿Qué significa esto?**	kay seegneefeekah aystoa

Su pasaporte, por favor.	May I see your passport, please?
¿Quiere llenar esta forma de registro?	Would you mind filling in this registration form?
Firme aquí, por favor.	Please sign here.
¿Cuánto tiempo piensa quedarse?	How long will you be staying?

What's my room number?	¿Cuál es el número de mi habitación?	kwahl ayss ayl noomayroa day mee ahbeetahssyoan
Will you have our luggage sent up?	¿Puede encargarse de que suban nuestro equipaje?	pwayday aynkahrgahrsay day kay soobahn nwaystroa aykeepahkhay
Where can I park my car?	¿Dónde puedo estacionar mi carro?	doanday pwaydoa aystahssyoanahr mee kahrroa
Does the hotel have a garage?	¿Tiene garaje el hotel?	tyaynay gahrahkhay ayl oatayl
I'd like to leave this in your safe.	Quisiera depositar esto en la caja fuerte.	keessyayrah daypoasseetahr aystoa ayn lah kahkhah fwayrtay

Hotel staff   *Personal del hotel*

hall porter	el conserje	ayl koansayrkhay
maid	la muchacha de servicio	lah moochahchah day sayrbeessyoa
manager	el gerente	ayl khayrayntay
page (bellboy)	el botones	ayl boatoanayss
porter	el mozo	ayl moassoa
receptionist	el recepcionista	ayl rayssaypssyoaneestah
switchboard operator	la telefonista	lah taylaylfoaneestah
waiter	el mesero	ayl mayssayroa
waitress	la mesera	lah mayssayrah

Call members of the staff *señorita* (sayñoa**ree**tah—Miss), *señora* (sayñoa**rah**—Madam) and *señor* (sayñoar—Sir).

TELLING THE TIME, see page 153

General requirements *Peticiones generales*

The key, please.	**La llave, por favor.**	lah yahbay poar fahboar
Will you please wake me at ...?	**¿Por favor, puede despertarme a las ...?**	poar fahboar pwayday dayspayrtahrmay ah lahss
Is there a bath on this floor?	**¿Hay baño en este piso?**	igh bahñoa ayn aystay peessoa
What's the voltage?	**¿Cuál es el voltaje?**	kwahl ayss ayl boaltahkhay
Where's the socket (outlet) for the shaver?	**¿Dónde está el enchufe para la máquina de afeitar?**	doanday aystah ayl aynchoofay pahrah lah mahkeenah day ahfaytahr
Can you find me a ...?	**¿Podría conseguirme ...?**	poadreeah koansaygeermay
baby-sitter	**una niñera**	oonah neeñayrah
secretary	**una secretaria**	oonah saykraytahryah
typewriter	**una máquina de escribir**	oonah mahkeenah day ayskreebeer
May I have a/an/some ...?	**¿Puede darme ...?**	pwayday dahrmay
ashtray	**un cenicero**	oon sayneessayroa
bath towel	**una toalla de baño**	oonah twahyah day bahñoa
extra blanket	**otra cobija**	oatrah koabeekhah
envelopes	**sobres**	soabrayss
(more) hangers	**(más) ganchos**	mahss gahnchoass
hot-water bottle	**una bolsa de agua caliente**	oonah boalsah day ahgwah kahlyayntay
needle and thread	**una aguja e hilo**	oonah ahgookhah ay eeloa
extra pillow	**otra almohada**	oatrah ahlmoaahdah
reading lamp	**una lámpara de mesa**	oonah lahmpahrah day mayssah
soap	**jabón**	khahboan
writing paper	**papel de cartas**	pahpayl day kahrtahss
Where's the ...?	**¿Dónde está ...?**	doanday aystah
bathroom	**el cuarto de baño**	ayl kwahrtoa day bahñoa
dining room	**el comedor**	ayl koamaydoar
emergency exit	**la salida de emergencia**	lah sahleedah day aymayr-khaynsyah
hairdresser's	**la peluquería**	lah paylookayreeah
lift (elevator)	**el elevador [ascensor]**	ayl aylaybahdoar [assaynsoar]
Where are the toilets?	**¿Dónde están los servicios?**	doanday aystahn loass sayrbeessyoass

BREAKFAST, see page 38

Telephone—Post (Mail)   *Teléfono—Correo*

Can you get me Mexico City 523-45-67?	**¿Puede comunicarme con el 523-45-67 de México?**	pwayday koamoonee-kahrmay koan ayl 523-45-67 day maykheekoa
Do you have stamps?	**¿Tiene estampillas?**	tyaynay aystahmpeeyahss
Would you please post (mail) this for me?	**¿Quiere mandar esto por correo, por favor?**	kyayray mahndahr aystoa poar koarrayoa poar fahboar
Is there any post (mail) for me?	**¿Hay correo para mí?**	igh koarrayoa pahrah mee
Are there any messages for me?	**¿Hay algún recado para mí?**	igh ahlgoon raykahdoa pahrah mee
How much are my telephone charges?	**¿Cuánto debo de llamadas telefónicas?**	kwahntoa dayboa day yah-mahdahss taylayfoanee-kahss

Difficulties   *Dificultades*

The ... doesn't work.	**... no funciona.**	... noa foonsyoanah
air conditioner	**el acondicionador de aire**	ayl ahkoandeessyoanahdoar day ighray
fan	**el ventilador**	ayl baynteelahdoar
heating	**la calefacción**	lah kahlayfahksyoan
light	**la luz**	lah looss
radio	**la radio**	lah rahdyoa
television	**el televisor**	ayl taylaybeessoar
The tap (faucet) is dripping.	**La llave [El grifo] del agua está goteando.**	lah yahbay [ayl greefoa] dayl ahgwah aystah goa-tayahndoa
There's no hot water.	**No hay agua caliente.**	noa igh ahgwah kahlyayntay
The wash-basin is blocked.	**El lavabo está tapado.**	ayl lahbahboa aystah tahpahdoa
The window is jammed.	**La ventana está atrancada.**	lah bayntahnah aystah ahtrahnkahdah
The curtains are stuck.	**Las cortinas están atrancadas.**	lahss koarteenahss aystahn ahtrahnkahdahss
The bulb is burnt out.	**El foco está fundido. [La bombilla está fundida.]**	ayl foakoa aystah foon-deedoa [lah boambeeyah aystah foondeedah]
My room has not been made up.	**No me han hecho la habitación.**	noa may ahn aychoa lah ahbeetahssyoan

POST OFFICE AND TELEPHONE, see page 132

The ... is broken.	... está roto(a).	... aystah roatoa(ah)
blind	la persiana	lah payrsyahnah
lamp	la lámpara	lah lahmpahrah
plug	la clavija de enchufe	lah klahbeekhah day aynchoofay
shutter	el postigo	ayl poasteegoa
switch	el interruptor	ayl eentayrrooptoar
Can you get it repaired?	¿Puede usted arreglarlo(la)?	pwayday oostayd ahrrayglahrloa(lah)

Laundry—Dry cleaner's   *Lavandería—Tintorería*

I want these clothes ...	Quiero que ... esta ropa.	kyayroa kay ... aystah roapah
cleaned	limpien	leempyayn
ironed/pressed	planchen	plahnchayn
washed	laven	lahbayn
When will they be ready?	¿Cuándo estará lista?	kwahndoa aystahrah leestah
I need them ...	La necesito para ...	lah nayssaysseetoa pahrah
today	hoy	oy
tonight	esta noche	aystah noachay
tomorrow	mañana	mahñahnah
before Friday	antes del viernes	ahntayss dayl byayrnayss
Can you ... this?	¿Puede ... esto?	pwayday ... aystoa
mend	zurcir	soorseer
patch	remendar	raymayndahr
stitch	coser	koassayr
Can you sew on this button?	¿Puede usted coser este botón?	pwayday oostayd koassayr aystay boatoan
Can you get this stain out?	¿Puede usted quitar esta mancha?	pwayday oostayd keetahr aystah mahnchah
Is my laundry ready?	¿Está lista mi ropa?	aystah leestah mee roapah
This isn't mine.	Esto no es mío.	aystoa noa ayss meeoa
There's something missing.	Falta algo.	fahltah ahlgoa
There's a hole in this.	Hay un hoyo aquí.	igh oon oayoa ahkee

Hairdresser—Barber *Peluquería—Barbería*

Is there a hairdresser/ beauty salon in the hotel?	¿Hay una peluquería/ un salón de belleza en el hotel?	igh oonah paylookayreeah/ oon sahloan day bayyay-ssah ayn ayl oatayl
Can I make an appointment for Thursday?	¿Puedo pedir turno para el jueves?	pwaydoa paydeer toornoa pahrah ayl khwaybayss
I'd like it cut and shaped.	Quiero un corte y marcado.	kyayroa oon koartay ee mahrkahdoa
I want a haircut, please.	Quiero un corte de pelo, por favor.	kyayroa oon koartay day payloa poar fahboar
bleach	un aclarado	oon ahklahrahdoa
blow-dry	un brushing	oon "brushing"
colour rinse	un enjuague de color	oon aynkhwahgay day koaloar
dye	un tinte [teñido]	oon teentay [tayñeedoa]
facepack	una máscara	oonah mahskahrah
manicure	una manicura	oonah mahneekoorah
parting (part) in the middle	una raya [partida] en medio	oonah rahyah [pahrteedah] ayn maydyoa
permanent wave	una permanente	oonah payrmahnayntay
setting lotion	un fijador	oon feekhahdoar
shampoo and set	lavado y marcado	lahbahdoa ee mahrkahdoa
with a fringe (bangs)	con un flequillo	koan oon flaykeeyoa
I'd like a shampoo for ... hair.	Quisiera un champú para pelo ...	keessyayrah oon chahmpoo pahrah payloa
normal/dry/ greasy (oily)	normal/seco/ grasoso	noarmahl/saykoa/ grahssoassoa
Do you have a colour chart?	¿Tiene usted un muestrario?	tyaynay oostayd oon mwaystrahryoa
Don't cut it too short.	No me lo corte mucho.	noa may loa koartay moochoa
A little more off the ...	Un poco más ...	oon poakoa mahss
back	por detrás	poar daytrahss
neck	en el cuello	ayn ayl kwayyoa
sides	en los lados	ayn loass lahdoass
top	arriba	ahrreebah
I don't want any hairspray.	No quiero laca.	noa kyayroa lahkah

DAYS OF THE WEEK, see page 151

I'd like a shave.	Quisiera que me afeite.	keessyayrah kay may ahfaytay
Would you trim my ..., please?	¿Quiere usted recortarme ...?	kyayray oostayd raykoartahrmay
beard	la barba	lah bahrbah
moustache	el bigote	ayl beegoatay
sideboards (sideburns)	las patillas	lahss pahteeyahss

Checking out *Al marcharse*

May I have my bill, please?	¿Me da la cuenta, por favor?	may dah lah kwayntah poar fahboar
I'm leaving early in the morning. Please have my bill ready.	Salgo mañana temprano. Por favor, tenga mi cuenta preparada.	sahlgoa mahñahnah taymprahnoa. poar fahboar tayngah mee kwayntah praypahrahdah
We'll be checking out around noon/soon.	Nos iremos alrededor de mediodía/pronto.	noass eeraymoass ahlraydaydoar day maydyoadeeah/proantoa
I must leave at once.	Tengo que irme inmediatamente.	tayngoa kay eermay eenmaydyahtahmayntay
Is everything included?	¿Está todo incluido?	aystah toadoa eenklweedoa
Can I pay by credit card?	¿Puedo pagar con la tarjeta [carta] de crédito?	pwaydoa pahgahr koan lah tahrkhaytah [kahrtah] day kraydeetoa
I think there's a mistake in the bill.	Creo que hay un error en la cuenta.	krayoa kay igh oon ayrroar ayn lah kwayntah
Can you get us a taxi?	¿Puede conseguir-nos un taxi?	pwayday koansaygeer-noass oon tahksee
Would you send someone to bring down our luggage?	¿Quiere mandar a alguien para bajar el equipaje?	kyayray mahndahr ah ahlgyayn pahrah bahkhahr ayl aykeepahkhay
Here's the forward-ing address.	Remita mis cartas a esta dirección.	raymeetah meess kahrtahss ah aystah deerayksyoan
You have my home address.	Tiene la dirección de mi domicilio.	tyaynay lah deerayksyoan day mee doameesseelyoa
It's been a very enjoyable stay.	Ha sido una estancia muy agradable.	ah seedoa oonah aystahn-syah mwee ahgrahdahblay

TIPPING, see inside back-cover

Camping *Camping*

In some parts of Latin America, camping isn't allowed without a permit. However, there are many authorized camp sites with excellent facilities. Camping and sleeping on the beach isn't recommended.

Is there a camp site near here?	¿Hay algún terreno de camping cerca de aquí?	igh ahl**goon** tayr**ray**noa day "camping" **sayr**kah day **ah**kee
Can we camp here?	¿Podemos acampar aquí?	poaday**moass** ahkahm**pahr** ah**kee**
Have you room for a tent/caravan (trailer)?	¿Tiene sitio para una tienda/caravana?	tyay**nay** **see**tyoa pahrah **oo**nah **tyayn**dah/kahrah**bah**nah
What's the charge ...?	¿Cuál es el precio ...?	kwahl ayss ayl **prayss**yoa
per day	por día	poar **dee**ah
per person	por persona	poar payr**soa**nah
for a car	por carro	poar **kah**rroa
for a tent	por tienda	poar **tyayn**dah
for a caravan (trailer)	por caravana	poar kahrah**bah**nah
Is the tourist tax included?	¿Está incluido el impuesto para turista?	ays**tah** eenk**lwee**doa ayl eemp**ways**toa **pah**rah too**ree**stah
Is/Are there (a) ...?	¿Hay ...?	igh
drinking water	agua potable	**ah**gwah poa**tah**blay
electricity	electricidad	aylayktreessee**dahd**
playground	un campo de juego	oon **kahm**poa day **khway**goa
restaurant	un restaurante	oon raystow**rahn**tay
shopping facilities	tiendas	**tyayn**dahss
swimming pool	una piscina [alberca]	**oo**nah pees**see**nah [ahl**bayr**kah]
Where are the showers/toilets?	¿Dónde están las duchas/los servicios?	**doan**day ays**tahn** lahss **doo**chahss/loass sayr**bees**syoass
Where can I get butane gas?	¿Dónde puedo conseguir gas butano?	**doan**day **pway**doa koan-say**geer** gahss boo**tah**noa
Is there a youth hostel near here?	¿Hay un albergue de juventud cerca de aquí?	igh oon ahl**bayr**gay day khoobayn**tood** **sayr**kah day **ah**kee

CAMPING EQUIPMENT, see page 106

Eating out

There are many types of places where you can eat and drink.

Bar
(bahr)

Serves drinks and *botanas* (appetizers). Some also serve hot drinks.

Cafetería
(kahfaytayreeah)

Not a self-service cafeteria in the English sense of the word, but a small café, serving both alcoholic and non-alcoholic drinks; varied menus. Sit at the counter or—for a little more money—choose a table. The *comida corrida* (set menu) may be very good.

Cantina
(kahnteenah)

Roughly equivalent to an English pub or an American tavern; standards vary; always a wide variety of appetizers on hand. A *cantina* is a great place for meeting friends and discussing the world. You'll find the people are hospitable, helpful and ... talkative. But one thing: *cantinas* are for men only.

Fonda
(foandah)

Similar to an inn; food plentiful, service usually good.

Fresquería
(frayskayreeah)

Serves refreshments and drinks. It may also be called *refresquería*.

Hacienda
(ahssyayndah)

Some old *haciendas* (big ranches), dating back to colonial times in Mexico, have been transformed into first class, luxurious restaurants. You will find fountains, gardens, tropical flowers and exotic birds in what may be compared to a real museum of old furniture and paintings. Regional and international dishes are served, music is played by *mariachi* orchestras.

Hostería
(oastayreeah)

Restaurant, often specializing in regional dishes.

Lonchería
(loanchayreeah)

Bar where you get snacks and small meals.

Pastelería (pahstaylayreeah)	A cake shop, also called *confitería*. Some serve coffee, tea and non-alcoholic drinks.
Posada (poassahdah)	Similar to *fondas*, these inns specialize in local cuisine.
Restaurante (raystowrahntay)	Classified according to the standard of cuisine and service: *de lujo* (de luxe); *de primera*, *de segunda* and *de tercera* (first, second and third class).
Restaurante de carretera (raystowrahntay day kahrraytayrah)	Modern buildings strategically situated on main highways. They offer the motorist good food and many other services in pleasant surroundings.
Salón de té (sahloan day tay)	Smart, expensive tea shop.
Snack-bar (''snack-bar'')	The English word has been taken over to describe fast-food establishments.

Meal times   *Horas de comida*

Breakfast (*el desayuno* – ayl dayssah**yoo**noa): from 8 to 10 a.m.

Lunch (*la comida* – lah koa**mee**dah): between 1 and 4 p.m.

Dinner (*la cena* – lah **say**nah): starts around 8 p.m. and continues until late.

Eating habits   *Costumbres de comida*

Breakfast is a light meal. A heartier second breakfast, *almuerzo* (ahl**mwayr**soa) is taken around 11 a.m. Lunch is the main meal, usually consisting of six or seven courses. Dinner is often replaced by a lighter meal, *merienda* (may-**ryayn**dah) between 6 and 9 p.m.

Latin-American cuisine *Cocina latinoamericana*

Latin-American cuisine in all its rich variety arose from a collision of two cooking worlds, that of the natives and the conquerors.

Avocado, chocolate, peanuts, potatoes, tomatoes and turkeys are some of the culinary gifts that Latin America has presented to the world.

Sweet corn (maize) and chillies form the basis of the cooking in all Latin-American countries. Here are some of the dishes using these two ingredients: *tacos* (Mexico), *tamales* (Colombia), *hallacas* (Venezuela).

Many delicious dishes are prepared with seafood: *cazuela de mariscos, ceviche,* etc.

¿Qué desea?	What would you like?
Le recomiendo esto.	I recommend this.
¿Qué desea beber?	What would you like to drink?
No tenemos ...	We haven't got ...
¿Desea ...?	Would you like ...?

Hungry? *¿Tiene hambre?*

I'm hungry/I'm thirsty.	**Tengo hambre/ Tengo sed.**	tayngoa ahmbray/ tayngoa sayd
Can you recommend a good restaurant?	**¿Puede recomendarme un buen restaurante?**	pwayday raykoamayn-dahrmay oon bwayn raystowrahntay
Are there any inexpensive restaurants around here?	**¿Hay algún restaurante barato cerca de aquí?**	igh ahlgoon raystow-rahntay bahrahtoa sayrkah day ahkee

If you want to be sure of getting a table in well-known restaurants, it may be better to telephone in advance.

Comidas y bebidas

I'd like to reserve a table for 4.	**Quiero reservar una mesa para 4.**	kyayroa raysayrbahr oonah mayssah pahrah 4
We'll come at 8.	**Llegaremos a las 8.**	yaygahraymoass ah lahss 8
Could we have a table ...?	**¿Puede darnos una mesa ...?**	pwayday dahrnoass oonah mayssah
in the corner	**en el rincón**	ayn ayl reenkoan
by the window	**cerca de la ventana**	sayrkah day lah bayntahnah
outside	**afuera**	ahfwayrah
on the terrace	**en la terraza**	ayn lah tayrrahssah
in a non-smoking area	**en la sección de no fumadores**	ayn lah sayksyoan day noa foomahdoarayss

Asking and ordering *Preguntando y pidiendo*

Waiter/Waitress!	**¡Mesero!/¡Mesera!**	mayssayroa/mayssayrah
I'd like something to eat/drink.	**Quisiera comer/ beber algo.**	keessyayrah koamayr/ baybayr ahlgoa
May I have the menu, please?	**¿Puedo ver la carta, por favor?**	pwaydoa bayr lah kahrtah poar fahboar
Do you have a set menu/local dishes?	**¿Tiene usted una comida corrida/ especialidades locales?**	tyaynay oostayd oonah koameedah koarreedah/ ayspayssyahleedahdayss loakahlayss
What do you recommend?	**¿Qué me aconseja?**	kay may ahkoansaykhah
I'd like ...	**Quisiera ...**	keessyayrah
Could we have a/ an ..., please?	**¿Puede darnos ..., por favor?**	pwayday dahrnoass poar fahboar
ashtray	**un cenicero**	oon sayneessayroa
cup	**una taza**	oonah tahssah
fork	**un tenedor**	oon taynaydoar
glass	**un vaso**	oon bahssoa
knife	**un cuchillo**	oon koocheeyoa
napkin (serviette)	**una servilleta**	oonah sayrbeeyaytah
plate	**un plato**	oon plahtoa
spoon	**una cuchara**	oonah koochahrah
May I have some ...?	**¿Puede darme ...?**	pwayday dahrmay
bread	**pan**	pahn
butter	**mantequilla**	mahntaykeeyah

NUMBERS, see page 147

lemon	**limón**	leemoan
oil	**aceite**	ahssaytay
pepper	**pimienta**	peemyayntah
salt	**sal**	sahl
seasoning	**condimentos**	koandeemayntoass
sugar	**azúcar**	ahssookahr
vinegar	**vinagre**	beenahgray

Some useful expressions for dieters and special requirements:

I'm on a diet.	**Sigo un régimen.**	seegoa oon raykheemayn
I don't drink alcohol.	**No bebo alcohol.**	noa bayboa ahlkoal
I mustn't eat food containing ...	**No debo comer alimentos que contengan ...**	noa dayboa koamayr ahleemayntoass kay koantayngahn
flour/fat	**harina/grasa**	ahreenah/grahssah
salt/sugar	**sal/azúcar**	sahl/ahssookahr
Do you have ... for diabetics?	**¿Tiene ... para diabéticos?**	tyaynay ... pahrah dyahbayteekoass
cakes	**pasteles**	pahstaylayss
fruit juice	**jugo de fruta**	khoogoa day frootah
a special menu	**un menú especial**	oon maynoo ayspayssyahl
Do you have any vegetarian dishes?	**¿Tiene platos vegetarianos?**	tyaynay plahtoass baykhaytahryahnoass
Could I have ... instead of the dessert?	**¿Podría tomar ... en lugar del postre?**	poadreeah toamahr ... ayn loogahr dayl poastray
Can I have an artificial sweetener?	**¿Puede darme un edulcorante?**	pwayday dahrmay oon aydoolkoarahntay

And ...

I'd like some more.	**Quisiera más.**	keessyayrah mahss
Can I have more ... please?	**¿Podría darme más ..., por favor?**	poadreeah dahrmay mahss ... poar fahboar
Just a small portion.	**Sólo una porción pequeña.**	soaloa oonah poarsyoan paykaynah
Nothing more, thanks.	**Nada más, gracias.**	nahdah mahss grahssyahss
Where are the toilets?	**¿Dónde están los servicios?**	doanday aystahn loass sayrbeessyoass

38

Breakfast *Desayuno*

The Latin-American breakfast is a light meal, consisting usually of a selection of sweet breads with milky coffee *(café con leche)* or hot chocolate *(chocolate caliente).*

I'd like breakfast, please.	**Quisiera desayunar, por favor.**	keessyayrah dayssahyoo-nahr poar fahboar
I'll have a/an some ...	**Tomaré ...**	toamahray
bacon and eggs	**huevos con tocino**	wayboass koan toasseenoa
boiled egg	**un huevo cocido**	oon wayboa koasseedoa
soft/hard	**blando/duro**	blahndoa/dooroa
cereal	**cereales**	sayrayahlayss
eggs	**huevos**	wayboass
fried eggs	**huevos fritos**	wayboass freetoass
scrambled eggs	**huevos revueltos**	wayboass raybwayltoass
fruit juice	**jugo de fruta**	khoogoa day frootah
grapefruit	**de toronja**	day toaroankhah
orange	**de naranja**	day nahrahnkhah
ham and eggs	**huevos con jamón**	wayboass koan khahmoan
jam	**mermelada**	mayrmaylahdah
marmalade	**mermelada de naranjas**	mayrmaylahdah day nahrahnkhah
toast	**pan tostado**	pahn toastahdoa
yoghourt	**yogur**	yoagoor
May I have some ...?	**¿Podría darme ...?**	poadreeah dahrmay
bread	**pan**	pahn
butter	**mantequilla**	mahntaykeeyah
(hot) chocolate	**chocolate (caliente)**	choakoalahtay (kahlyayntay)
coffee	**café**	kahfay
decaffeinated	**descafeinado**	dayskahfaynahdoa
black/with milk	**negro/con leche**	naygroa/koan laychay
honey	**miel**	myayl
milk	**leche**	laychay
cold/hot	**caliente/fría**	kahlyayntay/freeah
pepper	**pimienta**	peemyayntah
rolls	**bollitos**	boayeetoass
salt	**sal**	sahl
sugar	**azúcar**	ahssookahr
tea	**té**	tay
with milk	**con leche**	koan laychay
with lemon	**con limón**	koan leemoan
(hot) water	**agua (caliente)**	ahgwah (kahlyayntay)

What's on the menu?   *¿Qué hay en la carta?*

Many restaurants display a menu *(la carta)* outside. Besides ordering à la carte, you can have a set menu *(comida corrida),* a four- to six-course lunch, usually with two or more choices for each course.

Under the headings below you'll find alphabetical lists of dishes that might be offered on a Latin-American menu, with their English equivalent. You can simply show the book to the waiter. If you want some fruit, for instance, let *him* point to what's available on the appropriate list. Use pages 36 and 37 for ordering in general.

Reading the menu *Para leer la carta*

A elección	Of your choice
Comida corrida	Set menu
Especialidades de la casa	Specialities of the house
Especialidades locales	Local specialities
Menú del día	Set menu
Recomendamos ...	We recommend ...
Suplemento sobre ...	... extra

antojitos	ahntoakheetoass	starters
arroz	ahrroass	rice
aperitivos	ahpayreeteeboass	apéritifs
aves	ahbayss	poultry
barbacoas	bahrbahkoaahss	barbecue
bebidas	baybeedahss	drinks
carnes	kahrnayss	meat
caza	kahssah	game
enchiladas	ayncheelahdahss	meat pies
ensaladas	aynsahlahdahss	salads
entradas	ayntrahdahss	starters
frutas	frootahss	fruit
guisados	geessahdoass	stews
helados	aylahdoass	ice-cream
huevos	wayboass	eggs
legumbres	laygoombrayss	vegetables
mariscos	mahreeskoass	seafood
papas	pahpahss	potatoes
parrilladas	pahrreeyahdahss	grills
pasapalos	pahssahpahloass	starters
pastas	pahstahss	pasta
pastelería	pahstaylayreeah	pastries
patatas	pahtahtahss	potatoes
pescados	payskahdoass	fish
postres	poastrayss	dessert
quesos	kayssoass	cheese
refrescos	rayfrayskoass	cold drinks
sopas	soapahss	soups
verduras	bayrdoorahss	vegetables
vinos	beenoass	wine

Starters (Appetizers) *Entradas*

| I'd like an appetizer. | **Quisiera una entrada.** | keessyayrah oonah ayntrahdah |
| What do you recommend? | **¿Qué me aconseja?** | kay may ahkoansaykhah |

aceitunas	ahssaytoonahss	olives
aguacate	ahgwahkahtay	avocado
alcachofas	ahlkahchoafahss	artichokes
almejas	ahlmaykhahss	clams
anchoas	ahnchoaahss	anchovies
anguila (ahumada)	ahngeelah (ahoomahdah)	(smoked) eel
arenque	ahraynkay	herring
arenques ahumados	ahraynkayss ahoomahdoass	smoked herring
atún	ahtoon	tuna
camarones	kahmahroanayss	shrimps
camarones grandes	kahmahroanayss grahndayss	prawns
caracoles	kahrahkoalayss	snails
carne de cangrejo	kahrnay day kahngraykhoa	crab meat
cigalas	seegahlahss	crayfish
champiñones	chahmpeeñoanayss	mushrooms
chorizo	choareessoa	sausage made of pork and paprika
espárragos	ayspahrrahgoass	asparagus
fiambres	fyahmbrayss	cold meat
foie-gras	fwah grah	paté
gambas	gahmbahss	shrimps
hígados de pollo	eegahdoass day poayoa	chicken livers
hongos	oangoass	mushrooms
huevos	wayboass	eggs
jamón	khahmoan	ham
jamón cocido	khahmoan koasseedoa	boiled ham
jamón ahumado	khahmoan ahoomahdoa	smoked ham
jugo de fruta	khoogoa day frootah	fruit juice
naranja/piña	nahrahnkhah/peeñah	orange/pineapple
tomate/toronja	toamahtay/toaroankhah	tomato/grapefruit
langosta	lahngoastah	lobster
mejillones	maykheeyoanayss	mussels
menudencias	maynoodaynsyahss	chicken livers
menudo [mondongo]	maynoodoa [moandoangoa]	tripe
ostiones [ostras]	oastyoanayss [oastrahss]	oysters
palitos de queso	pahleetoass day kayssoa	cheese sticks (straws)
pepino	paypeenoa	cucumber

pimientos	peemyayntoass	peppers
rábanos	rahbahnoass	radishes
salchichón	sahlcheechoan	salami
salmón (ahumado)	sahlmoan (ahoomahdoa)	(smoked) salmon
sardinas	sahrdeenahss	sardines

When in Mexico, try some special starters and ask for *antojitos mexicanos* (ahntoa**khee**toass maykhee**kah**noass). A few examples:

guacamole (gwahkah**moa**lay)	mashed avocado with *tortilla*
tostadas (toa**stah**dahss)	*tortilla* with different fillings (a *tortilla* is a dry cornmeal pancake)
tacos (**tah**koass)	small *tortillas* doubled up and fried with a filling of meat, chicken, cheese or other fillings

Salads *Ensaladas*

A side dish of salad usually accompanies meat dishes, but other salads listed below may be ordered.

What salads do you have?	¿Qué clase de ensaladas tienen?	kay **klah**ssay day aynsah-**lah**dahss **tyay**nayn
Can you recommend a local speciality?	¿Puede aconsejarnos una especialidad local?	**pway**day ahkoansay**khahr**noass oonah ayspayssyah-lee**dahd** loa**kahl**
ensalada de camarones	aynsah**lah**dah day kahmah**roa**nayss	shrimp salad
ensalada de lechuga	aynsah**lah**dah day lay**choo**gah	green salad
ensalada de patatas [papas]	aynsah**lah**dah day pah**tah**tahss [**pah**pahss]	potato salad
ensalada de pepino	aynsah**lah**dah day pay**pee**noa	cucumber salad
ensalada de tomate	aynsah**lah**dah day toa**mah**tay	tomato salad

Soups and stews *Sopas y guisados*

You will find a great variety of soups in Latin America. Here are a few.

sopa de ajo	soapah day ahkhoa	with fried bread, paprika and garlic
sopa de arroz	soapah day ahrroass	rice
sopa de cebolla	soapah day sayboayah	onion
sopa de espárragos	soapah day ayspahrrah-goass	asparagus
sopa de fideos	soapah day feedayoass	vermicelli
sopa de frijoles	soapah day freekhoalayss	bean
sopa de mariscos	soapah day mahreeskoass	seafood
sopa de papas	soapah day pahpahss	potato, onion, parsley and sherry
sopa de pescado	soapah day payskahdoa	fish
sopa de tortuga	soapah day toartoogah	turtle
sopa de verduras	soapah day bayrdoorahss	green vegetable

And here is a choice of regional specialities:

cazuela de ave (kahswaylah day ahbay)	a rich chicken soup with green vegetables cooked in stock (Chile)
cazuela de mariscos (kahswaylah day mah-reeskoass)	a flavoursome seafood stew (Argentina)
chipi-chipi (cheepee cheepee)	a soup made with tiny clams (Venezuela)
chupe de camarones (choopay day kahmahroanayss)	a soup made of potatoes, milk, shrimp, hot chillies, peppers and eggs (Peru)
chupe de mariscos (choopay day mahreeskoass)	a superb shellfish dish (Chile and Peru)
cocido [sancocho] (koasseedoa [sahnkoachoa])	a stew made with chunks of beef, chicken or fish and local vegetables or roots
menudo (maynoodoa)	tripe; usually in chilli-pepper sauce
pozole (poassoalay)	pork and ground-corn soup (Mexico)

Fish and seafood   *Pescado y mariscos*

Don't miss the opportunity to sample some of the wide variety of fresh fish and seafood in coastal areas.

| I'd like some fish. | **Quisiera pescado.** | keessyayrah payskahdoa |
| What kind of seafood do you have? | **¿Qué tipo de mariscos tiene usted?** | kay teepoa day mahreeskoass tyaynay oostayd |

almejas	ahlmaykhahss	clams
anchoas	ahnchoaahss	anchovies
anguila	ahngeelah	eel
arenque	ahraynkay	herring
atún	ahtoon	tunny (tuna)
bacalao	bahkahlahoa	cod
besugo	bayssoogoa	(sea) bream
bonito	boaneetoa	striped tunny (tuna)
boquerones	boakayroanayss	whitebait
caballa	kahbahyah	mackerel
calamares	kahlahmahrayss	squid
camarones	kahmahroanayss	shrimps
camarones grandes	kahmahroanayss grahndayss	prawns
cangrejo	kahngraykhoa	crab
gambas	gahmbahss	shrimps
huachinango	wahcheenahngoa	red snapper
lamprea	lahmprayah	lamprey
langosta	lahngoastah	lobster
langostino	lahngoasteenoa	crayfish
lenguado	layngwahdoa	sole
merluza	mayrloossah	hake
mero	mayroa	bass
mújol	mookhoal	mullet
ostiones	oastyoanayss	oysters
ostras	oastrahss	oysters
perca	payrkah	perch
pescadilla	payskahdeeyah	whiting
pez espada	payss ayspahdah	swordfish
pulpo	poolpoa	octopus
rape	rahpay	monkfish
róbalo	roabahloa	haddock
rodaballo	roadahbahyoa	turbot
salmón (ahumado)	sahlmoan (ahoomahdoa)	(smoked) salmon
salmonetes	sahlmoanaytayss	red millet
sardinas	sahrdeenahss	sardines
trucha	troochah	trout

baked	**al horno**	ahl **o**arnoa
boiled	**cocido**	koa**see**doa
fried	**frito**	**free**toa
grilled (broiled)	**a la parrilla**	ah lah pahr**ree**yah
marinated	**en escabeche**	ayn ayskah**bay**chay
poached	**hervido**	ayr**bee**doa
raw	**crudo**	**kroo**doa
smoked	**ahumado**	ahoo**mah**doa

cazuela de mariscos
(kah**sswaylah day mahreeskoass)

a variety of shellfish in a bechamel sauce

cazuela de pescado
(kah**sswaylah day payskahdoa)

all kinds of fish in a very spicy sauce

ceviche
(say**bee**chay)

raw fish, marinated in lemon juice and served with onions and hot peppers

ceviche de langostinos
(say**bee**chay day lahngoa**stee**noass)

a *ceviche* (all kinds of shellfish) with crayfish as main ingredient

ceviche mixto
(say**bee**chay **meek**stoa)

a *ceviche* with a mixture of shrimp, fish and shellfish

pescado a la veracruzana
(pay**skahdoa** ah lah bayrah**kroossahnah**)

red snapper with tomatoes and pimientos

viudo de pescado
(**byoodoa** day pays**kahdoa**)

fish stew, traditionally cooked in holes dug in the ground and covered with hot stones (Colombia)

Meat   *Carne*

Many Latin-American countries are beef and pork producers. Lamb is common in mountainous countries and chicken is universal. Apart from the standard dishes there are, of course, lots of regional specialities.

I'd like some ...	Quisiera ...	keessyayrah
beef	carne de res [carne vacuna]	kahrnay day rayss [kahrnay bahkoonah]
lamb	cordero	koardayroa
pork	cerdo	sayrdoa
veal	ternera	tayrnayrah
asado	ahssahdoa	roast meat
bife	beefay	beefsteak
bistec	beestayk	beefsteak
carne molida	kahrnay moaleedah	minced meat
carnero	kahrnayroa	mutton
cerdo	sayrdoa	pork
cochinillo	koacheeneeyoa	suck(l)ing pig
cordero	koardayroa	lamb
costilla	koasteeyah	cutlet
criadillas	kryahdeeyahss	sweetbreads
chancho	chahnchoa	pork
chuleta	choolaytah	chop
filete	feelaytay	steak
hígado	eegahdoa	liver
jamón	khahmoan	ham
lechecillas	laychaysseeyahss	sweetbreads
lechón	laychoan	suck(l)ing pig
lengua	layngwah	tongue
lomo	loamoa	steak
lomo de cerdo	loamoa day sayrdoa	pork fillet
paleta de cordero	pahlaytah day koardayroa	breast of lamb
panceta	pahnsaytah	bacon
patas de cerdo	pahtahss day sayrdoa	pig's trotters (feet)
pierna de cordero	pyayrnah day koardayroa	leg of lamb
rabo de buey	rahboa day bway	oxtail
riñones	reeñoanayss	kidneys
salchichas	sahlcheechahss	sausages
solomillo	soaloameeyoa	pork fillet
ternera	tayrnayrah	veal
tocino	toasseenoa	bacon
tripas	treepahss	tripe
vaca	bahkah	beef

braised	**estofado**	aystoafahdoa
in casserole	**en salsa**	ayn sahlsah
fried	**frito**	freetoa
grilled (broiled)	**a la parrilla**	ah lah pahrreeyah
pot-roasted	**en su jugo**	ayn soo khoogoa
roast	**al horno**	ahl oarnoa
stewed	**estofado**	aystoafahdoa
rare	**poco hecho**	poakoa aychoa
medium	**término medio**	tayrmeenoa maydyoa
	[regular]	[raygoolahr]
well-done	**bien hecho**	byayn aychoa

The Mexican like it ...

asado	ahssahdoa	grilled
al carbón	ahl kahrboan	barbecued
en barbacoa	ayn bahrbahkoaah	barbecued, Mexican style

Meat dishes *Platos de carne*

anticucho
(ahnteekoochoa)
squares of beef heart on skewers, broiled over charcoal and served with hot sauce (Peru)

bife a caballo
(beefay ah kah-bahyoa)
"horseback beef"; a steak topped by two fried eggs (Argentina)

carbonada criolla
(kahrboanahdah kryoayah)
beef slices sautéed with courgette (zucchini), sweet potatoes, peaches and sweet corn (Argentina)

carne a la tampi-queña
(kahrnay ah lah tahmpeekayñah)
steak with *guacamole**, *tacos* and fried beans (Mexico)

cochinita pibil
(koacheeneetah peebeel)
suck(l)ing pig slowly baked in a banana-leaf wrapping (Mexico)

chile con carne
(cheelay koan kahrnay)
stew of kidney beans and minced beef, well spiced with chilli peppers (Mexico)

---

*In Mexico, meat dishes are often served with *guacamole* (mashed avocado), fried kidney beans and *tortilla*. A *tortilla* is a dry cornmeal pancake.

chorizo (choa**reess**oa)	a highly spiced type of pork sausage
empanada (aympah**nah**dah)	minced-meat turnover with onions and possibly potatoes or raisins; may be highly spiced (Argentina)
parrillada (pahrree**yah**dah)	mixed grill with everything from a steak to sausages grilled over charcoal (Argentina)
parrillada **Machu Picchu** (pahrree**yah**dah **mah**choo **pee**choo)	beefsteak garnished with avocado, pineapple and papayas (Peru)
taco (**tah**koa)	*tacos* are as popular in Mexico as hotdogs in the United States. They are made from *tortillas* stuffed with all kinds of meat fillings, then fried in hot oil and spiced with chilli-pepper sauce and *guacamole*. *Tacos* can be had in any kind of restaurant.

Game and poultry   *Caza y aves*

Chicken is found all over Latin America, in a wide range of preparations: whether grilled *(asado),* spit-roasted *(al espetón),* in sauces or in the form of stuffing or filling, it is always very tasty and quite inexpensive. Turkey, though more pricey, is excellent, above all in Mexico.

Game is difficult to find, especially in cities; but even in the country, restaurants serving game are rare.

I'd like some game.	**Quisiera caza.**	keess**yay**rah **kah**ssah
What poultry dishes do you have?	**¿Qué tipo de ave tiene usted?**	kay **tee**poa day **ah**bay **tyay**nay oo**stayd**
capón	kah**poan**	capon
codorniz	koadoar**neess**	quail
conejo	koa**nay**khoa	rabbit
faisán	figh**ssahn**	pheasant
ganso	**gahn**soa	goose
higaditos de pollo	eegah**dee**toass day **poa**yoa	chicken livers

liebre	lyaybray	hare
pato	pahtoa	duck
pavo	pahboa	turkey
perdiz	payrdeess	partridge
pichón	peechoan	pigeon
pollo	poayoa	chicken
muslo de pollo	moosloa day poayoa	chicken leg
pechuga de pollo	paychoogah day poayoa	chicken breast
pollo asado	poayoa ahssahdoa	roast chicken
venado	baynahdoa	venison

enchilada de pollo (aynchee**lah**dah day poayoa)	Mexican *tortilla* with a chicken filling in a red chilli-pepper sauce; served with cheese. In fact, an *enchilada* is a kind of *taco*. If you don't like the chilli-pepper sauce, ask for an *enchilada suiza* (aynchee**lah**dah **swee**ssah) and you'll get tomato sauce instead.
pollo en adobo (poayoa ayn ah**doa**boa)	chicken in a red-pepper sauce (Mexico)
pollo en mole (poayoa ayn moalay)	chicken in a *mole* (**moa**lay) sauce, made of chillies, oil, sugar, sesame seeds, peanuts, salt, cinnamon, cocoa and spices, with small pieces of toasted bread.

Omelets *Tortillas*

If you want an omelet, ask for a *tortilla* (toar**tee**yah). But be careful in Mexico: in this country a *tortilla* is a dry cornmeal pancake, so here you should ask for a *tortilla de huevo* (toar-**tee**yah day **way**boa).

pupusa	poopoossah	pancake with cheese or bacon
tortilla al ron	toarteeyah ahl roan	rum omelet
tortilla de cebolla	toarteeyah day sayboayah	onion omelet
tortilla de hongos	toarteeyah day oangoass	mushroom omelet
tortilla de jamón	toarteeyah day khahmoan	ham omelet
tortilla de papas	toarteeyah day pahpahss	potato omelet
tortilla de queso	toarteeyah day kayssoa	cheese omelet

Vegetables *Verduras*

achicoria	ahcheekoaryah	endive (Am. chicory)
ajo	ahkhoa	garlic
alcachofas	ahlkahchoafahss	artichokes
alcaparras	ahlkahpahrrahss	capers
apio	ahpyoa	celery
arvejas	ahrbaykhahss	peas
berenjena	bayraynkhaynah	eggplant (aubergine)
betabel	baytahbayl	beet(root)
calabaza	kahlahbahssah	marrow
cebollas	sayboayahss	onions
cebolletas	sayboayaytahss	chives
col	koal	cabbage
coles de Bruselas	koalayss day broossaylahss	Brussels sprouts
coliflor	koaleefloar	cauliflower
col morada	koal moarahdah	red cabbage
champiñones	chahmpeeñoanayss	mushrooms
chícharos	cheechahroass	peas
chile	cheelay	chilli
chirivías	cheereebeeahss	parsnips
choclo	choakloa	corn
ejotes	aykhoatayss	green (French) beans
elote	ayloatay	corn on the cob
escarola	ayskahroalah	endive (Am. chicory)
espárragos	ayspahrrahgoass	asparagus
espinacas	ayspeenahkahss	spinach
frijoles	freekhoalayss	beans
garbanzos	gahrbahnsoass	chickpeas
guisantes	geessahntayss	peas
lechuga	laychoogah	lettuce
lentejas	layntaykhahss	lentils
maíz	maheess	sweet corn
pepinillos	paypeeneeyoass	gherkins
pepino	paypeenoa	cucumber
pimientos	peemyayntoass	hot peppers
pimientos morrones	peemyayntoass moarroanayss	sweet peppers
puerros	pwayrroass	leeks
rábanos	rahbahnoass	radishes
remolacha	raymoalahchah	beet(root)
repollo	raypoayoa	cabbage
tomates	toamahtayss	tomatoes
zanahorias	sahnahoaryahss	carrots
zapallito	sahpahyeetoa	courgette (zucchini)
zapallo	sahpahyoa	pumpkin

A few vegetables that are a bit special:

nopalitos
(noapahleetoass)
cactus

chile
(cheelay)
chilli peppers, hot peppers or pimientos—call them what you like. They come in many varieties; the most popular are: *poblano chipotle, jalapeño, largo, piquín*

flor de calabaza
(floar day kahlah-**bah**ssah)
the flowers of courgettes (zucchini)

huitlacoche
(weetlah**koa**chay)
a kind of mushroom which grows on sweet corn

Potatoes, rice and noodles *Papas, arroz y pastas*

arroz	ahr**roass**	rice
batatas	bah**tah**tahss	sweet potatoes
camotes	kah**moa**tayss	sweet potatoes
croquetas	kroa**kay**tahss	croquettes
papas [patatas]	**pah**pahss [pah**tah**tahss]	potatoes
fritas	**free**tahss	chips (French fries)
hervidas	ayr**bee**dahss	boiled, steamed
puré de papas	poo**ray** day **pah**pahss	mashed potatoes
pastas	**pah**stahss	noodles
macarrones	mahkahr**roa**nayss	macaroni
yame	**yah**may	yam (sweet potato)
yuca	**yoo**kah	a type of potato

Herbs and spices *Condimentos y especias*

aceite	ah**ssay**tay	oil
ají	ah**khee**	red pepper
ajo	ah**khoa**	garlic
albahaca	ahlbah**hah**kah	basil

anís	ahneess	aniseed
azafrán	ahssahfrahn	saffron
canela	kahnaylah	cinnamon
cebolleta	sayboayaytah	chives
clavo	klahboa	cloves
comino	koameenoa	caraway
culantro [cilantro]	koolahntroa [seelahntroa]	coriander
chile	cheelay	chilli pepper
eneldo	aynayldoa	dill
estragón	aystrahgoan	tarragon
hoja de laurel	oakhah day lowrayl	bay leaf
menta	mayntah	mint
mostaza	moastahssah	mustard
nuez moscada	nwayss moaskahdah	nutmeg
orégano	oaraygahnoa	oregano
perejil	payraykheel	parsley
pimiento	peemyayntah	pepper
romero	roamayroa	rosemary
sal	sahl	salt
salvia	sahlbyah	sage
vinagre	beenahgray	vinegar

Sauces *Salsas*

In addition to the internationally known sauces found in all good restaurants, you may come across the following more typical preparations:

adobo (ahdoaboa)	a sauce made from two types of chilli peppers (*chile ancho* and *chile pasilla*), vegetable oil, sesame seeds, peanuts, sugar, salt and spices. It often contains small pieces of toasted bread
ajiaco (ahkhyahkoa)	a pimiento-based sauce
mole (moalay)	a composition of chilli peppers, oil, sugar, sesame seeds, peanuts, salt, cinnamon, cocoa and spices, with small pieces of toasted bread
pipián (peepyahn)	pumpkin seeds, chilli peppers, oil, sesame seeds, peanuts, salt, garlic, onions, coriander and caraway seeds, with small pieces of toasted bread

Cheese *Queso*

The most popular cheeses in Mexico are:

asadero (ahssahdayroa)	a soft, creamy cheese
queso añejo (kayssoa ahñaykhoa)	hand-pressed and salted. The flavour is sharp, the texture close-grained and hard with a few small holes; made from ewe's milk
queso de bola (kayssoa day boalah)	a soft cheese made in the form of a ball
queso de Chihuahua (kayssoa day cheewahwah)	a popular soft cheese named after the province from which it originates
queso de Oaxaca (kayssoa day wahkhahkah)	very popular in the south of Mexico
queso enchilado (kayssoa ayncheelahdoa)	same as *queso añejo* but a little sharper in taste; the exterior is coloured with red chilli peppers
queso fresco (kayssoa frayskoa)	fresh white cheese; made and sold the same day

In other Latin American countries, local cheese is of little importance.

Fruit *Fruta*

Do you have fresh fruit?	¿Tiene usted fruta fresca?	tyaynay oostayd frootah frayskah
I'd like a (fresh) fruit cocktail.	Quisiera una ensalada de fruta (fresca).	keessyayrah oonah aynsahlahdah day frootah (frayskah)
almendras	ahlmayndrahss	almonds
ananá[s]	ahnahnah[ss]	pineapple
avellanas	ahbayyahnahss	hazelnuts
banana	bahnahnah	banana
castañas	kahstahñahss	chestnuts
cacahuates	kahkahwahtayss	peanuts

cerezas	sayrayssahss	cherries
ciruelas	seerwaylahss	plums
ciruelas secas	seerwaylahss saykahss	prunes
coco	koakoa	coconut
chabacanos	chahbahkahnoass	apricots
damascos	dahmahskoass	apricots
dátiles	dahteelayss	dates
durazno	doorahsnoa	peach
frambuesas	frahmbwayssahss	raspberries
fresas	frayssahss	strawberries
granadas	grahnahdahss	pomegranates
higos	eegoass	figs
lima	leemah	lime
limón	leemoan	lemon
mandarina	mahndahreenah	tangerine
mango	mahngoa	mango
maníes	mahneeayss	peanuts
manzana	mahnsahnah	apple
melón	mayloan	melon
naranja	nahrahnkhah	orange
nueces	nwayssayss	walnuts
papaya	pahpahyah	papaya
pasas	pahssahss	raisins
pera	payrah	pear
piña	peeñah	pineapple
plátano	plahtahnoa	banana
pomelo	poamayloa	grapefruit
sandía	sahndeeah	watermelon
toronja	toaroankhah	grapefruit
uvas	oobahss	grapes

Here are a few tropical fruits, most of which will be new
to you. We find them hard to translate or describe. But try
them anyway, they're all delicious.

chirimoya	cheereemoayah
guanábana	gwahnahbahnah
guayaba	gwahyahbah
jícama	kheekahmah
mamoncillo	mahmoanseeyoa
nísperos	neespayroass
pitahayas	peetahyahss
tamarindo	tahmahreendoa
tunas	toonahss

Dessert   *Postre*

I'd like a dessert, please.	**Quisiera un postre, por favor.**	keessyayrah oon **poast**ray poar fah**boar**
What do you recommend?	**¿Qué me recomienda?**	kay may raykoam**yayn**dah
Something light, please.	**Algo ligero, por favor.**	**ahl**goa lee**khay**roa poar fah**boar**
Just a small portion.	**Una porción pequeña.**	oonah poars**yoan** pay**kay**ñah
alborotos	ahlboaroatoass	sweet made of roasted corn
ante	ahntay	pastry with coconut and almonds
arroz con leche	ahrroass koan laychay	rice pudding
bizcocho	beeskoachoa	sponge cake
buñuelos	booñwayloass	fritters
cocada	koakahdah	sweet made of coconut
espumilla	ayspoomeeyah	a sort of meringue
flan	flahn	caramel custard
flan casero	flahn kahssayroa	home-made
galletas	gahyaytahss	biscuits (cookies)
helado	aylahdoa	ice cream
de chocolate	day choakoalahtay	chocolate
de fresa	day frayssah	strawberry
de vainilla	day baheeneeyah	vanilla
masita	mahsseetah	pastries
melocotón melba	mayloakoatoan maylbah	peach melba
merengue	mayrayngay	meringue
con crema	koan kraymah	with cream
pastas	pahstahss	biscuits (cookies)
pastel	pahstayl	cake
de moca	day moakah	coffee cake
de queso	day kayssoa	cheese cake
pastelitos	pahstayleetoass	biscuits (cookies)
ponqué	poankay	layer cake
queque	kaykay	cake
tarta	tahrtah	tart
de almendras	day ahlmayndrahss	almond tart
de manzana	day mahnsahnah	apple tart
helada	aylahdah	ice cream tart
tarteletas	tahrtaylaytahss	small tarts
torta	toartah	cake

Drinks *Bebidas*

Local drinks may provide you with a new experience. They are usually made from tropical fruit, fermented, unfermented, or served hot. The most popular are:

Fermented

chicha (cheechah)	a strong drink made from fermented sweet corn and various kinds of fruit
pulque (poolkay)	fermented juice of the agave
tepache (taypahchay)	a drink made of *pulque,* pineapple, and cloves
tequila (taykeelah)	a drink reminiscent of gin, distilled from agave: ask your waiter how to drink it Mexican style

Unfermented

agua de jamaica (ahgwah day khahmighkah)	from a red flower
horchata (oarchahtah)	a cooling drink made from almonds and rice
tamarindo (tahmahreendoa)	from a sour kind of fruit

Hot drinks

atole (ahtoalay)	made from the same paste as *tortillas* and flavoured with walnuts, coconuts, etc.
café de olla (kahfay day oayah)	coffee with cane sugar, cinnamon and cloves
ponche (poanchay)	a fruit juice and rum punch

Wine *Vino*

You'll find imported European wines all over Latin America, but try the local ones as well, particularly in Chile, Argentina and Mexico: Latin America produces almost a tenth of the world's wines.

The best wines come from Chile, mainly from the central area round Santiago. Grapes and winegrowing methods are of French origin. You will find a smooth red wine, *Chilean Cabernet,* a dry but mellow *Sauvignon* and a good white *Riesling.*

Argentina's climate is less favourable for great wines, nevertheless this country is the largest wine-producer in South America. The red wine, of better quality than the white, is made from the *Malbec* grape, which is the most widely planted in Argentina. A variety called *Criollas* is used for white wine.

As the climate is too hot for the production of high quality wine, Mexico produces less than other Latin-American countries. Red wine is the most popular, for example *Cepa Urbiñon, Calafía* or *Chatillon,* but you will also find white *(blanco)* or rosé wine *(rosado).* If you want to sample a Champagne-type wine, try *Chambrule.*

As a general rule, white wine goes better with fish and light meats while red wine accompanies dark meats such as beef or lamb. If you need help in choosing a wine, don't hesitate to ask the waiter.

May I have the wine list, please?	**¿Puedo ver la carta de vinos, por favor?**	pwaydoa bayr lah kahrtah day beenoass poar fahboar
I'd like a bottle of white/red wine.	**Quisiera una botella de vino blanco/ tinto.**	keessyayrah oonah boatayyah day beenoa blahnkoa/teentoa
a half bottle	**media botella**	maydyah boatayyah
a carafe	**una jarra**	oonah khahrrah
half a litre	**medio litro**	maydyoa leetroa
a glass	**un vaso [una copa]**	oon bahssoa [oonah koapah]

A bottle of champagne, please.	Una botella de champán, por favor.	oonah boatayyah day chahmpahn poar fahboar
Please bring me another ...	Tráigame otro(a) ... ... por favor.	trighgahmay oatroa(ah) ... poar fahboar
Where does this wine come from?	¿De dónde viene este vino?	day doanday byaynay aystay beenoa

red	tinto	teentoa
white	blanco	blahnkoa
rosé	rosado	roassahdoa
dry	seco	saykoa
light	ligero	leekhayroa
full-bodied	fuerte	fwayrtay
sparkling	espumoso	ayspoomoassoa
sweet	dulce	doolsay
very dry	muy seco	mwee saykoa

Beer   *Cerveza*

Latin-American beer will be a pleasant surprise for you: Bolivia, Colombia, Peru and especially Mexico produce excellent local brands.

I'd like a beer, please.	Quisiera una cerveza, por favor.	keessyayrah oonah sayrbayssah poar fahboar
Do you have ... beer?	¿Tienen cerveza ...?	tyaynayn sayrbayssah
light	rubia	roobyah
dark	negra	naygrah
foreign	extranjera	aykstrahnkhayrah

Other alcoholic drinks

Don't expect to find exotic drinks in a small *posada*. For these you'll have to go to the more sophisticated bars and hotels. Here is a list of some standard drinks you'll find in most bars. Note that Mexican brandy is well worth drinking. It's the most popular spirit of that country.

aperitif	**un aperitivo**	oon ahpayreeteeboa
brandy	**un coñac**	oon koañahk
gin	**una ginebra**	oonah kheenaybrah
	[un gin]	[oon "gin"]
gin and tonic	**una tónica con**	oonah toaneekah koan
	ginebra	kheenaybrah
liqueur	**un licor**	oon leekoar
port	**un oporto**	oon oapoartoa
rum	**un ron**	oon roan
sherry	**un jerez**	oon khayrayss
vermouth	**un vermut**	oon bayrmoot
vodka	**un vodka**	oon boadkah
whisky	**un whisky**	oon "whisky"
whisky and soda	**un whisky con**	oon "whisky" koan soadah
	soda	

a glass	**un vaso [una**	oon bahssoa [oonah
	copa]	koapah]
a bottle	**una botella**	oonah boatayyah
ice cubes	**cubitos de**	koobeetoass day
	hielo	yayloa
neat (straight)	**solo**	soaloa
on the rocks	**con hielo**	koan yayloa
with water	**con agua**	koan ahgwah

¡SALUD!
(sahlood)
YOUR HEALTH/CHEERS!

For those whose journey is to lead them beyond Mexico, here are a few national specialities:

Colombia	*aguardiente,* a fiery spirit
	ron caldas, a rum comparable to the Jamaican type
	ron medellín, a lighter rum
Chile, Peru	*pisco,* a local brandy, served with lemon juice, bitters or syrup
	pisco sour, with ginger ale *(chilcano),* or with vermouth *(capitán)*
Puerto Rico	*ron* is the word for rum here and Puerto Ricans are justly proud of the wide variety available
Venezuela	*ponche crema,* an eggnog punch, spiced with liqueur

Non-alcoholic drinks *Bebidas sin alcohol*

(hot) chocolate	**chocolate (caliente)**	choakoalahtay (kahlyayntay)
coffee	**café**	kahfay
black	**solo [negro]**	soaloa [naygroa]
with cream	**con crema**	koan kraymah
with milk	**con leche**	koan laychay
decaffeinated	**descafeinado**	dayskahfaynahdoa
espresso	**exprés**	ayksprayss
fruit juice	**jugo de fruta**	khoogoa day frootah
grapefruit	**toronja**	toaroankhah
orange	**naranja**	nahrahnkhah
pineapple	**ananá[s]**	ahnahnah[ss]
lemonade	**limonada**	leemoanahdah
milk	**leche**	laychay
mineral water	**agua mineral**	ahgwah meenayrahl
fizzy (carbonated)	**con gas**	koan gahss
still	**sin gas**	seen gahss
tea	**té**	tay
with milk	**con leche**	koan laychay
with lemon	**con limón**	koan leemoan
iced tea	**helado**	aylahdoa
tonic water	**agua tónica**	ahgwah toaneekah

Complaints *Reclamaciones*

There is a plate/ glass missing.	**Falta un plato/ un vaso.**	fahltah oon plahtoa/ oon bahssoa
I don't have a knife/ fork/spoon.	**No tengo cuchillo/ tenedor/cuchara.**	noa tayngoa koocheeyoa/ taynaydoar/koochahrah
That's not what I ordered.	**Eso no es lo que pedí.**	ayssoa noa ayss loa kay paydee
I asked for ...	**He pedido ...**	ay paydeedoa
There must be some mistake.	**Debe haber algún error.**	daybay ahbayr ahlgoon ayrroar
May I change this?	**¿Puede cambiarme esto?**	pwayday kahmbyahrmay aystoa
I asked for a small portion (for the child).	**Pedí una porción pequeña (para el niño/la niña).**	paydee oonah poarsyoan paykayñah (pahrah ayl neeñoa/lah neeñah)
The meat is ...	**Esta carne está ...**	aystah kahrnay aystah
overdone	**demasiado hecha**	daymahssyahdoa aychah
underdone	**poco hecha**	poakoa aychah
too rare	**demasiado cruda**	daymahssyahdoa kroodah
too tough	**demasiado dura**	daymahssyahdoa doorah
This is too ...	**Esto está muy ...**	aystoa aystah mwee
bitter/salty/sweet	**amargo/salado/dulce**	ahmahrgoa/sahlahdoa/ doolsay
I don't like this.	**Esto no me gusta.**	aystoa noa may goostah
The food is cold.	**La comida está fría.**	lah koameedah aystah freeah
This isn't fresh.	**No está fresco.**	noa aystah frayskoa
What's taking so long?	**¿Por qué tarda tanto?**	poar kay tahrdah tahntoa
Have you forgotten our drinks?	**¿Se ha olvidado de nuestras bebidas?**	say ah oalbeedahdoa day nwaystrahss baybeedahss
The wine tastes of cork.	**El vino sabe a corcho.**	ayl beenoa sahbay ah koarchoa
This isn't clean.	**Esto no está limpio.**	aystoa noa aystah leempyoa
Would you ask the head waiter to come over?	**¿Quiere llamar al maître?**	kyayray yahmahr ahl maytray

The bill (check) *La cuenta*

A service charge is generally included in restaurant bills. Anything extra for the waiter is optional.

I'd like to pay.	**Quisiera pagar.**	kee**ss**yayrah pah**gah**r
We'd like to pay separately.	**Quisiéramos pagar por separado.**	kee**ss**yayrahmoass pah**gah**r poar saypahrahdoa
I think there is a mistake in this bill.	**Me parece que hay un error en esta cuenta.**	may pahrayssay kay igh oon ayrroar ayn aystah kwayntah
What's this amount for?	**¿A qué corresponde esta cifra?**	ah kay koarrays**poa**nday aystah seefrah
Is service included?	**¿Está incluido el servicio?**	aystah eenk**l**weedoa ayl sayrbeessyoa
Is the cover charge included?	**¿Está incluido el cubierto?**	aystah eenk**l**weedoa ayl koobyayrtoa
Is everything included?	**¿Está todo incluido?**	aystah toadoa eenk**l**weedoa
Do you accept traveller's cheques?	**¿Acepta usted cheques de viajero?**	ahss**ay**ptah oostayd chay-kayss day byah**kh**ayroa
Can I pay with this credit card?	**¿Puedo pagar con esta tarjeta de crédito?**	pwaydoa pah**gah**r koan aystah tahr**kh**aytah day kraydeetoa
Thank you, this is for you.	**Gracias, esto es para usted.**	grah**ss**yahss aystoa ayss pahrah oostayd
Keep the change.	**Quédese con el vuelto.**	kaydayssay koan ayl bwayltoa
That was a delicious meal.	**Ha sido una comida excelente.**	ah seedoa oonah koameedah ayksaylayntay
We enjoyed it, thank you.	**Nos ha gustado, gracias.**	noass ah goostahdoa grah**ss**yahss

---

SERVICIO INCLUIDO
SERVICE INCLUDED

TIPPING, see inside back-cover

Snacks—Picnic *Meriendas—Picnic*

You can get various snacks at any hour of the day at street-corner stands or in restaurants. The basis is the *tortilla*, a cornmeal pancake, which exists in endless delicious varieties: *tacos* (with meat, chicken or cheese filling), *tostada* (fried tortilla with sausage, beans or avocado), *enchilada* (tortilla with filling and sauce), *tamales* (steamed inside dried cornhusks).

I'll have one of those, please.	**Tomaré uno de éstos, por favor.**	toamah**ray** oonoa day ays**toass**, poar fah**boar**
Give me two of these and one of those.	**Déme dos de éstos y uno de ésos.**	**day**may doass day ays**toass** ee oonoa day ays**soass**
to the left	**a la izquierda**	ah lah eesky**ayr**dah
to the right	**a la derecha**	ah lah day**ray**chah
above/below	**encima/debajo**	ayn**see**mah/day**bah**khoa
It's to take away.	**Es para llevar.**	ayss **pah**rah yay**bahr**
I'd like a/some ...	**Quisiera ...**	kees**syayr**ah
chicken	**un pollo**	oon **poa**yoa
roast chicken	**pollo a la brasa**	**poa**yoa ah lah **brah**ssah
chips (french fries)	**papas fritas [a la francesa]**	pah**pahss free**tahss [ah lah frahn**say**ssah]
meat pie	**una empanada**	oonah aympah**nah**dah
salad	**una ensalada**	oonah aynsah**lah**dah
sandwich	**una torta [un sandwich]**	oonah **toar**tah [oon ''sandwich'']

Here's a basic list of food and drink that might come in useful when shopping for a picnic.

Please give me a/an/ some ...	**Déme ..., por favor.**	**day**may ... poar fah**boar**
apples	**manzanas**	mahn**sah**nahss
bananas	**bananas [plátanos]**	bah**nah**nahss [**plah**tahnoass]
biscuits (Br.)	**galletas**	gah**yay**tahss
beer	**cerveza**	sayr**bay**ssah

bread	pan	pahn
butter	mantequilla	mahntaykeeyah
cake	un pastel	oon pahstayl
candy	caramelos	kahrahmayloass
cheese	queso	kayssoa
chips (Am.)	papas fritas [chips]	pahpahss freetahss [chips]
chocolate bar	una tableta de chocolate	oonah tahblaytah day choakoalahtay
coffee	café	kahfay
cold cuts	fiambres	fyahmbrayss
cookies	galletas	gahyaytahss
crackers	galletas saladas	gahyaytahss sahlahdahss
crisps	papas fritas [chips]	pahpahss freetahss [chips]
cucumber	pepino	paypeenoa
eggs	huevos	wayboass
gherkins (pickles)	pepinillos	paypeeneeyoass
grapefruit	toronjas [pomelos]	toaroankhahss [poamayloass]
grapes	uvas	oobahss
ham	jamón	khahmoan
ice-cream	helado	aylahdoa
lemon	limón	leemoan
milk	leche	laychay
mineral water	agua mineral	ahgwah meenayrahl
mustard	mostaza	moastahssah
oranges	naranjas	nahrahnkhahss
pastries	pasteles	pahstaylayss
pepper	pimienta	peemyayntah
rolls	panecillos	pahnaysseeyoass
salt	sal	sahl
sausage	una salchicha	oonah sahlcheechah
soft drink	una bebida sin alcohol	oonah baybeedah seen ahlkoal
sugar	azúcar	ahssookahr
sweets	caramelos	kahrahmayloass
tea	té	tay
wine	vino	beenoa

Travelling around

Plane *Avión*

Is there a flight to Mexico City?	¿Hay algún vuelo a México?	igh ahl**goon** bwayloa ah may**khee**koa
Is it a direct flight?	¿Es un vuelo directo?	ayss oon **bway**loa dee**rayk**toa
When's the next flight to Lima?	¿Cuándo sale el próximo avión para Lima?	**kwahn**doa sahlay ayl **proak**seemoa ahb**yoan** pahrah **lee**mah
Is there a connection to La Paz?	¿Hay una conexión para La Paz?	igh oonah koanayk**syoan** pahrah lah pahss
I'd like a ticket to Acapulco.	Quiero un billete para Acapulco.	**kyay**roa oon beeyaytay pahrah ahkah**pool**koa
single (one-way)	ida	**ee**dah
return (roundtrip)	ida y vuelta	**ee**dah ee **bwayl**tah
What time do we take off?	¿A qué hora sale el avión?	ah kay **oa**rah sahlay ayl ahb**yoan**
What time do I have to check in?	¿A qué hora tengo que presentarme?	ah kay **oa**rah **tayn**goa kay prayssayn**tahr**may
Is there a bus to the airport/city terminal?	¿Hay un autobús que va al aeropuerto/a la terminal de la ciudad?	igh oon owtoa**booss** kay bah ahl ahayroap**wayr**toa/ah lah tayr**mee**nahl day lah **syoo**dahd
What's the flight number?	¿Cuál es el número del vuelo?	kwahl ayss ayl **noo**mayroa dayl **bway**loa
What time do we arrive?	¿A qué hora llegamos?	ah kay **oa**rah yay**gah**moass
I'd like to ... my reservation on flight no ...	Quisiera ... mi reservación para el vuelo ...	kee**ssyay**rah ... mee rayssayrbah**ssyoan** pahrah ayl **bway**loa
cancel	anular	ahnoo**lahr**
change	cambiar	kahm**byahr**
confirm	confirmar	koanfeer**mahr**

LLEGADA ARRIVAL	**SALIDA** DEPARTURE

Train *Tren*

Because of the vast distances and often difficult terrain encountered in South America, railway services are in general less developed than bus and air services. However, Mexico, Argentina and Chile have extensive railway networks.

If you have time to travel around, the train can be a convenient means of transport and it certainly gives you a better feel for the country and the people.
(In some countries, e.g. Peru or Paraguay, service is often unreliable.)

The following list describes the various types of trains:

Tren de lujo [de larga distancia]
(trayn day **look**hoa [day **lahr**gah deestahnsyah])

Long-distance expresses. Trains are generally very comfortable and well equipped, with bars, sleeping-cars and lounges. Compartments, with reclining seats, are airconditioned.

Tren directo
(trayn dee**rayk**toa)

Fast train stopping at main stations.

Autovía
(outoa**bee**ah)

Fast inter-city trains. In Mexico, they resemble track-bound buses rather than trains, and space is limited (3 cars).

Tren local [ómnibus]
(trayn loa**kahl** [**oam**neebooss])

Train stopping at all stations. Not very comfortable.

PRIMERA CLASE FIRST CLASS	**SEGUNDA CLASE** SECOND CLASS

Coche cama
(**koa**chay **kah**mah)

Sleeping car with individual compartments (single or double) and washing facilities.

Coche comedor
(**koa**chay koamay**doar**)

Dining car.

To the railway station   *A la estación*

Where's the railway station?	¿Dónde está la estación de ferro-carril?	doanday aystah lah aystahssyoan day fayrroa-kahrreel
Taxi!	¡Taxi!	tahksee
Take me to the railway station.	Lléveme a la estación de ferrocarril.	yaybaymay ah lah aystahssyoan day fayrroakahrreel
What's the fare?	¿Cuál es la tarifa?	kwahl ayss lah tahreefah

ENTRADA	ENTRANCE
SALIDA	EXIT
ANDENES	TO THE PLATFORMS

Where's the ...?   *¿Dónde está ...?*

Where is/are the ...?	¿Dónde está/están ...?	doanday aystah/aystahn
booking office	la oficina de reservaciones	lah oafeesseenah day rayssayrbahssyoanayss
currency exchange office	la oficina de cambio	lah oafeesseenah day kahmbyoa
left-luggage office (baggage check)	el depósito de equipajes	ayl daypoasseetoa day aykeepahkhayss
lost property (lost and found) office	la oficina de objetos perdidos	lah oafeesseenah day oabkhaytoass payrdeedoass
luggage lockers	la consigna automática	lah koanseegnah owtoamahteekah
newsstand	el puesto de periódicos	ayl pwaystoa day payryoadeekoass
platform 7	el andén 7	ayl ahndayn 7
reservations office	la oficina de reservaciones	lah oafeesseenah day raysayrbahssyoanayss
restaurant	el restaurante	ayl raystowrahntay
ticket office	la boletería	lah boalaytayreeah
waiting room	la sala de espera	lah sahlah day ayspayrah
Where are the toilets?	¿Dónde están los servicios?	doanday aystahn loass sayrbeessyoass

TAXI, see page 21

Inquiries *Información*

When is the ... train to Monterrey?	¿Cuándo sale el ... tren para Monterrey?	kwahndoa sahlay ayl ... trayn pahrah moantayrray
first/last	primer/último	preemayr/oolteemoa
next	próximo	proakseemoa
What time does the train to Mérida leave?	¿A qué hora sale el tren para Mérida?	ah kay oarah sahlay ayl trayn pahrah mayreedah
What's the fare to Guadalajara?	¿Cuál es el precio a Guadalajara?	kwahl ayss ayl prayssyoa ah gwahdahlahkharah
Is it a through train?	¿Es un tren directo?	ayss oon trayn deerayktoa
Is there a connection to ...?	¿Hay empalme en ...?	igh aympahlmay ayn
Do I have to change trains?	¿Tengo que cambiar de tren?	tayngoa kay kahmbyahr day trayn
How long will the train stop in Mazatlán?	¿Cuánto tiempo para el tren en Mazatlán?	kwahntoa tyaympoa pahrah ayl trayn ayn mahssahtlahn
Is there sufficient time to change?	¿Hay tiempo suficiente para transbordar?	igh tyaympoa soofeessyayntay pahrah trahnsboardahr
Is the train running on time?	¿Saldrá el tren puntualmente?	sahldrah ayl trayn poontwahlmayntay
What time does the train arrive in Veracruz?	¿A qué hora llega el tren a Veracruz?	ah kay oarah yaygah ayl trayn ah bayrahkrooss
Is there a dining car/ sleeping-car on the train?	¿Hay coche comedor/ coche cama en el tren?	igh koachay koamaydoar/ koachay kahmah ayn ayl trayn
Does the train stop in León?	¿Para el tren en León?	pahrah ayl trayn ayn layoan
What platform does the train to Tula leave from?	¿De qué andén sale el tren para Tula?	day kay ahndayn sahlay ayl trayn pahrah tooʻlah
What platform does the train from Mexicali arrive at?	¿A qué andén llega el tren de Mexicali?	ah kay ahndayn yaygah ayl trayn day maykhee-kahlee
I'd like to buy a timetable.	Quisiera comprar un horario.	keessyayrah koamprahr oon oarahryoa

Es un tren directo.	It's a through train.
Tiene que transbordar en ...	You have to change at ...
Transborde en ... y tome un tren local.	Change at ... and get a local train.
El andén 7 está ...	Platform 7 is ...
allí/arriba a la izquierda/derecha	over there/upstairs on the left/right
Hay un tren para ... a las ...	There's a train to ... at ...
El tren sale del andén 8.	Your train will leave from platform 8.
Habrá un retraso de ... minutos.	There'll be a delay of ... minutes.
Primera clase al frente/en medio/al final.	First class at the front/in the middle/at the end.

Tickets *Billetes*

I want a ticket to Puebla.	Quiero un billete a Puebla.	kyayroa oon beeyaytay ah pwayblah
single (one-way)	ida	eedah
return (roundtrip)	ida y vuelta	eedah ee bwayltah
first/second class	primera/segunda clase	preemayrah/saygoondah klahssay
half price	media tarifa	maydyah tahreefah

Reservation *Reservación*

I want to reserve a ...	Quiero reservar ...	kyayroa rayssayrbahr
seat (by the window)	un asiento (al lado de la ventana)	oon ahssyayntoa (ahl lahdoa day lah bayntahnah)
berth in the sleeping car	una litera en el coche cama	oonah leetayrah ayn ayl koachay kahmah
upper	superior	soopayryoar
lower	inferior	eenfayryoar

All aboard *¡Al tren!*

Is this the platform for the train to Mexico City?	¿Es éste el andén para el tren de México?	ayss **ay**stay ayl ahn**dayn** pah**rah** ayl trayn day may**khee**koa
Is this the train to Oaxaca?	¿Es éste el tren para Oaxaca?	ayss **ay**stay ayl trayn pah**rah** oaah**khah**kah
Excuse me. May I get by?	Perdone. ¿Puedo pasar?	payr**doa**nay. **pway**doa pah**ssahr**
Is this seat taken?	¿Está ocupado este asiento?	ay**stah** oakoo**pah**doa **ay**stay ahss**syayn**toa

FUMADORES	NO FUMADORES
SMOKER	NON SMOKER

I think that's my seat.	Creo que éste es mi asiento.	**kray**oa kay **ay**stay ayss mee ahss**syayn**toa
Would you let me know before we get to Rosario?	¿Me puede avisar antes de llegar a Rosario?	may **pway**day ahbee**ssahr ahn**tayss day yay**gahr** ah roa**ssahr**yoa
What station is this?	¿Qué estación es ésta?	kay aystahss**syoan** ayss **ay**stah
How long does the train stop here?	¿Cuánto tiempo se para el tren aquí?	**kwahn**toa **tyaym**poa say pah**rah** ayl trayn ah**kee**
When do we get to Buenos Aires?	¿Cuándo llegamos a Buenos Aires?	**kwahn**doa yay**gah**moass ah **bway**noass **igh**rayss

Sleeping *En el coche cama*

Are there any free compartments in the sleeping-car?	¿Hay algún compartimiento libre en el coche cama?	igh ahl**goon** koampahrtee-**myayn**toa **lee**bray ayn ayl **koa**chay **kah**mah
Where's the sleeping-car?	¿Dónde está el coche cama?	**doan**day ay**stah** ayl **koa**chay **kah**mah
Where's my berth?	¿Dónde está mi litera?	**doan**day ay**stah** mee lee**tay**rah
I'd like a lower berth.	Quisiera una litera en la parte inferior.	kee**ssyay**rah **oo**nah lee**tay**rah ayn lah **pahr**tay eenfayr**yoar**

| Would you make up our beds? | ¿Nos podrá hacer usted la cama? | noass poadrah ahssayr oostayd lah kahmah |
| Would you wake me at 7 o'clock? | ¿Me podrá despertar usted a las 7? | may poadrah dayspayrtahr oostayd ah lahss 7 |

Eating *En el coche comedor*

Before taking a long journey by rail, ask whether your train has a dining car. Not all do, and even if yours is a night train, that's no guarantee. However, trolley service is common, and there may be a small bar.

| Where's the dining car? | ¿Dónde está el coche comedor? | doanday aystah ayl koachay koamaydoar |

Baggage and porters *Equipaje y cargadores*

Porter!	¡Cargador! [¡Maletero!]	kahrgahdoar [mahlaytayroa]
Can you help me with my luggage?	¿Puede usted ayudarme con mi equipaje?	pwayday oostayd ahyoodahrmay koan mee aykeepahkhay
Where are the luggage trolleys (carts)?	¿Dónde están los carritos de equipaje?	doanday aystahn loass kahrreetoass day aykeepahkhay
Where are the luggage lockers?	¿Dónde está la consigna automática?	doanday aystah lah koanseegnah owtoamahteekah
Where's the left-luggage office (baggage check)?	¿Dónde está el depósito de equipajes?	doanday aystah ayl daypoasseetoa day aykeepahkhayss
I'd like to leave my luggage, please.	Quisiera dejar mi equipaje, por favor.	keessyayrah daykhahr mee aykeepahkhay poar fahboar
I'd like to register (check) my luggage.	Quisiera facturar mi equipaje.	keessyayrah fahktoorahr mee aykeepahkhay

---

FACTURACION
REGISTERING (CHECKING) BAGGAGE

PORTERS, see also page 18

Coach (Long-distance bus) *Autocar*

Mexico, Chile and Argentina provide good regional coach services. In other Latin-American countries, travel is likely to be more of an adventure than a convenience. Service is categorized as deluxe, first, second and third class. First class usually means comfortable seats, toilet facilities, etc. Second and third class services are less comfortable but much cheaper. Some buses operate long-distance, stopping only at roadside restaurants for snacks and a stretch.

When's the next coach to …?	¿A qué hora sale el próximo autobús a …?	ah kay oarah sahlay ayl proakseemoa owtoabooss ah
Does this coach stop in …?	¿Este autobús se detiene en …?	aystay owtoabooss say daytyaynay ayn
How long does the journey (trip) take?	¿Cuánto tiempo dura el trayecto?	kwahntoa tyaympoa doorah ayl trahyayktoa

Bus *Autobús*

Public transport in the cities is provided mainly by buses and trolley-buses. Regular bus services operate between cities and smaller towns and villages. You generally pay as you enter. In major cities it may be worth your while to get a pass or a booklet of tickets.

If a bus carries the sign *completo,* it means that it's full.

I'd like a pass/ booklet of tickets.	Quisiera un pase/ abono de billetes.	keessyayrah oon pahssay ahboanoa day beeyaytayss
Where can I get a bus to the opera?	¿Dónde puedo tomar un autobús para el Teatro de la Opera?	doanday pwaydoa toamahr oon owtoabooss pahrah ayl tayahtroa day lah oapayrah
Which bus do I take to the Zócalo?	¿Qué autobús tengo que tomar para el Zócalo?	kay owtoabooss tayngoa kay toamahr pahrah ayl soakahloa
Where's the bus stop?	¿Dónde está la parada de autobús?	doanday aystah lah pahrahdah day owtoabooss

When is the ... bus to the university?	¿Cuándo sale el ... autobús para la universidad?	kwahndoa sahlay ayl ... owtoabooss pahrah lah ooneebayrseedahd
first/last/next	primer/último/ próximo	preemayr/oolteemoa/ proakseemoa
How much is the fare to ...?	¿Cuánto es el precio para ...?	kwahntoa ayss ayl prayssyoa pahrah
Do I have to change buses?	¿Tengo que cambiar de autobús?	tayngoa kay kahmbyahr day owtoabooss
How many bus stops are there to ...?	¿Cuántas paradas de autobús hay hasta ...?	kwahntahss pahrahdahss day owtoabooss igh ahstah
Will you tell me when to get off?	¿Me dirá cuándo tengo que bajarme?	may deerah kwahndoa tayngoa kay bahkhahrmay
I want to get off at the cathedral.	Quiero bajarme en la catedral.	kyayroa bahkhahrmay ayn lay kahtaydrahl

| PARADA DE AUTOBUS | REGULAR BUS STOP |
| PARADA FACULTATIVA | STOPS ON REQUEST |

Underground (subway) *Metro*

The metros in Mexico, Buenos Aires, Santiago and Caracas correspond to the London Underground or the New York Subway. The fare is the same, irrespective of the distance travelled. You can buy a booklet of tickets (*un abono*—oon ah**boa**noa) which will mean a modest saving on fares if you use the metro frequently. The Mexico metro runs from 5 a.m. till midnight (7 a.m. on Sundays).

Where's the nearest underground station?	¿Dónde está la estación de Metro más cercana?	doanday aystah lah aystahssyoan day maytroa mahss sayrkahnah
Does this train go to ...?	¿Va este tren a ...?	bah aystay trayn ah
Is the next station ...?	¿Es ... la próxima parada?	ayss ... lah proakseemah pahrahdah
Which line should I take for ...?	¿Qué línea tengo que tomar para ...?	kay leenayah tayngoa kay toamahr pahrah

Boat service   *Barcos*

When does the next boat to ... leave?	¿Cuándo sale el próximo barco para ...?	kwahndoa sahlay ayl proakseemoa bahrkoa pahrah
Where's the embarkation point?	¿Dónde está el lugar de embarco?	doanday aystah ayl loogahr day aymbahrkoa
How long does the crossing take?	¿Cuánto dura la travesía?	kwahntoa doorah lah trahbaysseeah
At which port(s) do we stop?	¿En qué puerto(s) nos detenemos?	ayn kay pwayrtoass noass daytaynaymoass
I'd like to take a tour of the harbour/ cruise.	Quisiera dar una vuelta por el puerto en barco/hacer un crucero.	keessyayrah dahr oonah bwayltah poar ayl pwayrtoa ayn bahrkoa/ahssayr oon kroossayroa
boat	el barco	ayl bahrkoa
cabin	el camarote	ayl kahmahroatay
single/double	sencillo/doble	saynseeyoa/doablay
deck	la cubierta	lah koobyayrtah
ferry	el transbordador	ayl trahnsboardahdoar
hydrofoil	el hidroplano	ayl eedroaplahnoa
life belt/boat	el cinturón/bote salvavidas	ayl seentooroan/boatay sahlbahbeedahss
ship	la embarcación	lah aymbahrkahssyoan

Other means of transport   *Otros medios de transporte*

A familiar vehicle on Mexico City streets is the *pesero* (payssayroa). It's a kind of collective taxi which picks up passengers and stops at various official points, like the buses. You can recognize these vehicles by the *colectivo* sign on the roof.

bicycle	la bicicleta	lah beesseeklaytah
cable car	el funicular	ayl fooneekoolahr
helicopter	el helicóptero	ayl ayleekoaptayroa
moped	el velomotor	ayl bayloamoatoar
motorbike	la motocicleta	lah moatoasseeklaytah
scooter	el escúter	ayl ayskootayr

Or perhaps you prefer:

to hitchhike	hacer auto-stop	ahssayr owtoastoap
to walk	caminar	kahmeenahr

Car *Automóvil*

In general, roads are good in Mexico, Chile, Venezuela and Argentina, and adequate in the other Latin-American countries. It is best to check with the local Automobile Club regarding road conditions. Some motorways (expressways) are subject to tolls *(la cuota)*.

Take a spare can of petrol with you.

Where's the nearest filling station?	¿Dónde está la gasolinera [estación de servicio] más cercana?	doanday aystah lah gahssoaleenayrah [aystahssyoan day sayrbeessyoa] mahss sayrkahnah
Full tank, please.	Llénelo, por favor.	yaynayloa poar fahboar
Give me ... litres of petrol (gasoline).	Déme ... litros de gasolina.	daymay ... leetroass day gahssoaleenah
super (premium)/ regular	super/normal	soopayr/noarmahl
unleaded/diesel	sin plomo/diesel	seen ploamoa/deessayl
Please check the ...	Revise ..., por favor.	raybeessay ... poar fahboar
battery	la batería	lah bahtayreeah
brake fluid	el líquido de frenos	ayl leekeedoa day fraynoass
oil/water	el aceite/el agua	ayl ahssaytay/ayl ahgwah
Would you check the tyre pressure?	¿Puede controlar la presión de las llantas [gomas]?	pwayday koantroalahr lah prayssyoan day lahss yahntahss [goamahss]
1.6 front, 1.8 rear.	1,6 las delanteras, 1,8 las traseras.	1 koamah 6 lahss daylahntayrahss. 1 koamah 8 lahss trahssayrahss
Please check the spare tyre, too.	Mire también la llanta de repuesto, por favor.	meeray tahmbyayn lah yahntah day raypwaystoa poar fahboar
Can you mend this puncture (fix this flat)?	¿Puede arreglar esta llanta desinflada?	pwayday ahrrayglahr aystah yahntah daysseenflahdah
Would you change the ..., please?	¿Puede cambiar ..., por favor?	pwayday kahmbyahr poar fahboar
bulb	la bombilla [el foco]	lah boambeeyah [ayl foakoa]

CAR HIRE, see page 20

fan belt	la correa del ventilador	lah koarrayah dayl baynteelahdoar
spark(ing) plugs	las bujías	lahss bookheeahss
tyre	la llanta [goma]	lah yahntah [goamah]
wipers	los limpiapara-brisas	loass leempyahpahrah-breessahss
Would you clean the windscreen (windshield)?	¿Quiere limpiar el parabrisas?	kyayray leempyahr ayl pahrahbreessahss

Asking the way—Street directions *Preguntas—Direcciones*

Can you tell me the way to ...?	¿Puede indicarme el camino a ...?	pwayday eendeekahrmay ayl kahmeenoa ah
How do I get to ...?	¿Cómo puedo ir a ...?	koamoa pwaydoa eer ah
Are we on the right road for ...?	¿Es ésta la calle que va a ...?	ayss aystah lah kahyay kay bah ah
How far is the next village?	¿A qué distancia está el próximo pueblo?	ah kay deestahnsyah aystah ayl proakseemoa pwaybloa
Is there a road with little traffic?	¿Hay una carretera con poco tráfico?	igh oonah kahrrraytayrah koan poakoa trahfeekoa
How far is it to ... from here?	¿Qué distancia hay de aquí a ...?	kay deestahnsyah igh day ahkee ah
Is there a motorway (expressway)?	¿Hay una autopista?	igh oonah owtoapeestah
How long does it take by car/on foot?	¿Cuánto se tarda en automóvil/a pie?	kwahntoa say tahrdah ayn owtoamoabeel/ah pyay
Can I drive to the centre of town?	¿Puede conducir hasta el centro de la ciudad?	pwayday koandoosseer ahstah ayl sayntroa day lah syoodahd
Can you tell me where ... is?	¿Puede decirme dónde está ...?	pwayday daysseermay doanday aystah
How can I find this address?	¿Cómo puedo encontrar esta dirección?	koamoa pwaydoa aynkoan-trahr aystah deerayksyoan
Where's this?	¿Dónde está esto?	doanday aystah aystoa
Can you show me on the map where I am?	¿Puede enseñarme en el mapa dónde estoy?	pwayday aynsaynyahrmay ayn ayl mahpah doanday aystoy

Se ha equivocado usted de carretera.	You're on the wrong road.
Siga derecho.	Go straight ahead.
frente a/detrás de ...	opposite/behind ...
junto a/después de ...	next to/after ...
norte/sur/este/oeste	north/south/east/west
Vaya al primer/segundo cruce.	Go to the first/second crossroads (intersection).
Gire a la izquierda al llegar al semáforo.	Turn left at the traffic lights.
Gire a la derecha en la próxima esquina.	Turn right at the next corner.
Tome la carretera a ...	Take the road to ...
Tiene que regresar hasta ...	You have to go back to ...
Siga la indicación "Lima".	Follow signs for Lima.

Parking *Estacionamiento*

In general, town centres have parking meters. Car park attendants operate in other busy zones. You'll also find multistorey garages. In some countries, you should remove detachable accessories and screen wipers when parking.

Where can I park?	¿Dónde puedo estacionarme?	doanday pwaydoa aystahssyoanahrmay
Is there a car park nearby?	¿Hay un estacionamiento cerca de aquí?	igh oon aystahssyoanahmyayntoa sayrkah day ahkee
How long can I park here?	¿Cuánto tiempo puedo estacionarme aquí?	kwahntoa tyaympoa pwaydoa aystahssyoanahrmay ahkee
What's the charge per hour?	¿Cuánto cuesta por hora?	kwahntoa kwaystah poar oarah
Do you have some change for the parking meter?	¿Tiene suelto para el parquímetro?	tyaynay swayltoa pahrah ayl pahrkeemaytroa

Breakdown—Road assistance   *Averías—Policía de carretera*

Where's the nearest garage?	¿Dónde está el taller de reparaciones más cercano?	doanday aystah ayl tahyayr day raypahrahssyoanayss mahss sayrkahnoa
Excuse me. My car has broken down.	Perdone. Mi carro se ha descompuesto.	payrdoanay. mee kahrroa say ah dayskoampwaystoa
May I use your phone?	¿Puedo usar su teléfono?	pwaydoa oossahr soo taylayfoanoa
I've had a break-down at ...	Tengo un automóvil descompuesto en ...	tayngoa oon owtoamoabeel dayskoampwaystoa ayn
Can you send a mechanic?	¿Puede mandar a un mecánico?	pwayday mahndahr ah oon maykahneekoa
My car won't start.	Mi carro no quiere arrancar.	mee kahrroa noa kyayray ahrrahnkahr
The battery is dead.	La batería está descargada.	lah bahtayreeah aystah dayskahrgahdah
I've run out of petrol (gasoline).	Se ha terminado la gasolina.	say ah tayrmeenahdoa lah gahssoaleenah
I have a flat tyre.	Tengo una llanta desinflada.	tayngoa oonah yahntah daysseenflahdah
The engine is over-heating.	El motor está dema-sido caliente.	ayl moatoar aystah day-mahssyahdoa kahlyayntay
There is something wrong with the ...	Hay algo estropeado en ...	igh ahlgoa aystroapayahdoa ayn
brakes	los frenos	loass fraynoass
carburettor	el carburador	ayl kahrboorahdoar
exhaust pipe	el tubo de escape	ayl tooboa day ayskahpay
radiator	el radiador	ayl rahdyahdoar
wheel	la rueda	lah rwaydah
Can you send a breakdown van (tow truck)?	¿Puede mandar una grúa?	pwayday mahndahr oonah grooah

Accident—Police   *Accidente—Policía*

Please call the police.	Llamen a la policía, por favor.	yahmayn ah lah poaleesseeah poar fahboar
There's been an accident. It's about 2 km. from ...	Ha habido un acci-dente. Está a unos 2 kilómetros de ...	ah ahbeedoa oon ahkseedayntay. aystah ah oonoass 2 keeloamaytroass day

Where is there a telephone?	¿Dónde hay un teléfono?	doanday igh oon taylayfoanoa
Call a doctor/an ambulance quickly.	Llame a un doctor/una ambulancia, rápidamente.	yahmay ah oon doaktoar/oonah ahmboolahnsyah rahpeedahmayntay
There are people injured.	Hay gente herida.	igh khayntay ayreedah
Here's my driving licence.	Aquí está mi licencia de manejar.	ahkee aystah mee leessaynsyah day mahnaykhahr
What's your name and address?	¿Cuál es su nombre y dirección?	kwahl ayss soo noambray ee deerayksyoan
What's your insurance company?	¿Cuál es su compañía de seguros?	kwahl ayss soo koampahñeeah day saygooroass

Road signs *Señales de circulación*

AUTOPISTA	Motorway (expressway)
BAJADA-FRENE CON MOTOR	Steep hill, use low gear
CALLE DETERIORADA	Uneven surface
CALLE ESTRECHA	Road narrows
CAMINO EN REPARACION	Road under repair
CEDA EL PASO	Give way (yield)
CRUCE DE CAMINOS	Crossroads
CRUCE DE PEATONES	Pedestrian crossing
CUIDADO	Caution
CUOTA	Toll
CURVA	Bend (curve)
DESPACIO	Slow down
DESVIACION	Diversion (detour)
ENCENDER LOS FAROS	Switch on headlights
ESCUELA	School
OBRAS	Road works
PARE	Stop
PASO A NIVEL	Level (railroad) crossing
PELIGRO	Danger
PRECAUCION	Caution
PROHIBIDO ADELANTAR	No overtaking (passing)
PROHIBIDO EL PASO	No entry
PROHIBIDO ESTACIONAR	No parking
SALIDA DE CAMIONES	Lorry (truck) exit
SIGA EN UNA FILA	Stay in one lane
TRAFICO EN UN SOLO SENTIDO	One-way street
VIRAJE PELIGROSO	Dangerous bend (curve)

Sightseeing

Where's the tourist office?	¿Dónde está la oficina de turismo?	doanday aystah lah oafee-sseenah day tooreesmoa
What are the main points of interest?	¿Cuáles son los principales puntos de interés?	kwahlayss soan loass preenseepahlayss poontoass day eentayrayss
We're here for ...	Estamos aquí ...	aystahmoass ahkee
only a few hours	sólo unas pocas horas	soaloa oonahss poakahss oarahss
a day	un día	oon deeah
a week	una semana	oonah saymahnah
Can you recommend a sightseeing tour/ an excursion?	¿Puede usted recomendarme un recorrido turístico/ una excursión?	pwayday oostayd ray-koamayndahrmay oon ray-koarreedoa tooreesteekoa/oonah aykskoorsyoan
Where's the point of departure?	¿Cuál es el lugar de salida?	kwahl ayss ayl loogahr day sahleedah
Will the bus pick us up at the hotel?	¿Nos recogerá el autobús en el hotel?	noass raykoakhayrah ayl owtoabooss ayn ayl oatayl
How much does the tour cost?	¿Cuánto cuesta el recorrido?	kwahntoa kwaystah ayl raykoarreedoa
What time does the tour start?	¿A qué hora empieza el recorrido?	ah kay oarah aympyayssah ayl raykoarreedoa
Is lunch included?	¿Está incluida la comida?	aystah eenklweedah lah koameedah
What time do we get back?	¿A qué hora volvemos?	ah kay oarah boalbaymoass
Do we have free time in ...?	¿Tenemos tiempo libre en ...?	taynaymoass tyaympoa leebray ayn
Is there an English-speaking guide?	¿Hay algún guía que hable inglés?	igh ahlgoon geeah kay ahblay eenglayss
I'd like to hire a private guide for ...	Quisiera un guía particular para ...	keessyayrah oon geeah pahrteekoolahr pahrah
half a day	medio día	maydyoa deeah
a full day	todo el día	toadoa ayl deeah

Where is/are the ...?	¿Dónde está/ están ...?	doanday aystah/ aystahn
abbey	la abadía	lah ahbahdeeah
artists' quarter	el barrio de los artistas	ayl bahrryoa day loass ahrteestahss
botanical gardens	el jardín botánico	ayl khahrdeen boatahneekoa
building	el edificio	ayl aydeefeessyoa
business district	el barrio comercial	ayl bahrryoa koamayrsyahl
castle	el castillo	ayl kahsteeyoa
cathedral	la catedral	lah kahtaydrahl
cave	la cueva	lah kwaybah
cemetery	el cementerio	ayl saymayntayryoa
chapel	la capilla	lah kahpeeyah
church	la iglesia	lah eeglayssyah
city centre	el centro (de la ciudad)	ayl sayntroa (day lah syoodahd)
concert hall	la sala de conciertos	lah sahlah day koan- syayrtoass
convent	el convento	ayl koanbayntoa
court house	el palacio de justicia	ayl pahlahssyoa day khoosteessyah
downtown area	el centro (de la ciudad)	ayl sayntroa (day lah syoodahd)
exhibition	la exhibición	lah aykseebeessyoan
factory	la fábrica	lah fahbreekah
fair	la feria	lah fayryah
flea market	el mercado de ocasiones	ayl mayrkahdoa day oakahssyoanayss
fortress	la fortaleza	lah foartahlayssah
fountain	la fuente	lah fwayntay
gardens	los jardines públicos	loass khahrdeenayss poobleekoass
harbour	el puerto	ayl pwayrtoa
market	el mercado	ayl mayrkahdoa
memorial	el monumento	ayl moanoomayntoa
monastery	el monasterio	ayl moanahstayryoa
monument	el monumento	ayl moanoomayntoa
museum	el museo	ayl moossayoa
old town	la ciudad vieja	lah syoodahd byaykhah
opera house	el teatro de la ópera	ayl tayahtroa day lah oapayrah
palace	el palacio	ayl pahlahssyoa
park	el parque	ayl pahrkay
parliament building	el parlamento	ayl pahrlahmayntoa
planetarium	el planetario	ayl plahnaytahryoa
ruins	las ruinas	lahss rweenahss

shopping area	la zona de tiendas	lah soanah day tyayndahss
square	la plaza	lah plahssah
stadium	el estadio	ayl aystahdyoa
statue	la estatua	lah aystahtwah
stock exchange	la bolsa	lah boalsah
theatre	el teatro	ayl tayahtroa
tomb	la tumba	lah toombah
tower	la torre	lah toarray
town hall	el ayuntamiento [palacio de gobierno]	ayl ahyoontahmyayntoa [pahlahssyoa day goabyayrnoa]
university	la universidad	lah ooneebayrseedahd
zoo	el zoológico	ayl soaloakheekoa

Admission *Entrada*

Is ... open on Sundays?	¿Está abierto(a) ... los domingos?	aystah ahbyayrtoa(ah) ... loass doameengoass
What are the opening hours?	¿Cuáles son las horas de apertura?	kwahlayss soan lahss oarahss day ahpayrtoorah
When does it close?	¿Cuándo cierran?	kwahndoa syayrrahn
How much is the entrance fee?	¿Cuánto vale la entrada?	kwahntoa bahlay lah ayntrahdah
Is there any reduction for ...?	¿Hay alguna reducción para ...?	igh ahlgoonah raydooksyoan pahrah
children	niños	neeñoass
the disabled	incapacitados	eenkahpahsseetahdoass
groups	grupos	groopoass
pensioners	jubilados	khoobeelahdoass
students	estudiantes	aystoodyahntayss
Have you a guide-book (in English)?	¿Tiene usted una guía (en inglés)?	tyaynay oostayd oonah geeah (ayn eenglayss)
Can I buy a catalogue?	¿Puedo comprar un catálogo?	pwaydoa koamprahr oon kahtahloagoa
Is it all right to take pictures?	¿Se pueden tomar fotografías?	say pwaydayn toamahr foatoagrahfeeahss

---

| **ENTRADA LIBRE** | ADMISSION FREE |
| **PROHIBIDO TOMAR FOTOGRAFIAS** | NO CAMERAS ALLOWED |

Who — What — When? ¿Quién — Qué — Cuándo?

What's that building?	¿Qué es ese edificio?	kay ayss ayssay aydeefeessyoa
Who was the ...?	¿Quién fue el ...?	kyayn fway ayl
architect	arquitecto	ahrkeetayktoa
artist	artista	ahrteestah
painter	pintor	peentoar
sculptor	escultor	ayskooltoar
Who built it?	¿Quién lo construyó?	kyayn loa koanstrooyoa
Who painted that picture?	¿Quién pintó ese cuadro?	kyayn peentoa ayssay kwahdroa
When did he live?	¿En qué época vivió?	ayn kay aypoakah beebyoa
When was it built?	¿Cuándo se construyó?	kwahndoa say koanstrooyoa
Where's the house where ... lived?	¿Dónde está la casa en que vivió ...?	doanday aystah lah kahssah ayn kay beebyoa
We're interested in ...	Nos interesa(n) ...	noass eentayrayssah(n)
antiques	las antigüedades	lahss ahnteegwaydahdayss
archaeology	la arqueología	lah ahrkayoaloaakheeah
art	el arte	ayl ahrtay
botany	la botánica	lah boatahneekah
ceramics	la cerámica	lah sayrahmeekah
coins	las monedas	lahss moanaydahss
fine arts	las bellas artes	lahss bayyahss ahrtayss
furniture	los muebles	loass mwayblayss
geology	la geología	lah khayoaloaakheeah
handicrafts	la artesanía	lah ahrtayssahneeah
history	la historia	lah eestoaryah
medicine	la medicina	lah maydeesseenah
music	la música	lah moosseekah
natural history	la historia natural	lah eestoaryah nahtoorahl
ornithology	la ornitología	lah oarneetoaloaakheeah
painting	la pintura	lah peentoorah
pottery	la cerámica	lah sayrahmeekah
religion	la religión	lah rayleekhyoan
sculpture	la escultura	lah ayskooltoorah
zoology	la zoología	lah soaloaakheeah
Where's the ... department?	¿Dónde está el departamento de ...?	doanday aystah ayl daypahrtahmayntoa day

It's ...	Es ...	ayss
amazing	asombroso	ahssoambroassoa
awful	horrible	oarreeblay
beautiful	hermoso	ayrmoassoa
gloomy	lúgubre	loogoobray
impressive	impresionante	eemprayssyoanahntay
interesting	interesante	eentayrayssahntay
magnificent	magnífico	mahgneefeekoa
nice	bonito	boaneetoa
pretty	lindo	leendoa
strange	extraño	aykstrahñoa
superb	soberbio	soabayrbyoa
terrifying	aterrador	ahtayrrahdoar
tremendous	tremendo	traymayndoa
ugly	feo	fayoa

Religious services *Servicios religiosos*

Most churches and cathedrals are open to the public, except of course when a service is in progress.

In certain areas, women should still cover their heads when entering a church. Shorts and backless dresses should not be worn. If you're interested in taking pictures, get permission first.

Is there a ... near here?	¿Hay una ... cerca de aquí?	igh oonah ... sayrkah day ahkee
Catholic church	iglesia católica	eeglayssyah kahtoaleekah
Protestant church	iglesia protestante	eeglayssyah proataystahntay
synagogue	sinagoga	seenahgoagah
At what time is ...?	¿A qué hora hay ...?	ah kay oarah igh
mass/the service	misa/oficio	meessah/oafeessyoa
Where can I find a ... who speaks English?	¿Dónde puedo encontrar un ... que hable inglés?	doanday pwaydoa aynkoan-trahr oon ... kay ahblay eenglayss
priest/minister rabbi	sacerdote/ministro [pastor]/rabino	sahssayrdoatay/mee-neestroa [pahstoar]/ rahbeenoa
I'd like to visit the church.	Quisiera visitar la iglesia.	keessyayrah beesseetahr lah eeglayssyah

In the countryside *En el campo*

Is there a scenic route to ...?	¿Hay una carretera panorámica a ...?	igh oonah kahrraytayrah pahnoarahmeekah ah
How far is it to ...?	¿Qué distancia hay hasta ...?	kay deestahnsyah igh ahstah
Can we walk?	¿Podemos ir a pie?	poadaymoass eer ah pyay
How high is that mountain?	¿Qué altura tiene esa montaña?	kay ahltoorah tyaynay ayssah moantahñah
What's the name of that ...?	¿Cómo se llama ...?	koamoa say yahmah
animal/bird	ese animal/ese pájaro	ayssay ahneemahl/ ayssay pahkhahroa
flower/tree	esa flor/ese árbol	ayssah floar/ayssay ahrboal

Landmarks *Puntos de referencia*

bridge	el puente	ayl pwayntay
cliff	el acantilado	ayl ahkahnteelahdoa
farm	el estuario	ayl aystwahryoa
field	el campo	ayl kahmpoa
footpath	el sendero	ayl sayndayroa
forest	el bosque	ayl boaskay
garden	el jardín	ayl khahrdeen
hill	la colina	lah koaleenah
house	la casa	lah kahssah
lake	el lago	ayl lahgoa
meadow	el prado	ayl prahdoa
mountain	la montaña	lah moantahñah
(mountain) pass	el puerto	ayl pwayrtoa
path	el camino	ayl kahmeenoa
peak	el pico	ayl peekoa
pond	el estanque	ayl aystahnkay
river	el río	ayl reeoa
road	la carretera	lah kahrraytayrah
sea	el mar	ayl mahr
spring	el manantial	ayl mahnahntyahl
valley	el valle	ayl bahyay
village	el pueblo	ayl pwaybloa
vineyard	el viñedo	ayl beeñaydoa
wall	el muro	ayl mooroa
waterfall	la cascada	lah kahskahdah
wood	el bosque	ayl boaskay

ASKING THE WAY, see page 76

Visitas turísticas

Relaxing

Cinema (movies) — Theatre   *Cine — teatro*

You can find out what's playing from newspapers and entertainment guides.

Cinema performances are usually continuous. Most American and British films are dubbed. However, some cinemas show films in the original version with Spanish subtitles.

What's on at the cinema tonight?	¿Qué dan en el cine esta noche?	kay dahn ayn ayl seenay aystah noachay
What's playing at the ... Theatre?	¿Qué dan en el Teatro ...?	kay dahn ayn ayl tayahtroa
What sort of play is it?	¿Qué clase de pieza es?	kay klahssay day pyayssah ayss
Who's it by?	¿De quién es?	day kyayn ayss
Can you recommend (a) ...?	¿Puede usted recomendarme ...?	pwayday oostayd raykoamayndahrmay
good film	una buena película	oonah bwaynah payleekoolah
comedy	una comedia	oonah koamaydyah
musical	una comedia musical	oonah koamaydyah moosseekahl
Where's that new film by ... being shown?	¿Dónde dan esa nueva película de ...?	doanday dahn ayssah nwaybah payleekoolah day
Who's in it?	¿Quiénes son los artistas?	kyaynayss soan loass ahrteestahss
Who's playing the lead?	¿Quién es el/la protagonista?	kyayn ayss ayl/lah proatahgoaneestah
Who's the director?	¿Quién es el director?	kyayn ayss ayl deerayktoar
At which theatre is that new play by ... being performed?	¿En qué teatro dan esa nueva pieza de ...?	ayn kay tayahtroa dahn ayssah nwaybah pyayssah day
Is there a sound-and-light show?	¿Hay un espectáculo "luz y sonido"?	igh oon ayspayktahkooloa looss ee soaneedoa

What time does it begin?	¿A qué hora empieza?	ah kay oarah aympyayssah
Are there any seats for tonight?	¿Quedan localidades para esta noche?	kaydahn loakahleedahdayss pahrah aystah noachay
How much are the seats?	¿Cuánto cuestan las localidades?	kwahntoa kwaystahn lahss loakahleedahdayss
I'd like to reserve 2 seats for the show on Friday evening.	Quiero reservar 2 localidades para la función del viernes por la noche.	kyayroa raysayrbahr 2 loakahleedahdayss pahrah lah foonsyoan dayl byayrnayss poar lah noachay
Can I have a ticket for the matinée on Tuesday?	¿Puede usted darme una entrada para la función de tarde del martes?	pwayday oostayd dahrmay oonah ayntrahdah pahrah lah foonsyoan day tahrday dayl mahrtayss
I'd like a seat in the stalls (orchestra).	Quiero una localidad de luneta [platea].	kyayroa oonah loakahleedahd day loonaytah [plahtayah]
Not too far back.	No muy atrás.	noa mwee ahtrahss
Somewhere in the middle.	En algún lugar en el medio.	ayn ahlgoon loogahr ayn ayl maydyoa
How much are the seats in the circle (mezzanine)?	¿Cuánto cuestan las localidades de la galería [balcón]?	kwahntoa kwaystahn lahss loakahleedahdayss day lah gahlayreeah [bahlkoan]
May I have a programme, please?	¿Me da un programa, por favor?	may dah oon proagrahmah poar fahboar
Where's the cloakroom?	¿Dónde está el guardarropa?	doanday aystah ayl gwahrdahrroapah

---

Lo siento, está completo.	I'm sorry, we're sold out.
Sólo quedan algunas localidades de galería [balcón].	There are only a few seats left in the circle (mezzanine).
¿Me enseña su entrada?	May I see your ticket?
Aquí está su asiento.	This is your seat.

DAYS OF THE WEEK, see page 151

Opera—Ballet—Concert   *Opera—Ballet—Concierto*

Can you recommend a ...?	¿Puede usted recomendarme ...?	pwayday oostayd raykoamayndahrmay
ballet	un ballet	oon bahlayt
concert	un concierto	oon koansyayrtoa
opera	una ópera	oonah oapayrah
operetta	una opereta	oonah oapayraytah
Where's the opera house/the concert hall?	¿Dónde está el Teatro de la Opera/la Sala de Conciertos?	doanday aystah ayl tayahtroa day lah oapayrah/lah sahlah day koansyayrtoass
What's on at the opera tonight?	¿Qué ópera hay esta noche?	kay oapayrah igh aystah noachay
Who's singing/ dancing?	¿Quién canta/baila?	kyayn kahntah/bighlah
Which orchestra is playing?	¿Qué orquesta toca?	kay oarkaystah toakah
What are they playing?	¿Qué tocan?	kay toakahn
Who's the conductor/ soloist?	¿Quién es el director/ el/la solista?	kyayn ayss ayl deerayktoar/ ayl/lah soaleestah

Nightclubs   *Centros nocturnos*

Can you recommend a good nightclub?	¿Puede recomendarme un buen centro nocturno?	pwayday raykoamayndahrmay oon bwayn sayntroa noaktoornoa
Is there a floor show?	¿Hay atracciones?	igh ahtrahksyoanayss
What time does the show start?	¿A qué hora empieza el espectáculo?	ah kay oarah aympyayssah ayl ayspayktahkooloa
Is evening dress required?	¿Se necesita traje de noche?	say nayssaysseetah trahkhay day noachay

Discos   *Discotecas*

Where can we go dancing?	¿Dónde podemos ir a bailar?	doanday poadaymoass eer ah bighlahr
Is there a discotheque in town?	¿Hay alguna discoteca en la ciudad?	igh ahlgoonah deeskoataykah ayn lah syoodahd
Would you like to dance?	¿Quiere usted bailar?	kyayray oostayd bighlahr

Sports *Deportes*

Among the most popular sports in Latin America are hunting, fishing, swimming, riding, golf and baseball.

Football (soccer) and *jai alai* (*frontón* or *pelota vasca*) are as popular in Latin America as bullfighting. *Jai alai* is similar to handball but instead of wearing a glove, the players carry a kind of curved wicker basket or scoop (*cesta*). The ball (*pelota*) is hard and covered in goatskin.

The *corrida* (literally "running of the bulls") will either fascinate or appal you. In some ways the spectacle resembles a ballet. There are colourful moments when the procession (*paseo*) arrives. The entry of the bull into the arena is a moment of high tension. The movements of cape and bullfighter are graceful and precise.

The *matador* and his team of assistants goad the bull so as to assess its reactions to the cape. A *picador* weakens the bull by piercing its neck muscles with a lance.

A *banderillero* then confronts the animal and thrusts three sets of barbed sticks between its shoulder blades. The crowd will be watching critically, weighing the fearlessness of bull and man, the *matador's* skill as he executes a series of dangerous passes, leading up to the final climax of the kill.

You'll be asked whether you want a seat in the sun or shade (*sol o sombra*—soal oa **soam**brah). Be sure to specify *sombra,* for the sun is hot. Rent a cushion (*almohadilla*—ahlmoaah**dee**yah) for the hard concrete stands.

Charreada is the Mexican equivalent of an American rodeo. It can be seen mostly on Sunday mornings in Mexico City at the *Rancho del Charro.*

Even snow fans will find a place to go. There are wintersports resorts in Chile and Argentina (notably San Carlos de Bariloche).

I'd like to see a bullfight.	**Quisiera ver una corrida.**	keessyayrah bayr oonah koarreedah
Is there a football (soccer) match anywhere this Saturday?	**¿Hay algún partido de fútbol este sábado?**	igh ahlgoon pahrteedoa day footboal aystay sahbahdoa
Which teams are playing?	**¿Qué equipos juegan?**	kay aykeepoass khwaygahn
What's the admission charge?	**¿Cuánto cuesta la entrada?**	kwahntoa kwaystah lah ayntrahdah

basketball	**el baloncesto**	ayl bahloansaystoa
boxing	**el boxeo**	ayl boaksayoa
football (soccer)	**el fútbol**	ayl footboal
(horseback) riding	**la equitación**	lah aykeetahssyoan
skiing	**el esquí**	ayl ayskee
swimming	**la natación**	lah nahtahssyoan
tennis	**el tenis**	ayl tayneess
volleyball	**el balonvolea**	ayl bahloanboalayah

Where's the nearest golf course?	**¿Dónde está el campo de golf más cercano?**	doanday aystah ayl kahmpoa day goalf mahss sayrkahnoa
Where are the tennis courts?	**¿Dónde están las pistas de tenis?**	doanday aystahn lahss peestahss day tayneess
Can I hire (rent) rackets?	**¿Puedo alquilar raquetas?**	pwaydoa ahlkeelahr rahkaytahss
Is there any good fishing/hunting around here?	**¿Hay un buen lugar para pescar/cazar cerca de aquí?**	igh oon bwayn loogahr pahrah payskahr/kahssahr sayrkah day ahkee
Do I need a permit?	**¿Necesito un permiso?**	nayssaysseetoa oon payrmeessoa
Can one swim in the lake/river?	**¿Se puede nadar en el lago/río?**	say pwayday nahdahr ayn ayl lahgoa/reeoa
Is there a swimming pool here?	**¿Hay una piscina [alberca] por aquí?**	igh oonah peesseenah [ahlbayrkah] poar ahkee
Is it open-air or indoor?	**¿Está al descubierto o es cubierta?**	aystah ahl dayskoobyayrtoa oa ayss koobyayrtah

Is it heated?	¿Tiene calefacción?	tyaynay kahlayfahksyoan
What's the temperature of the water?	¿Cuál es la temperatura del agua?	kwahl ayss lah taympayrahtoorah dayl ahgwah
Is there a sandy beach?	¿Hay una playa de arena?	igh oonah plahyah day ahraynah

On the beach *En la playa*

Is it safe for swimming?	¿Se puede nadar sin peligro?	say pwayday nahdahr seen payleegroa
Is there a lifeguard?	¿Hay vigilante?	igh beekheelahntay
Is it safe for children?	¿Es segura para niños?	ayss saygoorah pahrah neeñoass
There are some big waves.	Hay algunas olas muy grandes.	igh ahlgoonahss oalahss mwee grahndayss
Are there any dangerous currents?	¿Hay alguna corriente peligrosa?	igh ahlgoonah koarryayntay payleegroassah
What time is high tide/low tide?	¿A qué hora es la marea alta/baja?	ah kay oarah ayss lah mahrayah ahltah/bahkhah
I'd like to hire a/an/some ...	Quiero alquilar ...	kyayroa ahlkeelahr
bathing hut (cabana)	una cabina	oonah kahbeenah
deckchair	una silla de lona	oonah seeyah day loanah
motorboat	una lancha	oonah lahnchah
rowing boat	una barca de remos	oonah bahrkah day raymoass
sailing boat	un velero	oon baylayroa
skin-diving equipment	un equipo de buceo	oon aykeepoa day boossayoa
sunshade (umbrella)	una sombrilla	oonah soambreeyah
surfboard	una tabla de surf	oonah tahblah day soorf
waterskis	unos esquíes acuáticos	oonoass ayskeeayss ahkwahteekoass
windsurfer	un patín de vela	oon pahteen day baylah

In the mountains *En la montaña*

I'd like to ski.	Quisiera esquiar.	keessyayrah ayskyahr
Are there any ski lifts?	¿Hay telesquí?	igh taylayskee
I'd like to hire skiing equipment.	Quisiera alquilar un equipo de esquí.	keessyayrah ahlkeelahr oon aykeepoa day ayskee

Making friends

Introductions *Presentaciones*

May I introduce ...?	**Quiero presentarle a ...**	kyayroa prayssayntahrlay ah
John, this is ...	**Juan, te presento a ...**	khwahn tay prayssayntoa ah
My name is ...	**Me llamo ...**	may yahmoa
Pleased to meet you.	**Tanto gusto.**	tahntoa goostoa
What's your name?	**¿Cómo se llama?**	koamoa say yahmah
How are you?	**¿Cómo está usted?**	koamoa aystah oostayd
Fine, thanks. And you?	**Bien, gracias. ¿Y usted?**	byayn grahssyahss. ee oostayd

Follow up *Continuación*

How long have you been here?	**¿Cuánto tiempo lleva usted aquí?**	kwahntoa tyaympoa yaybah oostayd ahkee
We've been here a week.	**Llevamos aquí una semana.**	yaybahmoass ahkee oonah saymahnah
Is this your first visit?	**¿Es la primera vez que viene?**	ayss lah preemayrah bayss kay byaynay
No, we came here last year.	**No, vinimos el año pasado.**	noa beeneemoass ayl ahñoa pahssahdoa
Are you enjoying your stay?	**¿Le gusta aquí?**	lay goostah ahkee
Yes, I like it very much.	**Sí, me gusta mucho.**	see may goostah moochoa
I like the land-scape/region a lot.	**Me gusta mucho el paisaje/la región.**	may goostah moochoa ayl paheessahkhay/lah raykhyoan
What do you think of the country/people?	**¿Qué opina usted del país/de la gente?**	kay oapeenah oostayd dayl paheess/day lah khayntay
Where do you come from?	**¿De dónde es usted?**	day doanday ayss oostayd
I'm from ...	**Soy de ...**	soy day
What nationality are you?	**¿Qué nacionalidad tiene?**	kay nahssyoanahleedahd tyaynay

COUNTRIES, see page 146

I'm ...	Soy ...	soy
American	americano(a)	ahmayreekahnoa(ah)
British	británico(a)	breetahneekoa(ah)
Canadian	canadiense	kahnahdyaynsay
English	inglés(a)	eenglayss(ah)
Irish	irlandés(a)	eerlahndayss(ah)
Where are you staying?	¿Dónde se hospeda?	doanday say oaspaydah
Are you on your own?	¿Ha venido usted solo(a)?	ah bayneedoa oostayd soaloa(ah)
I'm with my ...	Estoy con ...	aystoy koan
wife	mi mujer	mee mookhayr
husband	mi marido	mee mahreedoa
family	mi familia	mee fahmeelyah
parents	mis padres	meess pahdrayss
boyfriend/girlfriend	mi amigo/amiga	mee ahmeegoa/ahmeegah

father/mother	el padre/la madre	ayl pahdray/lah mahdray
son/daughter	el hijo/la hija	ayl eekhoa/lah eekhah
brother/sister	el hermano/la hermana	ayl ayrmahnoa/lah ayrmahnah
uncle/aunt	el tío/la tía	ayl teeoa/lah teeah
nephew/niece	el sobrino/la sobrina	ayl soabreenoa/lah soabreenah
cousin	el primo/la prima	ayl preemoa/lah preemah

Are you married/ single?	¿Está casado(a)/ soltero(a)?	aystah kahsahdoa(ah)/ soaltayroa(ah)
Do you have children?	¿Tiene hijos?	tyaynay eekhoass
What do you do?	¿Cuál es su ocupación?	kwahl ayss soo oakoopahssyoan
I'm a student.	Soy estudiante.	soy aystoodyahntay
What are you studying?	¿Qué estudia usted?	kay aystoodyah oostayd
I'm here on a business trip.	Estoy aquí en viaje de negocios.	aystoy ahkee ayn byahkhay day naygoassyoass
Do you travel a lot?	¿Viaja mucho?	byahkhah moochoa
Do you play cards/ chess?	¿Juega usted a las cartas/al ajedrez?	khwaygah oostayd ah lahss kahrtahss/ahl ahkhaydrayss

The weather *El tiempo*

What a lovely day!	**¡Qué día tan hermoso!**	kay **dee**ah tahn **ayr**moassoa
What awful weather!	**¡Qué tiempo tan malo!**	kay **tyaym**poa tahn **mah**loa
Isn't it cold/ hot today?	**¿Qué frío/calor hace hoy! ¿Verdad?**	kay **free**oa/kah**loar** ahssay oy. bayr**dah**d
Is it usually as warm as this?	**¿Hace normalmente este calor?**	ahssay noarmahl**mayn**tay **ays**tay kah**loar**
Do you think it's going to ... tomorrow?	**¿Cree usted que ... mañana?**	kray oo**stayd** kay ... mah**ñah**nah
be a nice day rain/snow	**hará buen tiempo lloverá/nevará**	ah**rah** bwayn **tyaym**poa yoabay**rah**/naybah**rah**
What is the weather forecast?	**¿Qué dice el boletín meteoro-lógico?**	kay **dee**ssay ayl boalay**teen** maytayoaroa-loa**khee**koa

cloud	**la nube**	lah **noo**bay
earthquake	**el terremoto**	ayl tayr**ray**moatoa
fog	**la niebla**	lah **nyay**blah
frost	**la helada**	lah ay**lah**dah
hurricane	**el huracán**	ayl oora**kahn**
lightning	**el relámpago [rayo]**	ayl ray**lahm**pahgoa [**rah**yoa]
moon	**la luna**	lah **loo**nah
rain	**la lluvia**	lah **yoo**byah
sky	**el cielo**	ayl **syay**loa
snow	**la nieve**	lah **nyay**bay
star	**la estrella**	lah ays**tray**yah
sun	**el sol**	ayl soal
thunder	**el trueno**	ayl **trway**noa
thunderstorm	**la tormenta**	lah toar**mayn**tah
wind	**el viento**	ayl **byayn**toa

Invitations *Invitaciones*

Would you like to have dinner with us on ...?	**¿Quiere acompañar-nos a cenar el ...?**	**kyay**ray ahkoampah**ñahr**noass ah say**nahr** ayl
May I invite you for lunch?	**¿Puedo invitarlo(a) a comer?**	**pway**doa eenbee**tahr**loa(ah) ah koa**mayr**

DAYS OF THE WEEK, see page 151

Can you come round for a drink this evening?	¿Puede usted venir a tomar una copa esta noche?	pwayday oostayd bayneer ah toamahr oonah koapah aystah noachay
There's a party. Are you coming?	Hay una fiesta. ¿Quiere usted venir?	igh oonah fyaysta kyayray oostayd bayneer
That's very kind of you.	Es usted muy amable.	ayss oostayd mwee ahmahblay
Great. I'd love to come.	¡Estupendo! Me encantaría ir.	aystoopayndoa. may aynkahntahreeah eer
What time shall we come?	¿A qué hora vamos?	ah kay oarah bahmoass
May I bring a friend?	¿Puedo llevar a un(a) amigo(a)?	pwaydoa yaybahr ah oon(ah) ahmeegoa(ah)
I'm afraid we have to leave now.	Lo siento, tenemos que irnos.	loa syayntoa taynaymoass kay eernoass
Next time you must come to visit us.	Otro día tienen que venir a vernos.	oatroa deeah tyaynayn kay bayneer ah bayrnoass
Thanks for the evening. It was great.	Muchas gracias por la velada. Ha sido estupenda.	moochahss grahssyahss poar lah baylahdah. ah seedoa aystoopayndah

Dating *Citas*

Do you mind if I smoke?	¿Le molesta si fumo?	lay moalaystah see foomoa
Would you like a cigarette?	¿Quiere usted un cigarrillo?	kyayray oostayd oon seegahrreeyoa
Do you have a light, please?	¿Tiene usted fuego [lumbre], por favor?	tyaynay oostayd fwaygoa [loombray] poar fahboar
Why are you laughing?	¿Por qué se ríe?	poar kay say reeay
Is my Spanish that bad?	¿Es tan malo mi español?	ayss tahn mahloa mee ayspahñoal
Do you mind if I sit down here?	¿Le molesta si me siento aquí?	lay moalaystah see may syayntoa ahkee
Can I get you a drink?	¿Quiere usted beber algo?	kyayray oostayd baybayr ahlgoa
Are you waiting for someone?	¿Está usted esperando a alguien?	aystah oostayd ayspayrahndoa ah ahlgyayn

Are you free this evening?	¿Está usted libre esta noche?	aystah oostayd leebray aystah noachay
Would you like to go out with me tonight?	¿Quisiera usted salir conmigo esta noche?	keessyayrah oostayd sahleer koanmeegoa aystah noachay
Would you like to go dancing?	¿Quisiera usted ir a bailar?	keessyayrah oostayd eer ah bighlahr
I know a good discotheque.	Conozco una buena discoteca.	koanoaskoa oonah bwaynah deeskoataykah
Shall we go to the cinema (movies)?	¿Quiere que vayamos al cine?	kyayray kay bahyahmoass ahl seenay
Would you like to go for a drive?	¿Le gustaría dar un paseo en coche?	lay goostahreeah dahr oon pahssayoa ayn koachay
Where shall we meet?	¿Dónde nos citamos?	doanday noass seetahmoass
I'll pick you up at your hotel.	Lo (la) recogeré en su hotel.	loa (lah) raykoakhayray ayn soo oatayl
I'll call for you at 8.	Iré a recogerlo(a) a las 8.	eeray ah raykoakhayrloa(ah) ah lahss 8
May I take you home?	¿Puedo acompañarlo(a) hasta su casa?	pwaydoa ahkoampahñahrloa(ah) ahstah soo kahssah
Can I see you again tomorrow?	¿Puedo verlo(a) mañana?	pwaydoa bayrloa(ah) mahñahnah
I hope we'll meet again.	Espero que nos veremos otra vez.	ayspayroa kay noass bayraymoass oatrah bayss

... and you might answer:

I'd love to, thank you.	Me encantaría, gracias.	may aynkahntahreeah grahssyahss
Thank you, but I'm busy.	Gracias, pero estoy ocupado(a).	grahssyahss payroa aystoy oakoopahdoa(ah)
No, I'm not interested, thank you.	No, no me interesa, gracias.	noa noa may eentayrayssah grahssyahss
Leave me alone, please!	¡Déjeme tranquilo(a), por favor!	daykhaymay trahnkeeloa(ah) poar fahboar
Thank you, it's been a wonderful evening.	Gracias, ha sido una velada maravillosa.	grahssyahss ah seedoa oonah baylahdah mahrahbeeyoassah
I've enjoyed myself.	Me he divertido mucho.	may ay deebayrteedoa moochoa

Shopping Guide

This shopping guide is designed to help you find what you want with ease, accuracy and speed. It features:

1. A list of all major shops, stores and services (p. 98)
2. Some general expressions required when shopping to allow you to be specific and selective (p. 100)
3. Full details of the shops and services most likely to concern you. Here you'll find advice, alphabetical lists of items and conversion charts listed under the headings below.

LAUNDRY, see page 29/HAIRDRESSER'S, see page 30

Guía de compras

Shops, stores and services *Comercios y servicios*

In Mexico and most Latin-American countries, smaller shops are usually open from 9 a.m. to 1 p.m. and from 3 to 7 p.m. Monday to Saturday. Department stores normally open at 10 a.m. and do not close for lunch. Very few shops are open on Sundays or public holidays.

Where's the nearest ...?	¿Dónde está ... más cercano(a)?	doanday aystah ... mahss sayrkahnoa(ah)
antique shop	la tienda de antigüedades	lah tyayndah day ahnteegwaydahdayss
art gallery	la galería de arte	lah gahlayreeah day ahrtay
baker's	la panadería	lah pahnahdayreeah
bank	el banco	ayl bahnkoa
barber's	la barbería	lah bahrbayreeah
beauty salon	el salón de belleza	ayl sahloan day bayyayssah
bookshop	la librería	lah leebrayreeah
butcher's	la carnicería	lah kahrneessayreeah
cake shop	la pastelería	lah pahstaylayreeah
camera shop	la tienda de fotografía	lah tyayndah day foatoagrahfeeah
chemist's	la farmacia [droguería]	lah fahrmahssyah [droagayreeah]
confectioner's	la confitería	lah koanfeetayreeah)
dairy	la lechería	lah laychayreeah
delicatessen	la tienda de especialidades	lah tyayndah day ayspayssyahleedahdayss
dentist	el dentista	ayl daynteestah
department store	los grandes almacenes	loass grahndayss ahlmahssaynayss
drugstore	la farmacia	lah fahrmahssyah
dry cleaner's	la tintorería	lah teentoarayreeah
electrician	el electricista	ayl aylayktreesseestah
fishmonger's	la pescadería	lah payskahdayreeah
florist's	la florería	lah floarayreeah
furrier's	la peletería	lah paylaytayreeah
greengrocer's	la verdulería	lah bayrdoolayreeah
grocery	la tienda de abarrotes	lah tyayndah day ahbahrroatayss
hairdresser's (ladies/men)	la peluquería	lah paylookayreeah
hardware store	la ferretería	lah fayrraytayreeah
health food shop	la tienda de alimentos dietéticos	lah tyayndah day ahleemayntoass deeaytayteekoass

hospital	**el hospital**	ayl oaspee**tahl**
ironmonger's	**la ferretería**	lah fayrraytay**ree**ah
jeweller's	**la joyería**	lah khoayay**ree**ah
launderette	**la lavandería**	lah lahbahnday**ree**ah
laundry	**la lavandería**	lah lahbahnday**ree**ah
library	**la biblioteca**	lah beebleeoa**tay**kah
market	**el mercado**	ayl mayr**kah**doa
newsstand	**el quiosco de periódicos**	ayl **kyoas**koa day payr**ryo**adeekoass
optician	**el óptico**	ayl **oap**teekoa
pastry shop	**la pastelería**	lah pahstaylay**ree**ah
photographer	**el fotógrafo**	ayl foa**toa**grahfoa
police station	**la comisaría**	lah koameessah**ree**ah
post office	**la oficina de correos**	lah oafee**ssee**nah day koar**ra**yoass
shoemaker's (repairs)	**el zapatero**	ayl sahpah**tay**roa
shoe shop	**la zapatería**	lah sahpahtay**ree**ah
shopping centre	**el centro comercial**	ayl **sayn**troa koamayr**syahl**
souvenir shop	**la tienda de regalos**	lah **tyayn**dah day ray**gah**loass
sporting goods shop	**la tienda de artículos deportivos**	lah **tyayn**dah day ahrtee**koo**loass daypoar**tee**boass
stationer's	**la papelería**	lah pahpaylay**ree**ah
supermarket	**el supermercado**	ayl soopayrmayr**kah**doa
tailor's	**la sastrería**	lah sahstray**ree**ah
telegraph office	**la oficina de telégrafos**	lah oafee**ssee**nah day tay**lay**grahfoass
telephone office	**la oficina de teléfonos**	lah oafee**ssee**nah day tay**lay**foanoass
tobacconist's	**la tabaquería [el estanquillo]**	lah tahbahkay**ree**ah [ayl aystahn**kee**yoa]
toy shop	**la juguetería**	lah khoogaytay**ree**ah
travel agency	**la agencia de viajes**	lah ah**khayn**syah day **byah**khayss
vegetable store	**la verdulería**	lah bayrdoolay**ree**ah
veterinarian	**el veterinario**	ayl baytayree**nah**ryoa
watchmaker's	**la relojería**	lah rayloakhay**ree**ah
wine merchant	**la tienda de vinos**	lah **tyayn**dah day **bee**noass

ENTRADA	ENTRANCE
SALIDA	EXIT
SALIDA DE EMERGENCIA	EMERGENCY EXIT

General expressions *Expresiones generales*

Where? *¿Dónde?*

Where's there a good ...?	¿Dónde hay un(a) buen(a) ...?	doanday igh oon(ah) bwayn(ah)
Where can I find a ...?	¿Dónde puedo encontrar un(a) ...?	doanday pwaydoa aynkoantrahr oon(ah)
Where's the main shopping area?	¿Dónde está la zona de tiendas más importante?	doanday aystah lah soanah day tyayndahss mahss eempoartahntay
Is it far from here?	¿Está lejos de aquí?	aystah laykhoass day ahkee
How do I get there?	¿Cómo puedo llegar allí?	koamoa pwaydoa yaygahr ahyee

---

REBAJAS   SALE

Service *Servicio*

Can you help me?	¿Puede usted atenderme?	pwayday oostayd ahtayndayrmay
I'm just looking.	Estoy sólo mirando.	aystoy soaloa meerahndoa
Do you sell ...?	¿Vende usted ...?	baynday oostayd
I'd like ...	Quisiera ...	keessyayrah
Where's the ... department?	¿Dónde está el departamento de ...?	doanday aystah ayl daypahrtahmayntoa day
Where is the lift (elevator)/escalator?	¿Dónde está el elevador [ascensor]/la escalera mecánica?	doanday aystah ayl aylaybahdoar [ahssaynsoar]/lah ayskahlayrah maykahneekah
Where do I pay?	¿Dónde está la caja?	doanday aystah lah kahkhah

That one *Ese*

Can you show me ...?	¿Puede usted enseñarme ...?	pwayday oostayd aynsayñahrmay
this/that	esto/eso	aystoa/ayssoa
the one in the window/in the display case	el del aparador/de la vitrina	ayl dayl ahpahrahdoar/day lah beetreenah

Preference *Preferencias*

Can you show me some more?	¿**Puede usted enseñarme algo más?**	pwayday oostayd aynsayñahrmay ahlgoa mahss
Haven't you anything ...?	¿**No tiene usted algo ...?**	noa tyaynay oostayd ahlgoa
cheaper/better	**más barato/mejor**	mahss bahrahtoa/maykhoar
larger/smaller	**más grande/más pequeño**	mahss grahnday/mahss paykayñoa

big	**grande***	grahnday
cheap	**barato**	bahrahtoa
dark	**oscuro**	oaskooroa
good	**bueno**	bwaynoa
heavy	**pesado**	payssahdoa
large	**grande**	grahnday
light (weight)	**ligero**	leekhayroa
light (colour)	**claro**	klahroa
oval	**oval**	oabahl
rectangular	**rectangular**	rayktahngoolahr
round	**redondo**	raydoandoa
small	**pequeño**	paykayñoa
square	**cuadrado**	kwahdrahdoa
sturdy	**resistente**	rayssseestayntay

How much? *¿Cuánto?*

How much is this?	¿**Cuánto cuesta?**	kwahntoa kwaystah
How much are they?	¿**Cuánto cuestan?**	kwahntoa kwaystahn
I don't understand.	**No comprendo.**	noa koamprayndoa
Please write it down.	**Escríbalo, por favor.**	ayskreebahloa poar fahboar
I don't want anything too expensive.	**No quiero algo muy caro.**	noa kyayroa ahlgoa mwee kahroa
I don't want to spend more than ... pesos.	**No quiero gastar más de ... pesos.**	noa kyayroa gahstahr mahss day ... payssoass

* For feminine and plural forms, see grammar section page 159 (adjectives).

COLOURS, see page 113

Decision *Decisión*

It's not quite what I want.	**No es exacta-mente lo que quiero.**	noa ayss ayksahktah-mayntay loa kay kyayroa
No, I don't like it.	**No, no me gusta.**	noa noa may goostah
I'll take it.	**Me lo llevo.**	may loa yayboa

Ordering *Encargo*

Can you order it for me?	**¿Podría usted en-cargarlo para mí?**	poadreeah oostayd ayn-kahrgahrloa pahrah mee
How long will it take?	**¿Cuánto tardará?**	kwahntoa tahrdahrah

Delivery *Entrega*

I'll take it with me.	**Me lo llevo.**	may loa yayboa
Deliver it to the ... Hotel.	**Entréguelo al hotel ...**	ayntraygayloa ahl oatayl
Please send it to this address.	**Por favor, mánde-lo a esta dirección.**	poar fahboar mahndayloa ah aystah deerayksyoan
Will I have any difficulty with the customs?	**¿Tendré alguna dificultad con la aduana?**	tayndray ahlgoonah deefeekooltahd koan lah ahdwahnah

Paying *Pagar*

How much is it?	**¿Cuánto es?**	kwahntoa ayss
Can I pay by traveller's cheque?	**¿Puedo pagar con un cheque de viajero?**	pwaydoa pahgahr koan oon chaykay day byahkhayroa
Do you accept dollars/pounds?	**¿Acepta usted dólares/libras?**	ahssayptah oostayd doalahrayss/leebrahss
Do you accept credit cards?	**¿Acepta usted tarjetas de crédito?**	ahssayptah oostayd tahr-khaytahss day kraydeetoa
Do I have to pay the VAT (sales tax)?	**¿Tengo que pagar el IVA?**	tayngoa kay pahgahr ayl eebah
I think there's a mistake in the bill.	**Me parece que hay un error en la cuenta.**	may pahrayssay kay igh oon ayrroar ayn lah kwayntah

Anything else?   *¿Algo más?*

No, thanks, that's all.	No gracias, eso es todo.	noa grahssyahss ayssoa ayss toadoa
Yes, I'd like ...	Sí, quisiera ...	see keessyayrah
Show me ...	Enséñeme ...	aynsayñaymay
May I have a bag, please?	¿Puede darme una bolsa, por favor?	pwayday dahrmay oonah boalsah poar fahboar
Could you wrap it up for me, please?	¿Podría envolverlo, por favor?	poadreeah aynboalbayr-loa poar fahboar

Dissatisfied?   *¿Descontento?*

Can you exchange this, please?	¿Podría cambiar-me esto, por favor?	poadreeah kahmbyahrmay aystoa poar fahboar
I want to return this.	Quisiera devolver esto.	keessyayrah dayboalbayr aystoa
I'd like a refund. Here's the receipt.	Quisiera que me devolviesen el dinero. Aquí está el recibo.	keessyayrah kay may dayboalbyayssayn ayl deenayroa. ahkee aystah ayl raysseeboa

¿En qué puedo servirle?	Can I help you?
¿Qué quiere usted?	What would you like?
¿Qué ... quiere usted?	What ... would you like?
color/forma calidad/cantidad	colour/shape quality/quantity
Lo siento, no tenemos ninguno.	I'm sorry, we haven't any.
Se nos ha agotado.	We're out of stock.
¿Quiere usted que se lo encarguemos?	Shall we order it for you?
¿Se lo lleva o quiere que se lo mandemos?	Will you take it with you or shall we send it?
¿Algo más?	Anything else?
Son ... pesos, por favor.	That's ... pesos, please.
Allá está la caja.	The cash desk is over there.

Bookshop—Stationer's *Librería—Papelería*

In Latin America, bookshops and stationers' are usually separate shops, though the latter will often sell paperbacks. Newspapers and magazines are sold at newsstands.

Where's the nearest ...?	¿Dónde está ... más cercano(a)?	doanday aystah ... mahss sayrkahnoa(ah)
bookshop	la librería	lah leebrayreeah
stationer's	la papelería	lah pahpaylayreeah
newsstand	el quiosco de periódicos	ayl kyoaskoa day payryoadeekoass
Where can I buy an English-language newspaper?	¿Dónde puedo comprar un periódico en inglés?	doanday pwaydoa koamprahr oon payryoadeekoa ayn eenglayss
Where's the guide-book section?	¿Dónde está la sección de guías (de viaje)?	doanday aystah lah sayksyoan day geeahss (day byahkhay)
Where do you keep the English books?	¿Dónde están los libros ingleses?	doanday aystahn loass leebroass eenglayssayss
Do you have second-hand books?	¿Tiene usted libros de segunda mano?	tyaynay oostayd leebroass day saygoondah mahnoa
I want to buy a/an/some ...	Quiero comprar ...	kyayroa koamprahr
address book	un librito de direcciones	oon leebreetoa day deerayksyoanayss
adhesive tape	cinta adhesiva	seentah ahdaysseebah
ball-point pen	un bolígrafo	oon boaleegrahfoa
book	un libro	oon leebroa
calendar	un calendario	oon kahlayndahryoa
carbon paper	papel carbón	pahpayl kahrboan
crayons	lápices de color	lahpeessayss day koaloar
dictionary	un diccionario	oon deeksyoanahryoa
Spanish-English	Español-Inglés	ayspahñoal-eenglayss
pocket	de bolsillo	day boalseeyoa
drawing paper	papel de dibujo	pahpayl day deebookhoa
drawing pins	chinchetas [chinches]	cheenchaytahss [cheenchayss]
envelopes	sobres	soabrayss
eraser	un borrador [una goma]	oon boarrahdoar [oonah goamah]
exercise book	un cuaderno	oon kwahdayrnoa
felt-tip pen	un rotulador	oon roatoolahdoar

fountain pen	una pluma fuente	oonah ploomah fwayntay
glue	cola de pegar	koalah day paygahr
grammar book	un libro de gra-mática	oon leebroa day grah-mahteekah
guidebook	una guía (de viaje)	oonah geeah (day byahkhay)
ink	tinta	teentah
black/red/blue	negra/roja/azul	naygrah/roakhah/ahssool
(adhesive) labels	unas etiquetas (adhesivas)	oonahss ayteekaytahss (ahdaysseebahss)
magazine	una revista	oonah raybeestah
map	un mapa	oon mahpah
map of the town	un plano de la ciudad	oon plahnoa day lah syoodahd
road map of ...	un mapa de carre-teras de ...	oon mahpah day kahrray-tayrahss day
newspaper	un periódico	oon payryoadeekoa
notebook	un cuaderno	oon kwahdayrnoa
note paper	papel de cartas	pahpayl day kahrtahss
paintbox	una caja de pinturas	oonah kahkhah day peentoorahss
paper	papel	pahpayl
paperback	un libro de bolsillo	oon leebroa day boalseeyoa
paperclips	sujetapapeles	sookhaytahpahpaylayss
paste	pasta para pegar	pahstah pahrah paygahr
pen	una pluma	oonah ploomah
pencil	un lápiz	oon lahpeess
pencil sharpener	un sacapuntas	oon sahkahpoontahss
playing cards	unos naipes	oonoass nighpayss
pocket calculator	una calculadora de bolsillo	oonah kahlkoolahdoarah day boalseeyoa
postcard	una tarjeta postal	oonah tahrkhaytah poastahl
refill (for a pen)	una carga (para pluma)	oonah kahrgah (pahrah ploomah)
rubber	un borrador [una goma]	oon boarrahdoar [oonah goamah]
ruler	una regla	oonah rayglah
staples	grapas	grahpahss
string	cordón [cuerda]	koardoan [kwayrdah]
thumbtacks	chinchetas [chinches]	cheenchaytahss [cheenchayss]
travel guide	una guía de viaje	oonah geeah day byahkhay
typewriter ribbon	una cinta para máquina de escribir	oonah seentah pahrah mahkeenah day ayskreebeer
typing paper	papel de máquina	pahpayl day mahkeenah
writing pad	un bloc de papel	oon bloak day pahpayl

Camping equipment   *Equipo de camping*

I'd like a/an/some ...	Quisiera ...	keessyayrah
backpack	una mochila	oonah moacheelah
bottle-opener	un destapador	oon daystahpahdoar
bucket	un cubo [balde]	oon kooboa [bahlday]
butane gas	gas butano	gahss bootahnoa
campbed	una cama de campaña	oonah kahmah day kahmpahñah
can opener	un abrelatas	oon ahbraylahtahss
candles	unas velas	oonahss baylahss
(folding) chair	una silla (plegable)	oonah seeyah (playgahblay)
charcoal	carbón	kahrboan
clothes pegs	pinzas	peensahss
compass	una brújula	oonah brookhoolah
cool box	una nevera portátil	oonah naybayrah poartahteel
corkscrew	un sacacorchos	oon sahkahkoarchoass
deck chair	una silla de lona	oonah seeyah day loanah
dishwashing detergent	detergente para la vajilla	daytayrkhayntay pahrah lah bahkheeyah
first-aid kit	un botiquín	oon boateekeen
fishing tackle	un equipo de pesca	oon aykeepoa day payskah
flashlight	una linterna	oonah leentayrnah
food box	una fiambrera	oonah fyahmbrayrah
frying pan	una sartén	oonah sahrtayn
groundsheet	una alfombra (de hule)	oonah ahlfoambrah (day oolay)
hammer	un martillo	oon mahrteeyoa
hammock	una hamaca	oonah ahmahkah
haversack	un morral	oon moarrahl
ice pack	un saco para hielo	oon sahkoa pahrah yayloa
kerosene	petróleo	paytroalayoa
lamp	una lámpara	oonah lahmpahrah
lantern	una linterna	oonah leentayrnah
matches	unos cerillos [fósforos]	oonoass sayreeyoass [foasfoaroass]
mattress	un colchón	oon koalchoan
methylated spirits	alcohol de quemar	ahlkoal day kaymahr
mosquito net	una red para mosquitos	oonah rayd pahrah moaskeetoass
pail	un cubo [balde]	oon kooboa [bahlday]
paper napkins	servilletas de papel	sayrbeeyaytahss day pahpayl
paraffin	petróleo	paytroalayoa
penknife	una navaja	oonah nahbahkhah

CAMPING, see page 32

picnic basket	una bolsa para merienda [picnic]	oonah boalsah pahrah mayryayndah ["picnic"]
plastic bag	una bolsa de plástico	oonah boalsah day plahsteekoa
rope	una cuerda [soga/un lazo]	oonah kwayrdah [soagah/oon lahssoa]
rucksack	una mochila	oonah moacheelah
saucepan	una cacerola	oonah kahssayroalah
scissors	unas tijeras	oonahss teekhayrahss
screwdriver	un destornillador	oon daystoarneeyahdoar
sleeping bag	un saco de dormir	oon sahkoa day doarmeer
(folding) table	una mesa (plegable)	oonah mayssah (playgahblay)
tent	una tienda de campaña	oonah tyayndah day kahmpahñah
tent pegs	estacas de tienda	aystahkahss day tyayndah
tent pole	un mástil de tienda	oon mahssteel day tyayndah
tinfoil	papel de estaño	pahpayl day aystahñoa
tin opener	un abrelatas	oon ahbraylahtahss
tongs	unas tenazas	oonahss taynahssahss
torch	una linterna	oonah leentayrnah
vacuum flask	un termo	oon tayrmoa
washing powder	jabón en polvo	khahboan ayn poalboa
washing-up liquid	detergente para la vajilla	daytayrkhayntay pahrah lah bahkheeyah
water flask	una cantimplora [garrafa]	oonah kahnteemploarah [gahrrahfah]
wood alcohol	alcohol de quemar	ahlkoal day kaymahr

Crockery *Vajilla*

cups	tazas	tahssahss
mugs	tazones con asa	tahssoanayss koan ahssah
plates	platos	plahtoass
saucers	platillos	plahteeyoass
tumblers	vasos	bahssoass

Cutlery *Cubiertos*

forks	tenedores	taynaydoarayss
knives	cuchillos	koocheeyoass
spoons	cucharas	koochahrahss
teaspoons	cucharillas	koochahreeyahss
(made of) plastic	(de) plástico	(day) plahsteekoa

Chemist's (Drugstore) *Farmacia*

Farmacias are normally open during shopping hours only. However, a number of pharmacies in the major cities offer 24-hour service. Hotel receptionists or taxi drivers have their addresses.

Go to a *perfumería* (payrfoomay**reea**h) for perfume and cosmetics.

This section is divided in two parts:
1. Pharmaceutical—medicine, first-aid, etc.
2. Toiletry—toilet articles, cosmetics

General *Generalidades*

Where's the nearest (all-night) chemist's?	**¿Dónde está la farmacia (de turno) más cercana?**	doan**day** ay**stah** lah fahr**mah**ssyah (day **toor**noa) mahss sayr**kah**nah
What time does the chemist's open/ close?	**¿A qué hora abre/ cierra la farma-cia?**	ah kay **oa**rah **ah**bray/ **syayr**rah lah fahr**mah**ssyah

1—Pharmaceutical *Productos farmacéuticos*

I want something for ...	**Quiero algo para ...**	**kyay**roa **ahl**goa **pah**rah
a cold/a cough	**un catarro/la tos**	oon kah**tahr**roa/lah toass
hay fever	**la fiebre del heno**	lah **fyay**bray dayl **ay**noa
insect bites	**las picaduras de insectos**	lahss peekah**doo**rahss day een**sayk**toass
a hangover	**la cruda**	lah **kroo**dah
sunburn	**las quemaduras del sol**	lahss kaymah**doo**rahss dayl soal
travel/altitude sickness	**el mareo/el soroche**	ayl mah**ray**oa/ ayl soa**roa**chay
an upset stomach	**las molestias de estómago**	lahss moa**lays**tyahss day ay**stoa**mahgoa
Can you make up this prescription for me?	**¿Puede usted prepararme esta receta?**	**pway**day oo**stayd** praypah**rahr**may ay**stah** ray**ssay**tah
Can I get it without a prescription?	**¿Puedo obtenerlo sin receta?**	**pway**doa oabtay**nayr**loa seen ray**ssay**tah
Shall I wait?	**¿Tengo que esperar?**	**tayn**goa kay ayspay**rahr**

DOCTOR, see page 137

Can I have a/an/ some ...?	¿Puede darme ...?	pwayday dahrmay
analgesic	un analgésico	oon ahnahlkhaysseekoa
antiseptic cream	una crema anti- séptica	oonah kraymah ahntee- saypteekah
aspirin	aspirinas	ahspeereenahss
bandage	una venda	oonah bayndah
elastic bandage	venda elástica	bayndah aylahsteekah
Band-Aids	esparadrapo	ayspahrahdrahpoa
contraceptives	unos anticoncep- tivos	oonoass ahnteekoansayp- teeboass
corn plasters	unos callicidas	oonoass kahyeesseedahss
cotton wool (absorbent cotton)	algodón	ahlgoadoan
cough drops	pastillas para la tos	pahsteeyahss pahrah lah toass
disinfectant	un desinfectante	oon daysseenfayktahntay
ear drops	gotas para los oídos	goatahss pahrah loass oaeedoass
Elastoplast	esparadrapo	ayspahrahdrahpoa
eye drops	gotas para los ojos	goatahss pahrah loass oakhoass
gauze	gasa	gahssah
insect repellent/ spray	un repelente/spray para insectos	oon raypaylayntay/"spray" pahrah eensayktoass
iodine	yodo	yoadoa
laxative	un laxante	oon lahksahntay
mouthwash	un gargarismo	oon gahrgahreesmoa
nose drops	gotas nasales	goatahss nahssahlayss
sanitary towels (napkins)	paños higiénicos	pahñoass eekhyayneekoass
sleeping pills	un somnífero	oon soamneefayroa
suppositories	unos supositorios	oonoass soopoasseetoaryoass
... tablets	unas tabletas para ...	oonahss tahblaytahss pahrah
tampons	Tampax	tahmpahks
thermometer	un termómetro	oon tayrmoamaytroa
throat lozenges	pastillas para la garganta	pahsteeyahss pahrah lah gahrgahntah
vitamin pills	vitaminas	beetahmeenahss

VENENO	POISON
SOLO PARA USO EXTERNO	FOR EXTERNAL USE ONLY

2—Toiletry *Artículos de tocador*

I'd like a/an/some ...	Quisiera ...	keessyayrah
after-shave lotion	una loción para después del afeitado	oonah loassyoan pahrah dayspwayss dayl ahfaytahdoa
astringent	un astringente	oon ahstreenkhayntay
bath salts	sales de baño	sahlayss day bahñoa
blusher (rouge)	colorete	koaloaraytay
bubble bath	un baño de espuma	oon bahñoa day ayspoomah
cosmetic	un cosmético	oon koasmayteekoa
cream	una crema	oonah kraymah
cleansing cream	limpiadora	leempyahdoarah
foundation cream	de maquillaje	day mahkeeyahkhay
moisturizing cream	hidratante	eedrahtahntay
night cream	de noche	day noachay
cuticle remover	un quita-cutículas	oon keetah kooteekoolahss
deodorant	un desodorante	oon dayssoadoarahntay
emery board	una lima de cartón	oonah leemah day kahrtoan
eye liner	un perfilador de ojos	oon payrfeelahdoar day oakhoass
eyebrow pencil	un lápiz de ojos	oon lahpeess day oakhoass
eye shadow	sombras	soambrahss
face powder	polvos para la cara	poalboass pahrah lah kahrah
foot cream	una crema para los pies	oonah kraymah pahrah loass pyayss
hand cream	una crema para las manos	oonah kraymah pahrah lahss mahnoass
lipsalve	cacao para los labios	kahkahoa pahrah loass lahbyoass
lipstick	un lápiz de labios	oon lahpeess day lahbyoass
make-up remover pads	toallitas de maquillaje	twahyeetahss day mahkeeyahkhay
nail brush	un cepillo de uñas	oon saypeeyoa day ooñahss
nail clippers	un cortador de uñas	oon koartahdoar day ooñahss
nail file	una lima de uñas	oonah leemah day ooñahss
nail polish	esmalte de uñas	aysmahltay day ooñahss
nail polish remover	un quita-esmalte	oon keetah aysmahltay
nail scissors	tijeras de uñas	teekhayrahss day ooñahss
perfume	un perfume	oon payrfoomay
powder	polvos	poalboass
powder puff	una borla	oonah boarlah
razor	una máquina de afeitar	oonah mahkeenah day ahfaytahr
razor blades	hojas de afeitar	oakhahss day ahfaytahr

safety pins	unos imperdibles [trabas]	oonoass eempayrdeeblayss [trahbahss]
shaving brush	una brocha	oonah broachah
shaving cream	crema de afeitar	kraymah day ahfaytahr
soap	jabón	khahboan
sponge	una esponja	oonah ayspoankhah
sun-tan cream	crema bronceadora	kraymah broansayahdoarah
sun-tan oil	aceite bronceador	ahssaytay broansayahdoar
talcum powder	talco	tahlkoa
tissues	pañuelos de papel	pahñwayloass day pahpayl
toilet paper	papel higiénico	pahpayl eekhyayneekoa
toilet water	agua de olor	ahgwah day oaloar
toothbrush	un cepillo de dientes	oon saypeeyoa day dyayn-tayss
toothpaste	una pasta de dientes	oonah pahstah day dyayn-tayss
towel	una toalla	oonah twahyah
tweezers	unas pinzas	oonahss peensahss

For your hair *Para el pelo*

bobby pins	pasadores	pahssahdoarayss
colour shampoo	un champú colorante	oon chahmpoo koaloararahntay
comb	un peine	oon paynay
curlers	tubos [ruleros]	tooboass [roolayroass]
dry shampoo	un champú seco	oon chahmpoo saykoa
hairbrush	un cepillo para el pelo	oon saypeeyoa pahrah ayl payloa
hairgrips	pasadores	pahssahdoarayss
hair lotion	una loción capilar	oonah loassyoan kahpeelahr
hair slide	un pasador	oon pahssahdoar
hair spray	laca	lahkah
setting lotion	un fijador	oon feekhahdoar
shampoo	un champú	oon chahmpoo
tint	coloración	koaloarahssyoan
wig	una peluca	oonah paylookah

For the baby *Para el bebé*

baby food	alimentos para bebé	ahleemayntoass pahrah baybay
dummy (pacifier)	un chupete [chupón]	oon choopaytay [choopoan]
feeding bottle	un biberón	oon beebayroan
nappies (diapers)	unos pañales [pañalines]	oonoass pahñahlayss [pahñahleenayss]

Clothing *Prendas de vestir*

If you want to buy something specific, prepare yourself in advance. Look at the list of clothing on page 116. Get some idea of the colour, material and size you want. They're all listed on the next few pages.

General *Generalidades*

I'd like ...	**Quisiera ...**	keessyayrah
I want ... for a 10-year-old boy/girl.	**Quiero ... para un niño/una niña de 10 años.**	kyayroa ... pahrah oon neeñoa/oonah neeñah day 10 ahñoass
I want something like this.	**Quiero algo como esto.**	kyayroa ahlgoa koamoa aystoa
I like the one in the window.	**Me gusta el del aparador [de la vitrina].**	may goostah ayl dayl ahpahrahdoar [day lah beetreenah]
How much is that per metre?	**¿Cuánto cuesta el metro?**	kwahntoa kwaystah ayl maytroa

1 centimetre (cm.)	= 0.39 in.	1 inch = 2.54 cm.
1 metre (m.)	= 39.37 in.	1 foot = 30.5 cm.
10 metres	= 32.81 ft.	1 yard = 0.91 m.

Colour *Color*

I want something in ...	**Quiero algo en ...**	kyayroa ahlgoa ayn
I want a darker/lighter shade.	**Quiero un tono más oscuro/más claro.**	kyayroa oon toanoa mahss oaskooroa/mahss klahroa
I want something to match this.	**Quiero algo que haga juego con esto.**	kyayroa ahlgoa kay ahgah khwaygoa koan aystoa
I don't like the colour.	**No me gusta el color.**	noa may goostah ayl koaloar

beige	beige	behzh
black	negro	naygroa
blue	azul	ahssool
brown	marrón [café]	mahrroan [kahfay]
fawn	marrón claro	mahrroan klahroa
golden	dorado	doarahdoa
green	verde	bayrday
grey	gris	greess
mauve	malva	mahlbah
orange	naranja	nahrahnkhah
pink	rosa	roassah
purple	purpúreo	poorpoorayoa
red	rojo	roakhoa
scarlet	escarlata	ayskahrlahtah
silver	plateado	plahtayahdoa
turquoise	turquesa	toorkayssah
white	blanco	blahnkoa
yellow	amarillo	ahmahreeyoa
light ...	... claro	... klahroa
dark ...	... oscuro	... oaskooroa

liso
(leessoa)

rayas
(rahyahss)

lunares
(loonahrayss)

cuadros
(kwahdroass)

estampado
(aystahmpahdoa)

Fabric *Tejido*

Do you have anything in ...?	¿Tiene usted algo en ...?	tyaynay oostayd ahlgoa ayn
Is that ...?	¿Es esto ...?	ayss aystoa
handmade	hecho a mano	aychoa ah mahnoa
imported	importado	eempoartahdoa
made here	hecho aquí	aychoa ahkee
I want something thinner.	Quiero algo más ligero.	kyayroa ahlgoa mahss leekhayroa
Do you have anything of better quality?	¿Tiene usted algo de mejor calidad?	tyaynay oostayd ahlgoa day maykhoar kahleedahd

What's it made of?	¿De qué está hecho?	day kay ay**stah** aychoa

cambric	**batista**	bah**tees**tah
camel-hair	**pelo de camello**	**pay**loa day kah**may**yoa
chiffon	**gasa [soplillo]**	**gah**ssah [soap**lee**yoa]
corduroy	**pana**	**pah**nah
cotton	**algodón**	ahlgoa**doan**
crepe	**crespón**	krays**poan**
denim	**dril de algodón**	dreel day ahlgoa**doan**
felt	**fieltro**	**fyayl**troa
flannel	**franela**	frah**nay**lah
gabardine	**gabardina**	gahbahr**dee**nah
lace	**encaje**	ayn**kah**khay
leather	**cuero**	**kway**roa
linen	**lino**	**lee**noa
poplin	**popelina**	poapay**lee**nah
satin	**raso**	**rah**ssoa
silk	**seda**	**say**dah
suede	**ante [gamuza]**	**ahn**tay [gah**moos**sah]
terrycloth	**albornoz**	ahlboar**noass**
velvet	**terciopelo**	tayrsyoapay**loa**
velveteen	**terciopelo de algodón**	tayrsyoapay**loa** day ahlgoa**doan**
wool	**lana**	**lah**nah
worsted	**estambre**	ay**stahm**bray

Is it ...?	¿Es ...?	ayss
pure cotton/wool	**puro algodón/ pura lana**	**poo**roa ahlgoa**doan**/ **poo**rah **lah**nah
synthetic	**sintético**	seen**tay**teekoa
colourfast	**de color permanente**	day koa**loar** payrmah**nayn**tay
wrinkle resistant	**inarrugable**	eenahrroo**gah**blay
Is it hand washable/ machine washable?	¿Puede ser lavado a mano/a máquina?	**pway**day sayr lah**bah**doa ah **mah**noa/ah **mah**keenah
Will it shrink?	¿Se encogerá?	say aynkoakhay**rah**

Size *Talla*

I take size 38.	Mi talla es 38.	mee **tah**yah ayss 38
Could you measure me?	¿Puede usted medirme?	**pway**day oo**stayd** may**deer**may
I don't know the Mexican sizes.	No conozco las tallas de México.	noa koa**noass**koa lahss **tah**yahss day **may**kheekoa

Sizes vary from country to country in Latin America. Some use the American system, some the British, or other European systems. In general, Mexico follows American practice.

Women *Señoras*

Dresses/Suits					
American	8	10	12	14	16	18
British	10	12	14	16	18	20
European	36	38	40	42	44	46

Stockings							Shoes				
American ⎫ British ⎬	8	8½	9	9½	10	10½	5½	6½	7½	8½	9½
							4	5	6	7	8
European	0	1	2	3	4	5	37	38	39	40	41

Men *Caballeros*

Suits/Overcoats							Shirts			
American ⎫ British ⎬	36	38	40	42	44	46	15	16	17	18
European	46	48	50	52	54	56	38	41	43	45

Shoes								
American ⎫ British ⎬	5	6	7	8	8½	9	9½	10	11
European	38	39	41	42	43	43	44	44	45

A good fit?   *¿Le queda bien?*

Can I try it on?	**¿Puedo probármelo?**	pwaydoa proabahrmayloa
Where's the fitting room?	**¿Dónde está el probador?**	doanday aystah ayl proabahdoar
Is there a mirror?	**¿Hay un espejo?**	igh oon ayspaykhoa
It fits very well.	**Me queda muy bien.**	may kaydah mwee byayn
It doesn't fit.	**No me queda bien.**	noa may kaydah byayn

NUMBERS, see page 147

It's too ...	**Es demasiado ...**	ayss daymah**ss**yahdoa
short/long	**corto/largo**	koartoa/lahrgoa
tight/loose	**ajustado/ancho**	ahkhoostahdoa/ahnchoa
How long will it take to alter?	**¿Cuánto tardarán en arreglarlo?**	kwahntoa tahrdahrahn ayn ahrrayglahrloa

Clothes and accessories *Ropa y accesorios*

I would like a/an some ...	**Quisiera ...**	kee**ss**yayrah
anorak	**un anorak**	oon ahnoa**rahk**
bathing cap	**un gorro de baño**	oon **g**oarroa day bah**ñ**oa
bathing suit	**un traje de baño**	oon **trahk**hay day bah**ñ**oa
bathrobe	**una bata de baño**	oonah bahtah day bah**ñ**oa
blouse	**una blusa**	oonah b**loo**ssah
bow tie	**una corbata de lazo**	oonah koarbahtah day lah**ss**oa
bra	**un sostén [brassiere]**	oon soa**stay**n [brah**ss**ayr]
braces	**unos tirantes**	oonoass teerahntayss
briefs	**unos calzoncillos**	oonoass kahlsoan**see**yoass
cap	**una gorra**	oonah **g**oarrah
cardigan	**una chaqueta de punto**	oonah chah**kay**tah day **poon**toa
coat	**un abrigo**	oon ah**bree**goa
dress	**un vestido**	oon bay**stee**doa
dressing gown	**una bata**	oonah **bah**tah
evening dress (woman's)	**un vestido de noche**	oon bay**stee**doa day **noa**chay
girdle	**una faja**	oonah **fah**khah
gloves	**unos guantes**	oonoass **g**wahntayss
handbag	**un bolso**	oon **boal**soa
handkerchief	**un pañuelo**	oon pah**ñ**wayloa
hat	**un sombrero**	oon soam**bray**roa
jacket	**un saco**	oon **sah**koa
jeans	**unos blue jeans**	oonoass "blue jeans"
jersey	**un jersey**	oon khay**r**say
jumper (Br.)	**un suéter**	oon **sway**tayr
nightdress	**un camisón**	oon kahmee**ss**oan
overalls	**un guardapolvo**	oon gwahrdah**poal**boa
pair of ...	**un par de ...**	oon pahr day
panties	**unas pantaletas [bragas]**	oonahss pahntah**lay**tahss [**brah**gahss]
pants (Am.)	**unos pantalones**	oonoass pahntah**loa**nayss
panty girdle	**una faja truga**	oonah **fah**khah **troo**gah
panty hose	**unos leotardos**	oonoass layoa**tahr**doass

pullover	un pullover	oon "pullover"
roll-neck (turtle-neck)	cuello vuelto	kwayyoa bwayltoa
round-neck	cuello redondo	kwayyoa raydoandoa
with long/short sleeves	con mangas largas/cortas	koan mahngahss lahrgahss/koartahss
sleeveless	sin mangas	seen mahngahss
pyjamas	una piyama	oonah peeyahmah
raincoat	un impermeable	oon eempayrmayahblay
scarf	una bufanda	oonah boofahndah
shirt	una camisa	oonah kahmeessah
shorts	unos shorts	oonoass "shorts"
skirt	una falda	oonah fahldah
slip	una combinación	oonah koambeenahssyoan
socks	unos calcetines	oonoass kahlsayteenayss
sports jacket	una chaqueta sport	oonah chahkaytah spoart
stockings	unas medias	oonahss maydyahss
suit (man's)	un traje [terno]	oon trahkhay [tayrnoa]
suit (woman's)	un traje sastre	oon trahkhay sahstray
suspenders (Am.)	unos tirantes	oonoass teerahntayss
sweater	un suéter	oon swaytayr
sweatshirt	un suéter de tela de punto	oon swaytayr day taylah day poontoa
swimming trunks	un bañador	oon bahñahdoar
swimsuit	un traje de baño	oon trahkhay day bahñoa
T-shirt	una camiseta	oonah kahmeessaytah
tie	una corbata	oonah koarbahtah
tights	unos leotardos	oonoass layoatahrdoass
tracksuit	un chandal de entrenamiento	oon chahndahl day ayntraynahmyayntoa
trousers	unos pantalones	oonoass pahntahloanayss
umbrella	un paraguas	oon pahrahgwahss
underpants	unos calzoncillos	oonoass kahlsoanseeyoass
undershirt	una camiseta	oonah kahmeessaytah
vest (Am.)	un chaleco	oon chahlaykoa
vest (Br.)	una camiseta	oonah kahmeessaytah
waistcoat	un chaleco	oon chahlaykoa

belt	un cinturón	oon seentooroan
buckle	una hebilla	oonah aybeeyah
button	un botón	oon boatoan
collar	un cuello	oon kwayyoa
press stud (snap fastener)	un broche de presión	oon broachay day prayssyoan
zip (zipper)	un cierre [zipper]	oon syayrray [seepayr]

Shoes *Zapatos*

I'd like a pair of ...	**Quisiera un par de ...**	keessyayrah oon pahr day
boots	**botas**	boatahss
moccasins	**mocasines**	moakahsseenayss
plimsolls (sneakers)	**zapatos de lona**	sahpahtoass day loanah
sandals	**sandalias**	sahndahlyahss
shoes	**zapatos**	sahpahtoass
flat	**planos**	plahnoass
with a heel	**con tacón**	koan tahkoan
with leather soles	**con suelas de cuero**	koan swaylahss day kwayroa
with rubber soles	**con suelas de goma**	koan swaylahss day goamah
slippers	**zapatillas**	sahpahteeyahss
These are too ...	**Estos son ...**	aystoass soan
narrow/wide	**estrechos/anchos**	aystraychoass/ahnchoass
Do you have a larger/smaller size?	**¿Tiene un número más grande/pequeño?**	tyaynay oon noomayroa mahss grahnday/paykayñoa
Do you have the same in black?	**¿Tiene los mismos en negro?**	tyaynay loass meesmoass ayn naygroa
cloth	**de tela**	day taylah
leather	**de cuero**	day kwayroa
rubber	**de goma**	day goamah
suede	**de ante**	day ahntay
Is it genuine leather?	**¿Es cuero verdadero?**	ayss kwayroa bayrdahdayroa
I need some shoe polish/shoelaces.	**Necesito crema/cordones [cintas] para zapatos.**	nayssaysseetoa kraymah/koardoanayss [seentahss] pahrah sahpahtoass

Shoes worn out? Here's the key to getting them fixed again:

Can you repair these shoes?	**¿Puede reparar estos zapatos?**	pwayday raypahrahr aystoass sahpahtoass
Can you stitch this?	**¿Puede coser esto?**	pwayday koassayr aystoa
I want new soles and heels.	**Quiero suelas y tacones nuevos.**	kyayroa swaylahss ee tahkoanayss nwayboass
When will they be ready?	**¿Cuándo estarán listos?**	kwahndoa aystahrahn leestoass

COLOURS, see page 113

Electrical appliances   *Aparatos eléctricos*

Check the voltage! It differs from country to country throughout the continent. In Mexico City the voltage is 125 volts, 60 cycles; elsewhere in the country 110 volts, 60 cycles. Argentina, Chile and Peru have 220 volts, Venezuela (Columbia, Ecuador) 110. You may need a transformer and perhaps also an adaptor plug.

What's the voltage?	¿Cuál es el voltaje?	kwahl ayss ayl boaltahkhay
Do you have a battery for this?	¿Tiene usted una pila para esto?	tyaynay oostayd oonah peelah pahrah aystoa
This is broken. Can you repair it?	Esto está roto. ¿Puede usted arreglarlo?	aystoa aystah roatoa. pwayday oostayd ahrrayglahrloa
Can you show me how it works?	¿Puede enseñarme cómo funciona?	pwayday aynsayñahrmay koamoa foonsyoanah
I'd like a/an/some ...	Quisiera ...	keessyayrah
adaptor	un adaptador	oon ahdahptahdoar
amplifier	un amplificador	oon ahmpleefeekahdoar
bulb	una ampolla [un foco]	oonah ahmpoayah [oon foakoa]
clock-radio	un radio-despertador	oon rahdyoa-dayspayr-tahdoar
electric toothbrush	un cepillo de dientes eléctrico	oon saypeeyoa day dyayn-tayss aylayktreekoa
extension lead (cord)	una extensión	oonah aykstaynsyoan
hair dryer	un secador de pelo	oon saykahdoar day payloa
headphones	un casco con auriculares	oon kahskoa koan owreekoolahrayss
(travelling) iron	una plancha (de viaje)	oonah plahnchah (day byahkhay)
lamp	una lámpara	oonah lahmpahrah
portable ...	... portátil	... poartahteel
radio	una radio	oonah rahdyoa
record player	un tocadiscos	oon toakahdeeskoass
speakers	unos altavoces	oonoass ahltahboassayss
(cassette) tape recorder	una grabadora (para cassettes)	oonah grahbahdoarah (pahrah kahssaytayss)
(colour) television	un televisor (de color)	oon taylaybeessoar (day koaloar)
transformer	un transformador	oon trahnsfoarmahdoar
video-recorder	una video-grabadora	oonah beedayoagrahbah-doarah

Grocery   *Tienda de abarrotes*

I'd like some bread, please.	**Quiero pan, por favor.**	kyayroa pahn poar fahboar
What sort of cheese do you have?	**¿Qué clases de queso tiene?**	kay klahssayss day kayssoa tyaynay
A piece of ...	**Un trozo ...**	oon troassoa
that one	**de ése**	day ayssay
the one on the shelf	**del que está en el estante**	dayl kay aystah ayn ayl aystahntay
May I help myself?	**¿Puedo servirme?**	pwaydoa sayrbeermay
I'd like ...	**Quisiera ...**	keessyayrah
a kilo of apples	**un kilo de manzanas**	oon keeloa day mahnsahnahss
half a kilo of tomatoes	**medio kilo de tomates**	maydyoa keeloa day toamahtayss
100 grams of butter	**100 gramos de mantequilla**	100 grahmoass day mahntaykeeyah
a litre of milk	**un litro de leche**	oon leetroa day laychay
4 slices of ham	**4 lonjas de jamón**	4 loankhahss day khahmoan
a packet of tea	**un paquete de té**	oon pahkaytay day tay
a jar of jam	**un tarro de mermelada**	oon tahrroa day mayrmaylahdah
a tin (can) of peaches	**una lata de duraznos**	oonah lahtah day doorahsnoass
a tube of mustard	**un tubo de mostaza**	oon tooboa day moastahssah
a box of chocolates	**una caja de chocolate**	oonah kahkhah day choakoalahtay

---

1 kilogram or kilo (kg.) = 1000 grams (g.)

100 g. = 3.5 oz.	½ kg. = 1.1 lb.
200 g. = 7.0 oz.	1 kg. = 2.2 lb.

1 oz. = 28.35 g.
1 lb. = 453.60 g.

---

1 litre (l.) = 0.88 imp. qt. or 1.06 U.S. qt.

1 imp. qt. = 1.14 l.	1 U.S. qt. = 0.95 l.
1 imp. gal. = 4.55 l.	1 U.S. gal. = 3.8 l.

FOOD, see also page 63

Jeweller's—Watchmaker's   *Joyería—Relojería*

Could I see that, please?	¿Puedo ver eso, por favor?	pwaydoa bayr ayssoa poar fahboar
Do you have anything in gold?	¿Tiene usted algo en oro?	tyaynay oostayd ahlgoa ayn oaroa
How many carats is this?	¿Cuántos quilates tiene esto?	kwahntoass keelahtayss tyaynay aystoa
Is this real silver?	¿Es plata verdadera?	ayss plahtah bayrdahdayrah
Can you repair this watch?	¿Puede arreglar este reloj?	pwayday ahrrayglahr aystay rayloakh
When will it be ready?	¿Cuándo estará listo?	kwahndoa aystahrah leestoa
I'd like a/an/some ...	Quisiera ...	keessyayrah

alarm clock	un despertador	oon dayspayrtahdoar
bangle	un brazalete	oon brahssahlaytay
battery	una pila	oonah peelah
bracelet	una pulsera	oonah poolsayrah
chain bracelet	de cadena	day kahdaynah
charm bracelet	con amuletos	koan ahmoolaytoass
brooch	un broche	oon broachay
chain	una cadena	oonah kahdaynah
charm	un amuleto	oon ahmoolaytoa
cigarette case	una pitillera	oonah peeteeyayrah
cigarette lighter	un encendedor	oon aynsayndaydoar
clip	un clip	oon kleep
clock	un reloj	oon rayloakh
cross	una cruz	oonah krooss
cuff links	unos gemelos	oonoass khaymayloass
cutlery	unos cubiertos	oonoass koobyayrtoass
earrings	unos aretes	oonoass ahraytayss
jewel	una joya	oonah khoayah
jewel box	un joyero	oon khoayayroa
mechanical pencil	un portaminas	oon poartahmeenahss
music box	una caja de música	oonah kahkhah day moosseekah
necklace	un collar	oon koayahr
pendant	un colgante	oon koalgahntay
pin	un alfiler	oon ahlfeelayr
pocket watch	un reloj de bolsillo	oon rayloakh day boalseeyoa
powder compact	una polvera	oonah poalbayrah
propelling pencil	un portaminas	oon poartahmeenahss

ring	**un anillo [una sortija]**	oon ahneeyoa [oonah soarteekhah]
engagement ring	**un anillo de compromiso**	oon ahneeyoa day koamproameessoa
signet ring	**un anillo de sello**	oon ahneeyoa day sayyoa
wedding ring	**un anillo de boda**	oon ahneeyoa day **boa**dah
rosary	**un rosario**	oon roasahryoa
silverware	**objetos de plata**	oabkhaytoass day **plah**tah
tie clip	**un pisacorbata**	oon peessahkoar**bah**tah
tie pin	**un alfiler de corbata**	oon ahl**fee**layr day koar**bah**tah
watch	**un reloj**	oon ray**loakh**
automatic	**automático**	owtoa**mah**teekoa
digital	**digital**	deekhee**tahl**
quartz	**de cuarzo**	day **kwahr**soa
with a second hand	**con segundero**	koan saygoon**day**roa
waterproof	**impermeable**	eempayrmay**ah**blay
watchstrap	**una correa de reloj**	oonah koar**ray**ah day ray**loakh**
wristwatch	**un reloj**	oon ray**loakh**

amber	**ámbar**	**ahm**bahr
amethyst	**amatista**	ahmah**tees**tah
chromium	**cromo**	**kroa**moa
coral	**coral**	koa**rahl**
crystal	**cristal**	krees**tahl**
cut glass	**cristal tallado**	krees**tahl** tah**yah**doa
diamond	**diamante**	dyah**mahn**tay
emerald	**esmeralda**	aysmay**rahl**dah
enamel	**esmalte**	ays**mahl**tay
gold	**oro**	**oa**roa
gold plate	**oro chapado**	**oa**roa chah**pah**doa
ivory	**marfil**	mahr**feel**
pearl	**perla**	**payr**lah
pewter	**peltre**	**payl**tray
platinum	**platino**	plah**tee**noa
ruby	**rubí**	roo**bee**
sapphire	**zafiro**	sah**fee**roa
silver	**plata**	**plah**tah
silver plate	**plata chapada**	**plah**tah chah**pah**dah
stainless steel	**acero inoxidable**	ah**ssay**roa eenoaksee**dah**blay
topaz	**topacio**	toa**pah**ssyoa
turquoise	**turquesa**	toor**kay**ssah

Optician   *El óptico*

I've broken my glasses.	Se me han roto los anteojos.	say may ahn **roa**toa loass ahn**tay**oa**khoass**
Can you repair them for me?	¿Me los puede arreglar?	may loass **pway**day ahr**ray**glahr
When will they be ready?	¿Cuándo estarán listos?	**kwahn**doa aysta**hrahn lees**toass
Can you change the lenses?	¿Puede cambiar los lentes?	**pway**day kahm**byahr** loass **layn**tayss
I want tinted lenses.	Quiero lentes ahumados.	**kyay**roa **layn**tayss ahoo**mah**doass
The frame is broken.	Está rota la armadura.	ays**tah roa**tah lah ahrmah**doo**rah
I'd like a spectacle case.	Quisiera un estuche para anteojos.	kees**syay**rah oon ays**too**chay **pah**rah ahn**tay**oa**khoass**
I'd like to have my eyesight checked.	Quisiera hacerme una revisión de la vista.	kees**syay**rah ah**ssayr**may **oo**nah raybees**syoan** day lah **bees**tah
I'm short-sighted/long-sighted.	Soy miope/présbite.	soy mee**oa**pay/**prays**beetay
I'd like some contact lenses.	Quisiera unos lentes de contacto.	kees**syay**rah **oo**noass **layn**tayss day koan**tahk**toa
I've lost one of my contact lenses.	He perdido un lente de contacto.	ay payr**dee**doa oon **layn**tay day koan**tahk**toa
Could you give me another one?	¿Me podría dar otro?	may poa**dree**ah dahr **oa**troa
I have hard/soft lenses.	Tengo lentes duros/blandos.	**tayn**goa **layn**tayss **doo**roass/**blahn**doass
Have you any contact-lens liquid?	¿Tiene líquido para lentes de contacto?	**tyay**nay **lee**keedoa **pah**rah **layn**tayss day koan**tahk**toa
I'd like to buy a pair of sunglasses.	Quisiera comprar unos anteojos de sol.	kees**syay**rah koam**prahr oo**noass ahn**tay**oa**khoass** day soal
May I look in a mirror?	¿Puedo mirarme en un espejo?	**pway**doa mee**rahr**may ayn oon ays**pay**khoa
I'd like to buy a pair of binoculars.	Quisiera comprar unos binoculares.	kees**syay**rah koam**prahr oo**noass beenoakoo**lah**rayss

Photography *Fotografía*

I'd like a/an ... camera.	Quisiera una cámara ...	keessyayrah oonah kahmahrah
automatic	automática	owtoamahteekah
inexpensive	barata	bahrahtah
simple	sencilla	saynseeyah
Show me some cine (movie) cameras, please.	Enséñeme unas cámaras de filmar, por favor.	aynsayñaymay oonahss kahmahrahss day feelmahr poar fahboar
I'd like to have some passport photos taken.	Quisiera que me hagan fotos para pasaporte.	keessyayrah kay may ahgahn foatoass pahrah pahssahpoartay

Film *Rollos/Películas*

I'd like a film for this camera.	Quiero un rollo para esta cámara.	kyayroa oon roayoa pahrah aystah kahmahrah
black and white	en blanco y negro	ayn blahnkoa ee naygroa
colour	en color	ayn koaloar
colour negative	negativo de color	naygahteeboa day koaloar
colour slide	diapositivas	deeahpoaseeteebahss
cartridge	un cartucho	oon kahrtoochoa
disc film	un disco-película	oon deeskoa payleekoolah
roll film	un carrete/rollo	oon kahrraytay/roayoa
video cassette	una video-cassette	oonah beedayoa kahssayt
24/36 exposures	24/36 exposiciones	24/36 aykspoasseessyoanayss
this size	de este tamaño	day aystay tahmahñoa
this ASA/DIN number	este número ASA/DIN	aystay noomayroa ahssah/deen
artificial light type	tipo luz artificial	teepoa looss ahrteefeessyahl
daylight type	tipo luz del día	teepoa looss dayl deeah
fast (high-speed)	grano rápido	grahnoa rahpeedoa
fine grain	grano fino	grahnoa feenoa

Processing *Revelado*

How much do you charge for developing?	¿Cuánto cuesta el revelado?	kwahntoa kwaystah ayl raybaylahdoa

I'd like ... prints of each negative.	Quiero ... copias de cada negativo.	kyayroa ... koapyahss day kahdah naygahteeboa
with a mat finish	con acabado mate	koan ahkahbahdoa mahtay
with a glossy finish	con acabado de brillo	koan ahkahbahdoa day breeyoa
Will you enlarge this, please?	¿Podría usted ampliar esto?	poadreeah oostayd ahmpleeahr aystoa
When will the photos be ready?	¿Cuándo estarán listas las fotos?	kwahndoa aystahrahn leestahss lahss foatoass

Accessories and repairs *Accesorios y reparaciones*

I'd like a/an/some ...	Quisiera ...	keessyayrah
battery	una pila	oonah peelah
cable release	un cable de disparador	oon kahblay day deespahrahdoar
camera case	una funda	oonah foondah
(electronic) flash	un flash (electrónico)	oon "flash" (aylayktroaneekoa)
filter	un filtro	oon feeltroa
for black and white	para blanco y negro	pahrah blahnkoa ee naygroa
for colour	para color	pahrah koaloar
lens	un objetivo	oon oabkhayteeboa
telephoto lens	un teleobjetivo	oon taylayoabkhayteeboa
wide-angle lens	un objetivo granangular	oon oabkhayteeboa grahnahngoolahr
lens cap	un capuchón para el objetivo	oon kahpoochoan pahrah ayl oabkhayteeboa
Can you repair this camera?	¿Puede usted reparar esta cámara?	pwayday oostayd raypahrahr aystah kahmahrah
The film is jammed.	El rollo está atorado.	ayl roayoa aystah ahtoarahdoa
There's something wrong with the ...	Hay algo que no va bien en ...	igh ahlgoa kay noa bah byayn ayn
exposure counter	la escala de exposición	lah ayskahlah day aykspoasseessyoan
film winder	el enrollador	ayl aynroayahdoar
flash attachment	la zapata para el flash	lah sahpahtah pahrah ayl "flash"
light meter	el exposímetro	ayl aykspoasseemaytroa
rangefinder	el telémetro	ayl taylaymaytroa
shutter	el obturador	ayl oabtoorahdoar

NUMBERS, see page 147

Tobacconist's *Tabaquería*

Cigarettes and tobacco are sold in *tabaquerías* (tahbahkay-reeahss—tobacconists'), supermarkets and street kiosks.

Throughout Latin America you will find a great variety of tobacco available. Almost every country produces its own cigarettes and cigars. American cigarettes will usually cost more than in the U.S.A.

A packet of cigarettes, please.	Una cajetilla de cigarrillos, por favor.	oonah kahkhayteeyah day seegahrreeyoass poar fahboar
Do you have any American/English cigarettes?	¿Tiene usted cigarrillos americanos/ingleses?	tyaynay oostayd seegahrreeyoass ahmayreekahnoass/eenglayssayss
I'd like a carton.	Quisiera un cartón.	keessyayrah oon kahrtoan
Give me a/some ... please.	Déme ..., por favor.	daymay ... poar fahboar
chewing gum	un chicle	oon cheeklay
chewing tobacco	tabaco para mascar	tahbahkoa pahrah mahskahr
cigarette case	una pitillera	oonah peeteeyayrah
cigarette holder	una boquilla	oonah boakeeyah
cigarettes	cigarrillos	seegahrreeyoass
filter-tipped/	con filtro	koan feeltroa
without filter	sin filtro	seen feeltroa
light/dark tobacco	tabaco rubio/negro	tahbahkoa roobyoa/naygroa
mild/strong	suaves/fuertes	swahbayss/fwayrtayss
menthol	mentolados	mayntoalahdoass
king-size	extra-grandes	aykstrah-grahndayss
cigars	unos puros	oonoass pooroass
lighter	un encendedor	oon aynsayndaydoar
lighter fluid/gas	gasolina/gas para encendedor	gahssoaleenah/gahss pahrah aynsayndaydoar
matches	cerillos [fósforos]	sayreeyoass [foasfoaroass]
pipe	una pipa	oonah peepah
pipe cleaners	unas limpiapipas	oonahss leempyahpeepahss
pipe tobacco	tabaco de pipa	tahbahkoa day peepah
postcard	una tarjeta postal	oonah tahrkhaytah poastahl
snuff	rapé	rahpay
wick	una mecha	oonah maychah

Miscellaneous *Diversos*

Souvenirs *Recuerdos*

Both Mexico and Latin America in general are rich in hand-icrafts of all kinds. Shopping can be a real delight, with something new and exciting round almost every corner. Ceramics, silverware, papier-mâché articles, textiles and a host of other handmade or handworked local products—all exude a sense of history, tradition, talent and imagination.

carpets	**tapetes [alfombras]**	tahpaytayss [ahlfoambrahss]
copperware	**cobres**	koabrayss
embroidery	**bordados**	boardahdoass
painted gourds	**calabazas pintadas**	kahlahbahssahss peentahdahss
hand-blown glass	**vidrio soplado**	beedryoa soaplahdoa
jewels	**joyas**	khoayahss
masks	**máscaras**	mahskahrahss
onyx	**ónix**	oaneeks
papier mâché	**papel maché**	pahpayl mahchay
poncho	**jorongo [poncho]**	khoaroangoa ["poncho"]
pottery	**cerámica**	sayrahmeekah
saddle	**silla de montar**	seeyah day moantahr
Mexican sandals	**huaraches**	wahrahchayss
woman's shawl	**rebozo**	rayboassoa
silver	**plata**	plahtah
sun hat	**sombrero**	soambrayroa
traditional ball game	**balero**	bahlayroa

Records—Cassettes *Discos—Cassettes*

Do you have any records by ...?	**¿Tiene algún disco de ...?**	tyaynay ahlgoon deeskoa day
I'd like a ...	**Quisiera ...**	keessyayrah
cassette	**una cassette**	oonah kahssayt
compact disc	**un disco compacto**	oon deeskoa koampahktoa
Have you any songs by ...?	**¿Tiene usted canciones de ...?**	tyaynay oostayd kahnsyoanayss day
Can I listen to this record?	**¿Puedo escuchar este disco?**	pwaydoa ayskoochahr aystay deeskoa

L.P. (33 rpm)	un disco de larga duración	oon deeskoa day lahrgah doorahssyoan
E.P. (45 rpm)	maxi 45	mahksee kwahrayntah ee seenkoa
single	un disco de corta duración	oon deeskoa day koartah doorahssyoan

chamber music	música de cámara	moosseekah day kahmahrah
classical music	música clásica	moosseekah klahsseekah
folk music	música folklórica	moosseekah foalkloareekah
instrumental music	música instrumental	moosseekah eenstroomayntahl
jazz	música de jazz	moosseekah day "jazz"
light music	música ligera	moosseekah leekhayrah
orchestral music	música de orquesta	moosseekah day oarkaystah
pop music	música pop	moosseekah "pop"

Toys *Juguetes*

I'd like a toy/game …	Quisiera un juguete/ un juego …	keessyayrah oon khoogaytay/oon khwaygoa
for a boy	para un niño	pahrah oon neeñoa
for a 5-year-old girl	para una niña de 5 años	pahrah oonah neeñah day 5 ahñoass
(beach) ball	una pelota (de playa)	oonah payloatah (day plahyah)
bucket and spade (pail and shovel)	un cubo y una pala	oon kooboa ee oonah pahlah
building blocks (bricks)	unos cubos de construcción	oonoass kooboass day koanstrooksyoan
card game	un juego de cartas	oon khwaygoa day kahrtahss
chess set	un ajedrez	oon ahkhaydrayss
doll	una muñeca	oonah mooñaykah
electronic game	un juego electrónico	oon khwaygoa aylayktroaneekoa
flippers	unas aletas para nadar	oonahss ahlaytahss pahrah nahdahr
roller skates	unos patines de ruedas	oonoass pahteenayss day rwaydahss
snorkel	un tubo respiratorio	oon tooboa rayspeerahtoaryoa

Your money: banks—currency

The basic unit of currency in Mexico and Chile is the *peso* (**pay**ssoa), divided into 100 *centavos* (sayn**tah**boass). *Peso* is abbreviated to $.

Other currency units are the *bolívar* (Venezuela), the *sol* (Peru) and the *austral* (Argentina).

In Mexico, there are coins of 10, 20 and 50 centavos and of 1, 5, 10, 20, 50 and 100 pesos. There are banknotes of 10, 20, 50, 100, 200, 500, 1000, 2000, 5000 and 10,000 pesos.

Though hours can vary, banks are generally open from 9 a.m. to 1.30 p.m. Change money at currency exchange offices (*oficinas* or *casa de cambio*), they often have better exchange rates than hotels or banks.

Credit cards are widely accepted in hotels, restaurants and tourist-related businesses.

Traveller's cheques are accepted by hotels, restaurants and many shops, although the exchange rate is invariably better at a bank. Don't forget to take your passport when going to cash a traveller's cheque.

Where's the nearest bank?	¿Dónde está el banco más cercano?	doanday aystah ayl bahnkoa mahss sayrkahnoa
Where's the nearest currency exchange office?	¿Dónde está la oficina de cambio más cercana?	doanday aystah lah oafeesseenah day kahmbyoa mahss sayrkahnah
What time does the bank open/close?	¿A qué hora abren/cierran el banco?	ah kay oarah ahbrayn/syayrrahn ayl bahnkoa
Where can I cash a traveller's cheque (check)?	¿Dónde puedo cobrar un cheque de viajero?	doanday pwaydoa koabrahr oon chaykay day byahkhayroa

At the bank   *En el banco*

I'd like to change some dollars/pounds.	**Quiero cambiar unos dólares/unas libras esterlinas.**	kyayroa kahmbyahr oonoass doalahrayss/oonahss leebrahss aystayrleenahss
I'd like to cash a traveller's cheque.	**Quiero cobrar un cheque de viajero.**	kyayroa koabrahr oon chaykay day byahkhayroa
What's the exchange rate?	**¿A cómo está el cambio?**	ah koamoa aystah ayl kahmbyoa
How much commission do you charge?	**¿Qué comisión cargan?**	kay koameessyoan kahrgahn
Can you telex my bank in London?	**¿Puede mandar un télex a mi banco en Londres?**	pwayday mahndahr oon taylayks ah mee bahnkoa ayn loandrayss
I have a/an/some ...	**Tengo ...**	tayngoa
bank card	**una tarjeta de banco**	oonah tahrkhaytah day bahnkoa
credit card	**una tarjeta de crédito**	oonah tahrkhaytah day kraydeetoa
Eurocheques	**unos eurocheques**	oonoass ayooroachaykayss
introduction from ...	**una carta de recomendación de ...**	oonah kahrtah day raykoamayndahssyoan day
letter of credit	**una carta de crédito**	oonah kahrtah day kraydeetoa
I'm expecting some money from New York. Has it arrived?	**Estoy esperando dinero de Nueva York. ¿Ha llegado ya?**	aystoy ayspayrahndoa deenayroa day nwaybah yoark. ah yaygahdoa yah
Please give me ... notes (bills) and some small change.	**Déme ... billetes y algo de suelto, por favor.**	daymay ... beeyaytayss ee ahlgoa day swayltoa poar fahboar
Give me ... large notes and the rest in small notes.	**Déme ... billetes grandes y el resto en billetes pequeños.**	daymay beeyaytayss grahndayss ee ayl raystoa ayn beeyaytayss paykayñoass

Deposits—Withdrawals   *Depósitos—Retiros*

I want to ...	**Quiero ...**	kyayroa
open an account	**abrir una cuenta**	ahbreer oonah kwayntah
withdraw ... pesos	**retirar ... pesos**	rayteerahr ... payssoass
Where should I sign?	**¿Dónde tengo que firmar?**	doanday tayngoa kay feermahr

NUMBERS, see page 147

| I want to deposit this in my account. | **Quiero depositar esto en mi cuenta.** | kyayroa daypoasseetahr aystoa ayn mee kwayntah |

Business terms *Expresiones de negocios*

My name is ...	**Me llamo ...**	may yahmoa
Here's my card.	**Aquí tiene mi tarjeta.**	ahkee tyaynay mee tahrkhaytah
I have an appointment with ...	**Tengo una cita con ...**	tayngoa oonah seetah koan
Can you give me an estimate of the cost?	**¿Puede darme una estimación del precio?**	pwayday dahrmay oonah aysteemahssyoan dayl prayssyoa
What's the rate of inflation?	**¿Cuál es el índice de inflación?**	kwahl ayss ayl eendeessay day eenflahssyoan
Can you provide me with an interpreter/ a secretary?	**¿Puede conseguirme un intérprete/ una secretaria?**	pwayday koansaygeermay oon eentayrpraytay/ oonah saykraytahryah
Where can I make photocopies?	**¿Dónde puedo hacer fotocopias?**	doanday pwaydoa ahssayr foatoakoapyahss

amount	**la suma**	lah soomah
balance	**el balance**	ayl bahlahnsay
bond	**la obligación**	lah oableegahssyoan
capital	**el capital**	ayl kahpeetahl
cheque book	**la chequera**	lah chaykayrah
contract	**el contrato**	ayl koantrahtoa
discount	**el descuento**	ayl dayskwayntoa
expenses	**los gastos**	loass gahstoass
interest	**el interés**	ayl eentayrayss
investment	**la inversión**	lah eenbayrsyoan
invoice	**la factura**	lah fahktoorah
loss	**la pérdida**	lah payrdeedah
mortgage	**la hipoteca**	lah eepoataykah
payment	**el pago**	ayl pahgoa
percentage	**el porcentaje**	ayl poarsayntahkhay
profit	**la ganancia**	lah gahnahnsyah
purchase	**la compra**	lah koamprah
sale	**la venta**	lah bayntah
share	**la acción**	lah ahksyoan
transfer	**la transferencia**	lah trahnsfayraynsyah
value	**el valor**	ayl bahloar

At the post office

You'll recognize a post office by the sign *Correos y Telégrafos*. Business hours may vary, but are generally from 8 a.m. to 7 p.m. The main post office in Mexico City is open from 7 a.m. to midnight, Monday–Friday, until 8 p.m. on Saturday and until 4 p.m. on Sunday.

Letterboxes, generally painted red, are often marked *Aéreo* for airmail items. *D.F.* (in Mexico City) or *local* for local mail, or *Terrestre* for surface mail.

Where's the nearest post office?	¿Dónde está la oficina de correos más cercana?	doanday aystah lah oafeesseenah day koarrayoass mahss sayrkahnah
What time does the post office open/ close?	¿A qué hora abren/ cierran correos?	ah kay oarah ahbrayn/ syayrrahn koarrayoass
Which window do I go to for stamps?	¿A qué ventanilla debo ir para comprar estampillas?	ah kay bayntahneeyah dayboa eer pahrah koamprahr aystahmpeeyahss
A stamp for this letter/postcard, please.	Una estampilla para esta carta/ tarjeta, por favor.	oonah aystahmpeeyah pahrah aystah kahrtah/ tahrkhaytah poar fahboar
A ...-peso stamp, please.	Una estampilla de ... pesos, por favor.	oonah aystahmpeeyah day ... payssoass poar fahboar
What's the postage for a letter to London?	¿Cuál es el franqueo para una carta para Londres?	kwahl ayss ayl frahnkayoa pahrah oonah kahrtah pahrah loandrayss
What's the postage for a postcard to Los Angeles?	¿Cuál es el franqueo para una tarjeta para Los Angeles?	kwahl ayss ayl frahnkayoa pahrah oonah tahrkhaytah pahrah "Los Angeles"
Where's the letterbox (mailbox)?	¿Dónde está el buzón?	doanday aystah ayl boossoan
I want to send this parcel.	Quiero mandar este paquete.	kyayroa mahndahr aystay pahkaytay

I want to send this (by) ...	Quiero mandar esto ...	kyayroa mahndahr aystoa
airmail	por correo aéreo	poar koarrayoa ahayrayoa
express (special delivery)	urgente	oorkhayntay
registered mail	certificado	sayrteefeekahdoa
At which counter can I cash an international money order?	¿En qué ventanilla puedo hacer efectivo un giro postal internacional?	ayn kay bayntahneeyah pwaydoa ahssayr ayfayktee-boa oon kheeroa poastahl eentayrnahssyoanahl
Where's the poste restante (general delivery)?	¿Dónde está la Lista de Correos [poste restante]?	doanday aystah lah leestah day koarrayoass [poastay raystahntay]
Is there any post for me? My name is ...	¿Hay correo para mí? Me llamo ...	igh koarrayoa pahrah mee. may yahmoa

ESTAMPILLAS	STAMPS
PAQUETES	PARCELS
GIROS POSTALES	MONEY ORDERS

Telegrams *Telegramas*

In Latin America, telegrams are sent by the post office.

I want to send a telegram/telex.	Quiero mandar un telegrama/télex.	kyayroa mahndahr oon taylaygrahmah/taylayks
May I have a form, please?	¿Me da un formulario, por favor?	may dah oon foarmoolahryoa poar fahboar
How much is it per word?	¿Cuánto cuesta por palabra?	kwahntoa kwaystah poar pahlahbrah
How long will a cable to Boston take?	¿Cuánto tardará un telegrama a Boston?	kwahntoa tahrdahrah oon taylaygrahmah ah boastoan
How much will this telex cost?	¿Cuánto costará este télex?	kwahntoa koastahrah aystay taylayks

Telephoning *Teléfonos*

In most Latin-American countries you will find public telephone booths. For long-distance calls it may be better to call from your hotel or go directly to the telephone office.

Where's the telephone?	**¿Dónde está el teléfono?**	doanday aystah ayl taylayfoanoa
I'd like a telephone token.	**Quisiera una ficha de teléfono.**	keessyayrah oonah feechah day taylayfoanoa
Where's the nearest telephone booth?	**¿Dónde está la cabina telefónica más cercana?**	doanday aystah lah kahbeenah taylayfoaneekah mahss sayrkahnah
May I use your phone?	**¿Puedo usar su teléfono?**	pwaydoa oossahr soo taylayfoanoa
Do you have a telephone directory for Mexico City?	**¿Tiene usted una guía de teléfonos para la ciudad de México?**	tyaynay oostayd oonah geeah day taylayfoanoass pahrah lah syoodahd day maykheekoa
I want to telephone to England.	**Quiero telefonear a Inglaterra.**	kyayroa taylayfoanayahr ah eenglahtayrrah
What's the dialling (area) code for ...?	**¿Cuál es el indicativo para ...?**	kwahl ayss ayl eendeekahteeboa pahrah
How do I get the international operator?	**¿Cómo puedo conseguir la telefonista internacional?**	koamoa pwaydoa koansaygeer lah taylayfoaneestah eentayrnahssyoanahl

Operator *La telefonista*

Good morning, I want Mexico City 512-34-56.	**Buenos días. Quiero hablar con el 512-34-56 de México.**	bwaynoass deeahss. kyayroa ahblahr koan ayl 512-34-56 day maykheekoa
Can you help me get this number?	**¿Puede usted ayudarme a conseguir este número?**	pwayday oostayd ahyoodahrmay ah koansaygeer aystay noomayroa
I want to place a personal (person-to-person) call.	**Quiero una llamada personal.**	kyayroa oonah yahmahdah payrsoanahl

NUMBERS, see page 147

Teléfono

| I'd like to reverse the charges (call collect). | **Quiero hacerlo por cobro rever- tido.** | kyayroa ahssayrloa poar **koa**broa raybayr- **tee**doa |

Speaking *Hablando*

Hello. This is ... speaking.	**Hola. Habla ...**	oalah. ahblah
I want to speak to ...	**Quiero hablar con ...**	kyayroa ah**blahr** koan
I want extension ...	**Quiero la extensión [el interno] ...**	kyayroa lah aykstayn**syoan** [ayl eentayrnoa]
Speak louder/more slowly, please.	**Hable más fuerte/más despacio, por favor.**	ahblay mahss **fwayr**tay/mahss day**spah**ssyoa poar fah**boar**

Bad luck *Mala suerte*

Would you try again later, please?	**¿Podría llamar más tarde, por favor?**	poa**dree**ah yah**mahr** mahss **tahr**day poar fah**boar**
Operator, you gave me the wrong number.	**Señorita, usted me dio un número equi- vocado.**	sayñoa**ree**tah oostayd may dyoa oon **noo**mayroa aykee- boa**kah**doa
Operator, we were cut off.	**Señorita, se cortó la comunicación.**	sayñoa**ree**tah say koar**toa** lah koamooneekah**ssyoan**

Telephone alphabet *Código de deletreo*

A	**Amalia**	ahmahlyah	N	**Nicaragua**	neekahrahgwah
B	**Beatriz**	bayahtreess	Ñ	**Ñoño**	ñoañoa
C	**Carmen**	kahrmayn	O	**Olimpo**	oaleempoa
D	**Domingo**	doameengoa	P	**Pablo**	pahbloa
E	**Enrique**	aynreekay	Q	**Quito**	keetoa
F	**Federico**	faydayreekoa	R	**Rafael**	rahfahayl
G	**Guatemala**	gwahtaymahlah	S	**Santiago**	sahntyahgoa
H	**Honduras**	oandoorahss	T	**Teresa**	tayrayssah
I	**Ida**	eedah	U	**Uruguay**	ooroogwigh
J	**José**	khoassay	V	**Venezuela**	baynaysswaylah
K	**Kilo**	keeloa	W	**Washington**	"Washington"
L	**Lima**	leemah	X	**Xilófono**	kseeloafoanoa
LL	**Llave**	yahbay	Y	**Yucatán**	yookahtahn
M	**México**	maykheekoa	Z	**Zorro**	soarroa

Not there *No está*

When will he/she be back?	¿Cuándo estará de vuelta?	kwahndoa aystahrah day bwayltah
Will you tell him/her I called? My name is ...	¿Quiere decirle que he llamado? Me llamo ...	kyayray daysseerlay kay ay yahmahdoa. may yahmoa
Would you ask him/her to call me?	¿Quiere pedirle que me llame?	kyayray paydeerlay kay may yahmay
Would you take a message, please?	¿Quiere tomar un recado, por favor?	kyayray toamahr oon raykahdoa poar fahboar

Charges *Tarifas*

| What was the cost of that call? | ¿Cuánto ha costado esta llamada? | kwahntoa ah koastahdoa aystah yahmahdah |
| I want to pay for the call. | Quiero pagar por la llamada. | kyayroa pahgahr poar lah yahmahdah |

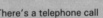

Hay una llamada para usted.	There's a telephone call for you.
¿Qué número está usted marcando?	What number are you calling?
La línea está ocupada.	The line's engaged.
No contestan.	There's no answer.
Se ha equivocado de número.	You've got the wrong number.
El teléfono no funciona.	The phone is out of order.
Un momento.	Just a moment.
Espere, por favor.	Hold on, please.
No está en este momento.	He's/She's out at the moment.

Doctor

Make sure your health insurance policy covers any illness or accident while on holiday. If it doesn't, ask your insurance representative, automobile association or travel agent for details of special health insurance.

General   *Generalidades*

Can you get me a doctor?	¿Puede usted conseguirme un médico?	pwayday oostayd koansaygeermay oon maydeekoa
Is there a doctor here?	¿Hay un médico aquí?	igh oon maydeekoa ahkee
I need a doctor, quickly.	Necesito un médico rápidamente.	nayssaysseetoa oon maydeekoa rahpeedahmayntay
Where can I find a doctor who speaks English?	¿Dónde hay un médico que hable inglés?	doanday igh oon maydeekoa kay ahblay eenglayss
Where's the surgery (doctor's office)?	¿Dónde está el consultorio?	doanday aystah ayl koansooltoaryoa
What are the surgery (office) hours?	¿Cuáles son las horas de consulta?	kwahlayss soan lahss oarahss day koansooltah
Could the doctor come to see me here?	¿Podría el médico venir a reconocerme aquí?	poadreeah ayl maydeekoa bayneer ah raykoanoassayrmay ahkee
What time can the doctor come?	¿A qué hora puede venir el médico?	ah kay oarah pwayday bayneer ayl maydeekoa
Can you recommend a/an ...?	¿Puede recomendar un ...?	pwayday raykoamayndahr oon
general practitioner	generalista	khaynayrahleestah
children's doctor	pediatra	paydyahtrah
eye specialist	oculista	oakooleestah
gynaecologist	ginecólogo	kheenaykoaloagoa
surgeon	cirujano	seerookhahnoa
Can I have an appointment ...?	¿Me puede dar una cita ...?	may pwayday dahr oonah seetah
tomorrow	mañana	mahñahnah
as soon as possible	cuanto antes	kwahntoa ahntayss

CHEMIST'S, see page 108

Parts of the body *Partes del cuerpo*

arm	el brazo	ayl **brahs**soa
artery	la arteria	lah ahr**tayr**ryah
back	la espalda	lah ays**pahl**dah
bladder	la vesícula	lah bay**sseek**oolah
bone	el hueso	ayl **way**ssoa
bowel	el intestino	ayl eentay**stee**noa
breast	el pecho	ayl **pay**choa
chest	el pecho	ayl **pay**choa
ear	la oreja	lah oa**ray**khah
eye	el ojo	ayl **oak**hoa
face	la cara	lah **kah**rah
finger	el dedo	ayl **day**doa
foot	el pie	ayl **pyay**
gland	la glándula	lah **glahn**doolah
hand	la mano	lah **mah**noa
head	la cabeza	lah kah**bay**ssah
heart	el corazón	ayl koarah**ssoan**
jaw	la mandíbula	lah mahn**dee**boolah
joint	la articulación	lah ahrteekoolah**ssyoan**
kidney	el riñón	ayl ree**ñoan**
knee	la rodilla	lah roa**dee**yah
leg	la pierna	lah **pyayr**nah
lip	el labio	ayl **lahb**yoa
liver	el hígado	ayl **eeg**ahdoa
lung	el pulmón	ayl pool**moan**
mouth	la boca	lah **boa**kah
muscle	el músculo	ayl **moos**kooloa
neck	el cuello	ayl **kwayy**oa
nerve	el nervio	ayl **nayrb**yoa
nervous system	el sistema nervioso	ayl see**stay**mah **nayrb**yoassoa
nose	la nariz	lah nah**reess**
rib	la costilla	lah koa**stee**yah
shoulder	la espalda	lah ays**pahl**dah
skin	la piel	lah **pyayl**
spine	la columna	lah koa**loom**nah
stomach	el estómago	ayl ay**stoa**mahgoa
tendon	el tendón	ayl tayn**doan**
thigh	el muslo	ayl **moos**loa
throat	la garganta	lah gahr**gahn**tah
thumb	el pulgar	ayl pool**gahr**
toe	el dedo del pie	ayl **day**doa dayl **pyay**
tongue	la lengua	lah **layng**wah
tonsils	las amígdalas	lahss ah**meeg**dahlahss
vein	la vena	lah **bay**nah

Accident—Injury *Accidente—Herida*

There has been an accident.	**Ha habido un accidente.**	ah ahbeedoa oon ahkseedaynтay
My child has had a fall.	**Se ha caído mi hijo/hija.**	say ah kaheedoa mee eekhoa/eekhah
He/She has hurt his/her head.	**Está herido(a) en la cabeza.**	aystah ayreedoa(ah) ayn lah kahbayssah
He's/She's unconscious.	**Está inconsciente.**	aystah eenkoansyayntay
He's/She's bleeding (heavily).	**Está sangrando (mucho).**	aystah sahngrahndoa (moochoa)
He's/She's (seriously) injured.	**Está (gravemente) herido(a).**	aystah (grahbaymayntay) ayreedoa(ah)
His/Her arm is broken.	**Se ha roto el brazo.**	say ah roatoa ayl brahssoa
His/Her ankle is swollen.	**Su tobillo está hinchado.**	soo toabeeyoa aystah eenchahdoa
I've been stung.	**Tengo una picadura.**	tayngoa oonah peekahdoorah
I've got something in my eye.	**Me ha entrado algo en el ojo.**	may ah ayntrahdoa ahlgoa ayn ayl oakhoa
I've got a/an ...	**Tengo ...**	tayngoa
blister	**una ampolla**	oonah ahmpoayah
boil	**un furúnculo**	oon fooroonkooloa
bruise	**un cardenal [un moretón]**	oon kahrdaynahl [oon moaraytoan]
burn	**una quemadura**	oonah kaymahdoorah
cut	**una cortadura**	oonah koartahdoorah
graze	**un arañazo**	oon ahrahñahssoa
insect bite	**una picadura de insecto**	oonah peekahdoorah day eensayktoa
lump	**un bulto**	oon booltoa
rash	**un salpullido**	oon sahlpooyeedoa
sting	**una picadura**	oonah peekahdoorah
swelling	**una hinchazón**	oonah eenchahssoan
wound	**una herida**	oonah ayreedah
Could you have a look at it?	**¿Podría examinarlo?**	poadreeah ayksahmeenahrloa
I can't move my ...	**No puedo mover el/la ...**	noa pwaydoa moabayr ayl/lah
It hurts.	**Me duele.**	may dwaylay

¿Dónde le duele?	Where does it hurt?
¿Qué clase de dolor es?	What kind of pain is it?
apagado/agudo/palpitante constante/intermitente	dull/sharp/throbbing constant/on and off
Está ...	It's ...
roto/torcido dislocado/desgarrado	broken/sprained dislocated/torn
Quiero que le hagan una radiografía.	I want you to have an X-ray.
Le pondrán yeso.	You'll get a plaster.
Está infectado.	It's infected.
¿Lo han vacunado contra el tétanos?	Have you been vaccinated against tetanus?
Le daré un antiséptico/ un analgésico.	I'll give you an antiseptic/ a painkiller.

Illness *Enfermedad*

I'm not feeling well.	No me siento bien.	noa may **syayntoa** byayn
I'm ill.	Estoy enfermo(a).	aystoy ayn**fayr**moa(ah)
I feel ...	Tengo ...	**tayng**oa
dizzy	mareos	mah**ray**oass
nauseous	náuseas	**now**ssayahss
shivery	escalofríos	ayskahloa**free**oass
I've got a fever.	Tengo fiebre.	**tayng**oa **fyay**bray
My temperature is 38 degrees.	Tengo 38 grados de calentura.	**tayng**oa 38 **grah**doass day kahlayn**too**rah
I've been vomiting.	He tenido vómitos.	ay tay**nee**doa **boa**meetoass
I'm constipated/ I've got diarrhoea.	Estoy estreñido(a)/ Tengo diarrea.	aystoy aystray**ñee**doa(ah)/ **tayng**oa dyah**rray**ah
My ... hurt(s).	Me duele(n) ...	may **dway**lay(n)

Médico

NUMBERS, see p. 147

I've got (a/an) ...	Tengo ...	tayngoa
asthma	asma	ahsmah
backache	dolor de espalda	doaloar day ayspahldah
cold	un resfriado	oon raysfreeahdoa
cough	la tos	lah toass
cramps	calambres	kahlahmbrayss
earache	dolor de oídos	doaloar day oaeedoass
headache	dolor de cabeza	doaloar day kahbayssah
indigestion	indigestión	eendeekhaystyoan
nosebleed	una hemorragia nasal	oonah aymoarrahkhyah nahssahl
palpitations	palpitaciones	pahlpeetahssyoanayss
rheumatism	reumatismo	rayoomahteesmoa
sore throat	la garganta irritada	lah gahrgahntah eerreetahdah
stiff neck	tortícolis	toarteekoaleess
stomach ache	dolor de estómago	doaloar day aystoamahgoa
sunstroke	una insolación	oonah eensoalahssyoan

I have difficulties breathing.	Me duele al respirar.	may dwaylay ahl rayspeerahr
I have a pain in my chest.	Tengo un dolor en el pecho.	tayngoa oon doaloar ayn ayl paychoa
I had a heart attack ... years ago.	Tuve un ataque al corazón hace ... años.	toobay oon ahtahkay ahl koarahssoan ahssay ... ahñoass
My blood pressure is too high/too low.	Mi presión sanguínea es demasiado alta/baja.	mee prayssyoan sahngeenayah ayss daymahssyahdoa ahltah/bahkhah
I'm diabetic.	Soy diabético(a).	soy deeahbayteekoa(ah)

Women's section *Asuntos de la mujer*

I have period pains.	Tengo dolores menstruales.	tayngoa doaloarayss maynstrwahlayss
I have a vaginal infection.	Tengo una infección vaginal.	tayngoa oonah eenfayksyoan bahkheenahl
I'm on the pill.	Tomo la píldora.	toamoa lah peeldoarah
I haven't had my period for 2 months.	Hace dos meses que no tengo reglas.	ahssay doass mayssayss kay noa tayngoa rayglahss
I'm (3 months) pregnant.	(Hace 3 meses que) estoy embarazada.	(ahssay 3 mayssayss kay) aystoy aymbahrahssahdah

¿Cuánto tiempo hace que se siente así?	How long have you been feeling like this?
¿Es la primera vez que ha tenido esto?	Is this the first time you've had this?
Le voy a tomar la temperatura/la presión.	I'll take your temperature/ blood pressure.
Súbase la manga, por favor.	Roll up your sleeve, please.
Desvístase (hasta la cintura), por favor.	Please undress (down to the waist).
Acuéstese ahí, por favor.	Please lie down over here.
Abra la boca.	Open your mouth.
Respire hondo.	Breathe deeply.
Tosa, por favor.	Cough, please.
Tiene ...	You've got (a/an) ...
apendicitis	appendicitis
cistitis	cystitis
una enfermedad venérea	venereal disease
gastritis	gastritis
gripe	flu
ictericia	jaundice
una inflamación de ...	inflammation of ...
una intoxicación por alimentos	food poisoning
neumonía	pneumonia
sarampión	measles
(No) es contagioso.	It's (not) contagious.
Le pondré una inyección.	I'll give you an injection.
Quiero una muestra de sangre/heces/orina.	I want a specimen of your blood/stools/urine.
Debe quedarse en cama durante ... días.	You must stay in bed for ... days.
Quiero que consulte a un especialista.	I want you to see a specialist.
Quiero que vaya al hospital para un reconocimiento general.	I want you to go to the hospital for a general check-up.

Prescription — Treatment *Prescripción — Tratamiento*

This is my usual medicine.	**Esta es la medicina que tomo normalmente.**	aystah ayss lah maydee-sseenah kay toamoa noarmahlmayntay
Can you give me a prescription for this?	**¿Puede darme una receta para esto?**	pwayday dahrmay oonah rayssaytah pahrah aystoa
Can you prescribe a/an/some ...?	**¿Puede recetarme un ...?**	pwayday rayssaytahrmay oon
antidepressant sleeping pills tranquillizer	**antidepresivo somnífero tranquilizante**	ahnteedaypraysseeboa soamneefayroa trahnkeeleessahntay
I'm allergic to antibiotics/penicillin.	**Soy alérgico(a) a los antibióticos/la penicilina.**	soy ahlayrkheekoa(ah) ah loass ahnteebyoateekoass/lah payneesseeleenah
I don't want anything too strong.	**No quiero algo muy fuerte.**	noa kyayroa ahlgoa mwee fwayrtay
How many times a day should I take it?	**¿Cuántas veces al día tengo que tomarlo?**	kwahntahss bayssayss ahl deeah tayngoa kay toamahrloa
Must I swallow them whole?	**¿Debo tragármelas enteras?**	dayboa trahgahrmaylahss ayntayrahss

---

¿Qué tratamiento está siguiendo?	What treatment are you having?
¿Qué medicina toma?	What medicine are you taking?
¿En inyección u oral?	By injection or orally?
Tome ... cucharaditas de esta medicina ...	Take ... teaspoons of this medicine ...
Tome una píldora con un vaso de agua ...	Take one pill with a glass of water ...
cada ... horas	every ... hours
... veces al día	... times a day
antes/después de cada comida	before/after each meal
por la mañana/por la noche	in the morning/at night
en caso de dolor	if there is any pain
durante ... días	for ... days

CHEMIST'S, see page 108

Fee *Honorarios*

How much do I owe you?	**¿Cuánto le debo?**	kwahntoa lay dayboa
May I have a receipt for my health insurance?	**¿Puede darme un recibo para mi seguro?**	pwayday dahrmay oon raysseeboa pahrah mee saygooroa
Can I have a medical certificate?	**¿Puede darme un certificado médico?**	pwayday dahrmay oon sayrteefeekahdoa maydeekoa
Would you fill in this health insurance form, please?	**¿Quiere llenar esta hoja de seguro, por favor?**	kyayray yaynahr aystah oakhah day saygooroa poar fahboar

Hospital *Hospital*

Please notify my family.	**Avise a mi familia, por favor.**	ahbeessay ah mee fah-meelyah poar fahboar
What are the visiting hours?	**¿Cuáles son las horas de visita?**	kwahlayss soan lahss oarahss day beessseetah
When can I get up?	**¿Cuándo puedo levantarme?**	kwahndoa pwaydoa laybahntahrmay
When will the doctor come?	**¿Cuándo viene el médico?**	kwahndoa byaynay ayl maydeekoa
I'm in pain.	**Me duele.**	may dwaylay
I can't eat/sleep.	**No puedo comer/ dormir.**	noa pwaydoa koamayr/ doarmeer
Where is the bell?	**¿Dónde está el timbre?**	doanday aystah ayl teembray

nurse	**la enfermera**	lah aynfayrmayrah
patient	**el/la paciente**	ayl/lah pahssyayntay
anaesthetic	**el anestésico**	ayl ahnaystaysseekoa
blood transfusion	**la transfusión de sangre**	lah trahnsfoossyoan day sahngray
injection	**la inyección**	lah eenyayksyoan
operation	**la operación**	lah oapayrahssyoan
bed	**la cama**	lah kahmah
bedpan	**la silleta**	lah seeyaytah
thermometer	**el termómetro**	ayl tayrmoamaytroa

Dentist *Dentista*

Can you recommend a good dentist?	¿Puede recomendarme un buen dentista?	pwayday raykoamayndahrmay oon bwayn daynteestah
Can I make an (urgent) appointment to see Dr...?	¿Puedo pedir cita (urgente) para ver al Doctor ...?	pwaydoa paydeer seetah (oorkhayntay) pahrah bayr ahl doaktoar
Could you make it earlier than that?	¿No sería posible antes?	noa sayreeah poasseeblay ahntayss
I have a broken tooth.	Me he roto un diente.	may ay roatoa oon dyayntay
I have a toothache.	Tengo dolor de muelas.	tayngoa doaloar day mwaylahss
I have an abscess.	Tengo un flemón.	tayngoa oon flaymoan
This tooth hurts.	Me duele este diente.	may dwaylay aystay dyayntay
at the top/bottom in the front at the back	arriba/abajo delante detrás	ahrreebah/ahbahkhoa daylahntay daytrahss
Can you fix it temporarily?	¿Puede usted arreglarlo temporalmente?	pwayday oostayd ahrrayglahrloa taympoarahlmayntay
I don't want it taken out.	No quiero que me la saque.	noa kyayroa kay may lah sahkay
Could you give me an anaesthetic?	¿Podría darme un anestésico?	poadreeah dahrmay oon ahnaystaysseekoa
I've lost a filling.	He perdido un empaste.	ay payrdeedoa oon aympahstay
The gum ...	Las encías están ...	lahss aynseeahss aystahn
is very sore is bleeding	muy inflamadas sangrando	mwee eenflahmahdahss sahngrahndoa
I've broken this denture.	Se me ha roto la dentadura.	say may ah roatoa lah dayntahdoorah
Can you repair this denture?	¿Puede usted arreglar esta dentadura?	pwayday oostayd ahrrayglahr aystah dayntahdoorah
When will it be ready?	¿Cuándo estará lista?	kwahndoa aystahrah leestah

Reference section

Where do you come from?   *¿De dónde viene usted?*

Africa	**Africa**	ahfreekah
Asia	**Asia**	ahssyah
Australia	**Australia**	owstrahlyah
Europe	**Europa**	ayooroapah
North America	**América del Norte**	ahmayreekah dayl **noar**tay
South America	**América del Sur**	ahmayreekah dayl soor
Argentina	**Argentina**	ahrkhaynteenah
Bolivia	**Bolivia**	boaleebyah
Brazil	**Brasil**	brah**sseel**
Canada	**Canadá**	kahnah**dah**
Colombia	**Colombia**	koaloambyah
Cuba	**Cuba**	koobah
Chile	**Chile**	cheelay
China	**China**	cheenah
Ecuador	**Ecuador**	aykwah**doar**
El Salvador	**El Salvador**	ayl sahlbah**doar**
England	**Inglaterra**	eenglahtayrrah
France	**Francia**	frahnsyah
Germany	**Alemania**	ahlaymahnyah
Great Britain	**Gran Bretaña**	grahn braytahñah
Guatemala	**Guatemala**	gwahtaymahlah
Guyana	**Guayana**	gwahyahnah
Honduras	**Honduras**	oandoorahss
India	**India**	eendyah
Ireland (Eire)	**Irlanda**	eerlahndah
Israel	**Israel**	eesrahayl
Japan	**Japón**	khahpoan
Mexico	**México**	maykheekoa
New Zealand	**Nueva Zelandia**	nwaybah saylahndyah
Nicaragua	**Nicaragua**	neekahrahgwah
Panama	**Panamá**	pahnah**mah**
Paraguay	**Paraguay**	pahrah**gwigh**
Peru	**Perú**	pay**roo**
Scotland	**Escocia**	ayskoassyah
South Africa	**Africa del Sur**	ahfreekah dayl soor
Soviet Union	**Unión Soviética**	oonyoan soabyaayteekah
Spain	**España**	ayspahñah
United States	**Estados Unidos**	aystahdoass ooneedoass
Uruguay	**Uruguay**	ooroogwigh
Venezuela	**Venezuela**	baynayswaylah
Wales	**Gales**	gahlayss

Numbers *Números*

0	cero	**sayr**oa
1	uno	**oon**oa
2	dos	**doass**
3	tres	**trayss**
4	cuatro	**kwaht**roa
5	cinco	**seenk**oa
6	seis	**sayss**
7	siete	**syay**tay
8	ocho	**oach**oa
9	nueve	**nway**bay
10	diez	**dyayss**
11	once	**oan**say
12	doce	**doass**say
13	trece	**trayss**say
14	catorce	**kaht**oarssay
15	quince	**keen**say
16	dieciséis	dyaysseess**ayss**
17	diecisiete	dyaysseess**yay**tay
18	dieciocho	dyayss**yoach**oa
19	diecinueve	dyaysseen**way**bay
20	veinte	**bayn**tay
21	veintiuno	baynteeoonoa
22	veintidós	bayntee**doass**
23	veintitrés	bayntee**trayss**
24	veinticuatro	bayntee**kwaht**roa
25	veinticinco	bayntee**sseenk**oa
26	veintiséis	bayntee**ssayss**
27	veintisiete	bayntee**ssyay**tay
28	veintiocho	bayn**tyoach**oa
29	veintinueve	baynteen**way**bay
30	treinta	**trayn**tah
31	treinta y uno	**trayn**tah ee **oon**oa
32	treinta y dos	**trayn**tah ee **doass**
33	treinta y tres	**trayn**tah ee **trayss**
40	cuarenta	kwah**rayn**tah
41	cuarenta y uno	kwah**rayn**tah ee **oon**oa
42	cuarenta y dos	kwah**rayn**tah ee **doass**
43	cuarenta y tres	kwah**rayn**tah ee **trayss**
50	cincuenta	seen**kwayn**tah
51	cincuenta y uno	seen**kwayn**tah ee **oon**oa
52	cincuenta y dos	seen**kwayn**tah ee doass
53	cincuenta y tres	seen**kwayn**tah ee trayss
60	sesenta	sayss**ayn**tah
61	sesenta y uno	sayss**ayn**tah ee **oon**oa
62	sesenta y dos	sayss**ayn**tah ee **doass**

63	**sesenta y tres**	say**ssayntah** ee trayss
70	**setenta**	say**tayntah**
71	**setenta y uno**	say**tayntah** ee oonoa
72	**setenta y dos**	say**tayntah** ee doass
73	**setenta y tres**	say**tayntah** ee trayss
80	**ochenta**	oa**chayntah**
81	**ochenta y uno**	oa**chayntah** ee oonoa
82	**ochenta y dos**	oa**chayntah** ee doass
83	**ochenta y tres**	oa**chayntah** ee trayss
90	**noventa**	noa**bayntah**
91	**noventa y uno**	noa**bayntah** ee oonoa
92	**noventa y dos**	noa**bayntah** ee doass
93	**noventa y tres**	noa**bayntah** ee trayss
100	**cien/ciento***	syayn/**syayntoa**
101	**ciento uno**	**syayntoa** oonoa
102	**ciento dos**	**syayntoa** doass
110	**ciento diez**	**syayntoa** dyayss
120	**ciento veinte**	**syayntoa** bayntay
130	**ciento treinta**	**syayntoa trayntah**
140	**ciento cuarenta**	**syayntoa** kwah**rayntah**
150	**ciento cincuenta**	**syayntoa** seen**kwayntah**
160	**ciento sesenta**	**syayntoa** say**ssayntah**
170	**ciento setenta**	**syayntoa** say**tayntah**
180	**ciento ochenta**	**syayntoa** oa**chayntah**
190	**ciento noventa**	**syayntoa** noa**bayntah**
200	**doscientos**	doa**ssayntoass**
300	**trescientos**	trays**syayntoass**
400	**cuatrocientos**	kwahtroa**ssyayntoass**
500	**quinientos**	keen**yayntoass**
600	**seiscientos**	says**syayntoass**
700	**setecientos**	saytays**syayntoass**
800	**ochocientos**	oachoa**ssyayntoass**
900	**novecientos**	noabays**syayntoass**
1,000	**mil**	meel
1,100	**mil cien**	meel syayn
1,200	**mil doscientos**	meel doa**ssyayntoass**
2,000	**dos mil**	doass meel
5,000	**cinco mil**	**seen**koa meel
10,000	**diez mil**	dyayss meel
50,000	**cincuenta mil**	seen**kwayntah** meel
100,000	**cien mil**	syayn meel
1,000,000	**un millón**	oon mee**yoan**
1,000,000,000	**mil millones**	meel mee**yoanayss**

*** *cien* is used before nouns and adjectives.**

first	primero	preemayroa
second	segundo	saygoondoa
third	tercero	tayrsayroa
fourth	cuarto	kwahrtoa
fifth	quinto	keentoa
sixth	sexto	saykstoa
seventh	séptimo	saypteemoa
eighth	octavo	oaktahboa
ninth	noveno	noabaynoa
tenth	décimo	daysseemoa
once	una vez	oonah bayss
twice	dos veces	doass bayssayss
three times	tres veces	trayss bayssayss
a half	una mitad	oonah meetahd
half a ...	medio ...	maydyoa
half of ...	la mitad de ...	lah meetahd day
half (adj.)	medio	maydyoa
a quarter/one third	un cuarto/un tercio	oon kwahrtoa/oon tayrsyoa
a pair of	un par de	oon pahr day
a dozen	una docena	oonah doassaynah
one per cent	uno por ciento	oonoa poar syayntoa
3.4%	3,4 por ciento	3 koamah 4 poar syayntoa
1981	mil novecientos ochenta y uno	meel noabayssyayntoass oachayntah ee oonoa
2003	dos mil tres	doass meel trayss

Year and age *Año y edad*

year	el año	ayl ahñoa
leap year	el año bisiesto	ayl ahñoa beessyaystoa
decade	la década	lah daykahdah
century	el siglo	ayl seegloa
this year	este año	aystay ahñoa
last year	el año pasado	ayl ahñoa pahssahdoa
next year	el año próximo	ayl ahñoa proakseemoa
each year	cada año	kahdah ahñoa
2 years ago	hace 2 años	ahssay 2 ahñoass
in one year	dentro de un año	dayntroa day oon ahñoa
in the eighties	en los años ochenta	ayn loass ahñoass oachayntah
the 16th century	el siglo XVI	ayl seegloa 16
in the 20th century	en el siglo XX	ayn ayl seegloa 20
He/She was born in 1960.	Nació en mil novecientos sesenta.	nahssyoa ayn meel noabayssyayntoass sayssayntah

How old are you?	¿Cuántos años tiene?	kwahntoass ahñoass tyaynay
I'm 30 years old.	Tengo 30 años.	tayngoa 30 ahñoass
What is his/her age?	¿Cuál es su edad?	kwahl ayss soo aydahd
Children under 16 are not admitted.	No se admiten niños menores de 16 años.	noa say ahdmeetayn neeñoass maynoarayss day 16 ahñoass

Seasons *Estaciones*

spring/summer	la primavera/el verano	lah preemahbayrah/ayl bayrahnoa
autumn (fall)/winter	el otoño/el invierno	ayl oatoañoa/ayl eenbyayrnoa
in spring	en primavera	ayn preemahbayrah
during the summer	durante el verano	doorahntay ayl bayrahnoa
in autumn	en otoño	ayn oatoañoa
during the winter	durante el invierno	doorahntay ayl eenbyayrnoa
high season	alta estación	ahltah aystahssyoan
low season	baja estación	bahkhah aystahssyoan

Months *Meses*

January	enero*	aynayroa
February	febrero	faybrayroa
March	marzo	mahrsoa
April	abril	ahbreel
May	mayo	mahyoa
June	junio	khoonyoa
July	julio	khoolyoa
August	agosto	ahgoastoa
September	septiembre	sayptyaymbray
October	octubre	oaktoobray
November	noviembre	noabyaymbray
December	diciembre	deessyaymbray
in September	en septiembre	ayn sayptyaymbray
since October	desde octubre	daysday oaktoobray
the beginning of January	a principios de enero	ah preenseepyoass day aynayroa
the middle of February	a mediados de febrero	ah maydyahdoass day faybrayroa
the end of March	a finales de marzo	ah feenahlayss day mahrsoa

* The names of months aren't capitalized in Spanish.

Days and Date *Días y fechas*

What day is it today?	¿Qué día es hoy?	kay **dee**ah ayss oy
Sunday	domingo*	doa**meen**goa
Monday	lunes	**loo**nayss
Tuesday	martes	**mahr**tayss
Wednesday	miércoles	**myayr**koalayss
Thursday	jueves	**khway**bayss
Friday	viernes	**byayr**nayss
Saturday	sábado	**sah**bahdoa
It's ...	Es ...	ayss
July 1	el primero de julio	ayl pree**may**roa day **khool**yoa
March 10	el 10 de marzo	ayl 10 day **mahr**soa
in the morning	por la mañana	poar lah mah**ñah**nah
during the day	durante el día	doo**rahn**tay ayl **dee**ah
in the afternoon	por la tarde	poar lah **tahr**day
in the evening	por la tarde	poar lah **tahr**day
at night	por la noche	poar lah **noa**chay
the day before yesterday	anteayer	ahntayah**yayr**
yesterday	ayer	ah**yayr**
today	hoy	oy
tomorrow	mañana	mah**ñah**nah
the day after tomorrow	pasado mañana	pah**ssah**doa mah**ñah**nah
the day before	el día anterior	ayl **dee**ah ahntay**ryoar**
the next day	el día siguiente	ayl **dee**ah seeg**yayn**tay
two days ago	hace dos días	**ah**ssay doass **dee**ahss
in three days' time	en tres días	ayn trayss **dee**ahss
last week	la semana pasada	lah say**mah**nah pah**ssah**dah
next week	la semana próxima	lah say**mah**nah **proak**seemah
for a fortnight (two weeks)	durante quince días	doo**rahn**tay **keen**say **dee**ahss
birthday	el cumpleaños	ayl koomplay**ah**ñoass
day off	el día libre	ayl **dee**ah **lee**bray
holiday	el día feriado	ayl **dee**ah fay**ryah**doa
holidays/vacation	las vacaciones	lahss bahkah**ssyoa**nayss
week	la semana	lah say**mah**nah
weekend	el fin de semana	ayl feen day say**mah**nah
working day	el día laborable	ayl **dee**ah lahboa**rah**blay

* The names of days aren't capitalized in Spanish.

Public holidays   *Días festivos*

January 1	**Año Nuevo**	New Year's Day
May 1	**Día del trabajo**	Labour Day
October 12	**Día de la Raza**	Columbus Day
December 25	**Navidad**	Christmas Day
Movable date:	**Viernes Santo**	Good Friday

Only holidays celebrated in all Latin American countries are cited above. In addition, every country has its own special holidays, e.g. the Independence Day *(Día de la Independencia)* which is different from country to country. (On September 16 in Mexico, on July 9 in Argentina, and so on.)

Greetings and wishes   *Saludos y deseos*

Merry Christmas!	**¡Feliz Navidad!**	fayleess nahbeedahd
Happy New Year!	**¡Feliz Año Nuevo!**	fayleess ahñoa nwayboa
Happy Easter!	**¡Felices Pascuas!**	fayleessayss pahskwahss
Happy birthday!	**¡Feliz cumpleaños!**	fayleess koomplayahñoass
Best wishes!	**¡Mejores deseos!**	maykhoarayss dayssayoass
Congratulations!	**¡Enhorabuena!**	aynoarahbwaynah
Good luck/ All the best!	**¡Buena suerte!/¡Qué todo salga bien!**	bwaynah swayrtay/kay toadoa sahlgah byayn
Have a good trip!	**¡Buen viaje!**	bwayn byahkhay
Have a nice holiday!	**¡Buenas vacaciones!**	bwaynahss bahkahssyoanayss
Best regards from ...	**Recuerdos de ...**	raykwayrdoass day
My regards to ...	**Recuerdos a ...**	raykwayrdoass ah
Give my love to ...	**Saludos cariñosos a ...**	sahloodoass kahreeñoassoass ah

What time is it? *¿Qué hora es?*

Excuse me. Can you tell me the time?	**Perdone. ¿Puede decirme la hora?**	payrdoanay. pwayday daysseermay lah oarah
It's ...	**Es/Son ...**	ayss/soan
five past one	**la una y cinco***	lah oonah ee seenkoa
ten past two	**las dos y diez**	lahss doass ee dyayss
a quarter past three	**las tres y cuarto**	lahss trayss ee kwahrtoa
twenty past four	**las cuatro y veinte**	lahss **kwah**troa ee bayntay
twenty-five past five	**las cinco y venti-cinco**	lahss **seen**koa ee bayntee-seenkoa
half past six	**las seis y media**	lahss sayss ee maydyah
twenty-five to seven	**veinticinco para las siete**	baynteeseenkoa pahrah lahss syaytay
twenty to eight	**veinte para las ocho**	bayntay pahrah lahss oachoa
a quarter to nine	**cuarto para las nueve**	kwahrtoa pahrah lahss nwaybay
ten to ten	**diez para las diez**	dyayss pahrah lahss dyayss
five to eleven	**cinco para las once**	seenkoa pahrah lahss oansay
twelve o' clock (noon/midnight)	**las doce (medio-día/medianoche)**	lahss doassay (maydyoa-deeah/maydyahnoachay)
in the morning	**de la mañana**	day lah mahñahnah
in the afternoon	**de la tarde**	day lah tahrday
in the evening	**de la tarde**	day lah tahrday
The train leaves at ...	**El tren sale a ...**	ayl trayn sahlay ah
13.04 (1.04 p.m.)	**las trece y cuatro**	lahss **tray**ssay ee **kwah**troa
0.40 (0.40 a.m.)	**las cero y cuarenta**	lahss sayroa ee kwahrayntah
in five minutes	**en cinco minutos**	ayn seenkoa meenootoass
in a quarter of an hour	**en un cuarto de hora**	ayn oon kwahrtoa day oarah
half an hour ago	**hace media hora**	ahssay maydyah oarah
about two hours	**aproximadamente dos horas**	ahproakseemahdah**mayn**tay doass oarahss
more than 10 minutes	**más de diez minutos**	mahss day dyayss meenootoass
less than 30 seconds	**menos de treinta segundos**	maynoass day trayntah saygoondoass
The clock is fast/slow.	**El reloj adelanta/atrasa.**	ayl rayloakh ahdaylahntah/ahtrahssah

---
* In ordinary conversation, time is expressed as shown here. However, for official time a 24-hour clock is used which means that after noon hours are counted from 13 to 24.

Common abbreviations *Abreviaturas corrientes*

A.C.	año de Cristo	A.D.
a/c	al cuidado de	c/o
a. de J.C.	antes de Jesucristo	B.C.
adj.	adjunto	enclosed
A.M.A.	Asociación Mexicana de Automovilistas	Mexican Automobile Association
Av., Avda.	Avenida	avenue
C., Cía.	Compañía	company
cta.	cuenta	account
cte.	corriente	of the present month
cts.	centavos	cents
C.V.	caballos de vapor	horsepower
D.	Don	courtesy title (men)
Da., Dª	Doña	courtesy title (women)
dto.	descuento	discount
EE.UU.	Estados Unidos	United States
f.c.	ferrocarril	railway
F.M.I.	Fondo Monetario Internacional	IMF (International Monetary Fund)
h.	hora	hour
hab.	habitantes	population
M.F.	modulación de frecuencia	FM (frequency modulation)
MX	Compañía Mexicana de Aviación	Mexican Airline Company
n.º, núm.	número	number
O.E.A.	Organización de los Estados Americanos	OAS (Organization of American States)
O.M.S.	Organización Mundial de la Salud	WHO (World Health Organization)
O.N.U.	Organización de las Naciones Unidas	UNO (United Nations Organization)
p.ej.	por ejemplo	for example, e.g.
provª	provincia	province
S., Sta.	San, Santa	Saint
S.A.	Sociedad Anónima	Ltd., Inc.
S.A. de C.V.	Sociedad Anónima de Capital Variable	Limited liability company with variable capital
Sr.	Señor	Mr.
Sra.	Señora	Mrs.
Sres., Srs.	Señores	Messrs.
Srta.	Señorita	Miss
Ud., Vd.	Usted	you (singular)
Uds., Vds.	Ustedes	you (plural)

Signs and Notices *Letreros e indicaciones*

Abierto	Open
Arriba	Up
Ascensor	Lift (elevator)
Averiado	Out of order
Caballeros	Gentlemen
Caja	Cashier
Caliente	Hot
Carretera particular	Private road
Cerrado	Closed
Cierre la puerta	Close the door
Completo	Full/No vacancies
Cuidado	Caution
Cuidado con el perro	Beware of the dog
Debajo	Down
Elevador	Lift (elevator)
Empujar	Push
Entrada	Entrance
Frío	Cold
Libre	Vacant
No molestar	Do not disturb
No obstruya la entrada	Do not block entrance
No tocar	Do not touch
Ocupado	Occupied
Peligro	Danger
Peligro de muerte	Danger of death
Permitido fumar	Smoking allowed
Pintura fresca	Wet paint
Privado	Private
... prohibido	... forbidden
Prohibido arrojar basuras	No littering
Prohibido entrar	No entrance
Prohibido fumar	No smoking
Prohibida la entrada a personas no autorizadas	No trespassing
Rebajas	Sale
Reservado	Reserved
Salida	Exit
Salida de emergencia	Emergency exit
Se alquila	To let (for rent)
Se vende	For sale
Sendero para bicicletas	Bicycle path
Señoras	Ladies
Tirar	Pull
Toque el timbre por favor	Please ring

Emergency *Urgencia*

Call the police	**Llame a la policía**	yahmay ah lah poalee-sseeah
Consulate	**Consulado**	koansoolahdoa
DANGER	**PELIGRO**	payleegroa
Embassy	**Embajada**	aymbahkhahdah
FIRE	**FUEGO**	fwaygoa
Gas	**Gas**	gahss
Get a doctor	**Llame a un doctor**	yahmay ah oon doaktoar
HELP	**SOCORRO**	soakoarroa
Get help quickly	**Busque ayuda rápido**	booskay ahyoodah rahpeedoa
I'm ill	**Estoy enfermo**	aystoy aynfayrmoa
LOOK OUT	**CUIDADO**	kweedahdoa
Poison	**Veneno**	baynaynoa
POLICE	**POLICIA**	poaleesseeah
Quick	**Rápido**	rahpeedoa
STOP	**DETENGASE**	daytayngahssay
STOP THIEF	**AL LADRON**	ahl lahdroan

Emergency telephone numbers *Números de urgencia*

	Mexico (City area)
Fire	768-37-00
Ambulance	06
Police	588-51-00

Lost! *¡Perdido!*

Where's the ...?	**¿Dónde está la ...?**	doanday aystah lah
lost property (lost and found) office	**oficina de objetos perdidos**	oafeesseenah day oabkhaytoass payrdeedoass
police station	**comisaría de policía**	koameessahreeah day poaleesseeah
I want to report a theft.	**Quiero denunciar un robo.**	kyayroa daynoonsyahr oon roaboa
My ... has been stolen.	**Me han robado mi ...**	may ahn roabahdoa mee
I've lost my ...	**He perdido mi ...**	ay payrdeedoa mee
passport	**pasaporte**	pahssahpoartay
wallet	**cartera**	kahrtayrah

CAR ACCIDENTS, see page 78

Conversion tables

Centimetres and inches

To change centimetres into inches, multiply by .39.

To change inches into centimetres, multiply by 2.54.

	in.	feet	yards
1 mm.	0.039	0.003	0.001
1 cm.	0.39	0.03	0.01
1 dm.	3.94	0.32	0.10
1 m.	39.40	3.28	1.09

	mm.	cm.	m.
1 in.	25.4	2.54	0.025
1 ft.	304.8	30.48	0.305
1 yd.	914.4	91.44	0.914

(32 metres = 35 yards)

Temperature

To convert centigrade into degrees Fahrenheit, multiply centigrade by 1.8 and add 32.

To convert degrees Fahrenheit into centigrade, subtract 32 from Fahrenheit and divide by 1.8.

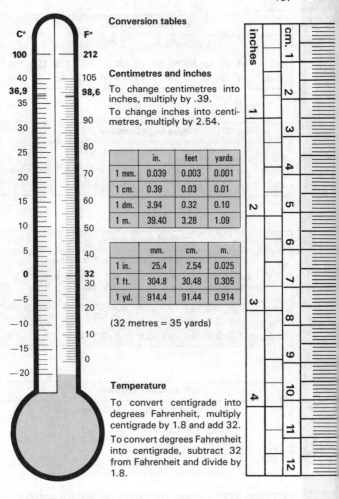

C°	F°
100	212
40	105
36,9	98,6
35	90
30	80
25	70
20	60
15	50
10	40
5	32
0	30
−5	20
−10	10
−15	0
−20	

Kilometres into miles

1 kilometre (km.) = 0.62 miles

km.	10	20	30	40	50	60	70	80	90	100	110	120	130
miles	6	12	19	25	31	37	44	50	56	62	68	75	81

Miles into kilometres

1 mile = 1.609 kilometres (km.)

miles	10	20	30	40	50	60	70	80	90	100
km.	16	32	48	64	80	97	113	129	145	161

Fluid measures

1 litre (l.) = 0.88 imp. quart or 1.06 U.S. quart

1 imp. quart = 1.14 l.	1 U.S. quart = 0.95 l.
1 imp. gallon = 4.55 l.	1 U.S. gallon = 3.8 l.

litres	5	10	15	20	25	30	35	40	45	50
imp. gal.	1.1	2.2	3.3	4.4	5.5	6.6	7.7	8.8	9.9	11.0
U.S. gal.	1.3	2.6	3.9	5.2	6.5	7.8	9.1	10.4	11.7	13.0

Weights and measures

1 kilogram or kilo (kg.) = 1000 grams (g.)

100 g. = 3.5 oz.	½ kg. = 1.1 lb.
200 g. = 7.0 oz.	1 kg. = 2.2 lb.

1 oz. = 28.35 g.
1 lb. = 453.60 g.

CLOTHING SIZES, see page 115/YARDS AND INCHES, see page 112

Basic Grammar

Articles

Nouns in Spanish are either masculine or feminine. Articles agree in gender and number with the noun.

1. Definite article (the):

	singular		plural
masc.	**el tren**	the train	**los trenes**
fem.	**la casa**	the house	**las casas**

2. Indefinite article (a/an):

masc.	**un lápiz**	a pencil	**unos lápices**
fem.	**una carta**	a letter	**unas cartas**

Nouns

1. Most nouns which end in **o** are masculine. Those ending in **a** are generally feminine.

2. Normally, nouns which end in a vowel add **s** to form the plural; nouns ending in a consonant add **es**.

3. To show possession, use the preposition **de** (of).

el fin de la fiesta	the end of the party
el principio del* mes	the beginning of the month
las maletas de los viajeros	the travellers' suitcases
los ojos de las niñas	the girls' eyes
la habitación de Roberto	Robert's room

* (**del** is the contraction of **de** + **el**)

Adjectives

1. Adjectives agree with the noun in gender and number. If the masculine form ends in **o** the feminine ends in **a**. As a rule, the adjective comes after the noun.

el niño pequeño	the small boy
la niña pequeña	the small girl

If the masculine form ends in **e** or with a consonant, the feminine keeps in general the same form.

el muro/la casa grande	the big wall/house
el mar/la flor azul	the blue sea/flower

2. Most adjectives form their plurals in the same way as nouns.

un coche inglés	an English car
dos coches ingleses	two English cars

3. Possessive adjectives: They agree with the thing possessed, not with the possessor.

	sing.	plur.
my	**mi**	**mis**
your (fam.)	**tu**	**tus**
your (polite form)	**su**	**sus**
his/her/its	**su**	**sus**
our	**nuestro(a)**	**nuestros(as)**
your	**vuestro(a)**	**vuestros(as)**
their	**su**	**sus**

su hijo	*his* or *her* son
su habitación	*his* or *her* or *their* room
sus maletas	*his* or *her* or *their* suitcases

4. Comparative and superlative: These are formed by adding **más** (more) or **menos** (less) and **lo más** or **lo menos**, respectively, before the adjective.

alto	high	**más alto**	**lo más alto**

Adverbs

These are generally formed by adding **-mente** to the feminine form of the adjective (if it differs from the masculine); otherwise to the masculine. (Adjectives are sometimes used as adverbs, e.g., **alto** can mean loud or loudly.)

cierto(a)	sure	**fácil**	easy
ciertamente	surely	**fácilmente**	easily

Possessive pronouns

	sing.	plur.
mine	**mío(a)**	**míos(as)**
yours (fam. sing.)	**tuyo(a)**	**tuyos(as)**
yours (polite form)	**suyo(a)**	**suyos(as)**
his/hers/its	**suyo(a)**	**suyos(as)**
ours	**nuestro(a)**	**nuestros(as)**
yours (fam. pl.)	**vuestro(a)**	**vuestros(as)**
theirs	**suyo(a)**	**suyos(as)**

Demonstrative pronouns

	masc.	fem.	neut.
this	**éste**	**ésta**	**esto**
these	**éstos**	**éstas**	**estos**
that	**ése/aquél**	**ésa/aquélla**	**eso/aquello**
those	**ésos/aquéllos**	**ésas/aquéllas**	**esos/aquellos**

The above masculine and feminine forms are also used as demonstrative adjectives, but accents are dropped. The two forms for "that" designate difference in place; **ése** means "that one", **aquél** "that one over there".

Esos libros no me gustan.   I don't like those books.

Eso no me gusta.   I don't like that.

Personal pronouns

	subject	direct object	indirect object
I	**yo**	**me**	**me**
you	**tú**	**te**	**te**
you	**usted**	**lo**	**le**
he	**él**	**lo**	**le**
she	**ella**	**la**	**le**
it	**él/ella**	**lo/la**	**le**
we	**nosotros(as)**	**nos**	**nos**
you	**vosotros(as)**	**os**	**os**
	ustedes	**los**	**les**
they	**ellos(as)**	**los**	**les**

Subject pronouns are generally omitted, except in the polite form (**usted, ustedes**) which corresponds to "you". **Tú** (sing.) and **vosotros** (plur.) are used when talking to relatives, close friends and children and between young people; **usted** and the plural **ustedes** (often abbreviated to **Vd./Vds.**) are used in all other cases. In some countries (e.g. Argentina, Uruguay) **vos** is used instead of **tú** in informal address.

Verbs

Here we are concerned only with the infinitive and the present tense.

	ser* (to be)	estar* (to be)	haber** (to have)
yo	soy	estoy	he
tú	eres	estás	has
usted	es	está	ha
él/ella	es	está	ha
nosotros(as)	somos	estamos	hemos
vosotros(as)	sois	estáis	habéis
ustedes	son	están	han
ellos(as)	son	están	han

* There are two verbs in Spanish for "to be". **Ser** is used to describe a permanent condition. **Estar** is used to describe location or a temporary condition.

** **haber** is used *only* in compound tenses.

Here are three of the main categories of regular verbs:

	ends in **ar** hablar (to speak)	ends in **er** comer (to eat)	ends in **ir** reír (to laugh)
yo	hablo	como	río
tú	hablas	comes	ríes
usted	habla	come	ríe
él/ella	habla	come	ríe
nosotros(as)	hablamos	comemos	reímos
vosotros(as)	habláis	coméis	reís
ustedes	hablan	comen	ríen
ellos(as)	hablan	comen	ríen

Irregular verbs: As in all languages, these have to be learned. Here are four you will find useful.

	poder (to be able)	ir (to go)	ver (to see)	tener (to have)
yo	puedo	voy	veo	tengo
tú	puedes	vas	ves	tienes
usted	puede	va	ve	tiene
él/ella	puede	va	ve	tiene
nosotros(as)	podemos	vamos	vemos	tenemos
vosotros(as)	podéis	vais	veis	tenéis
ustedes	pueden	van	ven	tienen
ellos(as)	pueden	van	ven	tienen

Negatives

Negatives are formed by placing **no** before the verb.

Es nuevo.　　It's new.　　　　**No es nuevo.**　　It's not new.

Questions

In Spanish, questions are often formed by changing the intonation of your voice. Very often, the personal pronoun is left out, both in affirmative sentences and in questions.

Hablo español.　　　　I speak Spanish.
¿Habla español?　　　Do you speak Spanish?

Note the double question mark used in Spanish. The same is true of exclamation marks.

¡Qué tarde se hace!　　　　How late it's getting!

DICTIONARY

Dictionary
and alphabetical index

English–Latin-American Spanish

f feminine   *m* masculine   *pl* plural

Alternatives are given in brackets [ ]; see page 2.

a un(a) 159
abbey abadía *f* 81
abbreviation abreviatura *f* 154
able, to be poder 163
about *(approximately)* aproximadamente 153
above encima 15
abscess flemón *m* 145
absorbent cotton algodón *m* 109
accept, to aceptar 62, 102
accessories accesorios *m/pl* 116, 125
accident accidente *m* 78, 139
accommodation alojamiento *m* 22
account cuenta *f* 130, 131
ache dolor *m* 141
adaptor adaptador *m* 119
address dirección *f* 21, 31, 76, 79, 102
address book librito de direcciones *m* 104
adhesive adhesivo(a) 105
adhesive tape cinta adhesiva *f* 104
admission entrada *f* 82, 90
admit, to admitir 150
Africa Africa *f* 146
after después 15, 77
afternoon tarde *f* 10, 151, 153
after-shave lotion loción para después del afeitado *f* 110

against contra 140
age edad *f* 149
ago hace 149, 151
air conditioner acondicionador de aire *m* 28
air conditioning aire acondicionado *m* 23
airmail por correo aéreo 133
airplane avión *m* 65
airport aeropuerto *m* 21, 65
alarm clock despertador *m* 121
alcohol alcohol *m* 37
all todo 103
allergic alérgico(a) 143
almond almendra *f* 53
alphabet alfabeto *m* 9
also también 15
alter, to *(garment)* arreglar 116
amazing asombroso(a) 84
amber ámbar *m* 122
ambulance ambulancia *f* 79, 156
American americano(a) 93, 105, 126
American plan pensión completa *f* 24
amethyst amatista *f* 122
amount cifra *f* 62; suma *f* 131
amplifier amplificador *m* 119
anaesthetic anestésico *m* 144, 145

Diccionario

analgesic analgésico m 109
anchovy anchoa f 41, 44
and y 15
animal animal m 85
aniseed anís m 52
ankle tobillo m 139
anorak anorak m 116
another otro(a) 123
answer, to contestar 136
antibiotic antibiótico m 143
antidepressant antidepresivo m 143
antiques antigüedades f/pl 83
antique shop tienda de antigüedades f 98
antiseptic antiséptico(a) 109
antiseptic antiséptico m 140
any alguno(a) 15
anyone alguien 12
anything algo 17, 25, 103, 113
apartment *(flat)* apartamento m 22
aperitif aperitivo m 59
appendicitis apendicitis f 142
appetizer entrada f 41
apple manzana f 54, 63
appliance aparato m 119
appointment cita f 131, 137, 145; turno m 30
apricot damasco [chabacano] m 54
April abril m 150
archaeology arqueología f 83
architect arquitecto m 83
area code indicativo m 134
Argentina Argentina f 146
arm brazo m 138, 139
arrival llegada f 16, 65
arrive, to llegar 65, 68, 130
art arte m 83
artery arteria f 138
art gallery galería de arte f 98
artichoke alcachofa f 41, 50
artificial artificial 124
artist artista m/f 81, 83
ashtray cenicero m 27, 36
Asia Asia f 146
ask, to preguntar 36, 76; *(for)* pedir 25, 136
asparagus espárrago m 41, 50
aspirin aspirina f 109
asthma asma m 141
astringent astringente m 110
at a, en 15
at least por lo menos 24
at once inmediatamente 31
aubergine berenjena f 50
August agosto m 150

aunt tía f 93
Australia Australia f 146
automatic automático(a) 20, 122, 124
autumn otoño m 150
avocado aguacate m 41
awful horrible, malo(a) 84, 94

B

baby bebé m 24, 111
baby food alimentos para bebé m/pl 111
babysitter niñera f 27
back espalda f 138
backache dolor de espalda m 141
backpack mochila f 106
bacon tocino m 38, 46
bacon and eggs huevos con tocino m/pl 38
bad malo(a) 14, 95
bag bolsa f 17, 18, 103
baggage equipaje m 18, 26, 31, 71
baggage cart carrito de equipaje m 18, 71
baggage check depósito de equipajes m 67, 71
baked al horno 45
baker's panadería f 98
balance *(account)* balance m 131
balcony balcón m 23
ball *(inflated)* pelota f 128
ballet ballet m 88
ball-point pen bolígrafo m 104
banana banana f 53, 63
bandage venda f 109
Band-Aid esparadrapo m 109
bangle brazalete m 121
bangs flequillo m 30
bank *(finance)* banco m 98, 129
bank card tarjeta de banco f 130
banknote billete m 130
bar bar m 33; *(chocolate)* tableta f 64
barber's barbería f 30, 98
basil albahaca f 52
basketball baloncesto m 90
bass *(fish)* mero m 44
bath *(hotel)* baño m 23, 25, 27
bathing cap gorro de baño m 116
bathing hut cabina f 91
bathing suit traje de baño m 116
bathrobe bata de baño f 116
bathroom cuarto de baño m 27
bath salts sales de baño f/pl 110

bath towel toalla de baño *f* 27
battery pila *f* 119, 121, 125; *(car)* batería *f* 75, 78
bay leaf hoja de laurel *f* 52
be, to ser, estar 162
beach playa *f* 91
beach ball pelota de playa *f* 128
bean ejote *m* 49
beard barba *f* 31
beautiful hermoso(a) 14, 84
beauty salon salón de belleza *m* 30, 98
bed cama *f* 23, 24, 71, 142, 144
bed and breakfast habitación y desayuno *f* 24
bedpan silleta *f* 144
beef carne de res [carne vacuna] *f* 46
beer cerveza *f* 58, 63
beet(root) betabel [remolacha] *f* 50
before *(place)* delante 15; *(time)* antes 15
begin, to empezar 80, 87, 88
beginning principio *m* 150
behind detrás 15, 77
beige beige 113
bell *(electric)* timbre *m* 144
bellboy botones *m* 26
below debajo 15
belt cinturón *m* 117
bend *(road)* curva *f* [viraje *m*] 79
berth litera *f* 69, 70
better mejor 14, 25, 101, 113
between entre 15
beverage bebida *f* 61
bicycle bicicleta *f* 74, 155
big grande 14, 25, 101
bill cuenta *f* 31, 62, 102; *(banknote)* billete *m* 130
billion *(Am.)* mil millones *m/pl* 148
binoculars binoculares *m/pl* 123
bird pájaro *m* 85
birth nacimiento *m* 25
birthday cumpleaños *m* 151, 152
biscuit *(Br.)* galleta *f* 63
bitter amargo(a) 61
black negro(a) 38, 105, 113, 118
bladder vesícula *f* 138
blade hoja *f* 110
blanket cobija *f* 27
bleach aclarado *m* 30
bleed, to sangrar 139, 145
blind *(window)* persiana *f* 29
blister ampolla *f* 139
block, to obstruir 155; tapar 28

blood sangre *f* 142
blood pressure presión sanguínea *f* 141, 142
blood transfusion transfusión de sangre *f* 144
blouse blusa *f* 116
blow-dry brushing *m* 30
blue azul 105, 113
blusher colorete *m* 110
boarding house pensión *f* 19, 22
boat barco *m* 74
bobby pin pasador *m* 111
body cuerpo *m* 138
boil furúnculo *m* 139
boiled cocido(a) 45
boiled egg huevo cocido *m* 38
Bolivia Bolivia *f* 146
bond *(finance)* obligación *f* 131
bone hueso *m* 138
book libro *m* 12, 104
book, to reservar 69
booking office oficina de reservaciones *f* 19, 67
booklet *(of tickets)* abono *m* 72
bookshop librería *f* 98, 104
boot bota *f* 118
born, to be nacer 149
botanical gardens jardín botánico *m* 81
botany botánica *f* 83
bottle botella *f* 17, 58
bottle-opener destapador *m* 106
bowel intestino *m* 138
bow tie corbata de lazo *f* 116
box caja *f* 120
boxing boxeo *m* 90
boy niño *m* 112, 128
boyfriend amigo *m* 93
bra sostén [brassiere] *m* 116
bracelet pulsera *f* 121
braces *(suspenders)* tirantes *m/pl* 116
braised estofado(a) 47
brake freno *m* 78
brake fluid líquido de frenos *m* 75
brandy coñac *m* 59
Brazil Brasil *m* 146
bread pan *m* 36, 38, 64
break, to romper 29, 119, 123, 139, 145
breakdown avería *f* 78
breakdown van grúa *f* 78
breakfast desayuno *m* 24, 34, 38
breast pecho *m* 138
breathe, to respirar 141

bricks *(toy)* cubos de construcción m/pl 128
bridge puente m 85
briefs calzoncillos m/pl 116
bring, to traer 13
British británico(a) 93
broken roto(a) 29, 119, 140
brooch broche m 121
brother hermano m 93
brown marrón [café] 113
bruise cardenal [moretón] m 139
brush cepillo m 111
Brussels sprouts coles de Bruselas f/pl 50
bubble bath baño de espuma m 110
bucket cubo [balde] m 106, 128
buckle hebilla f 117
build, to construir 83
building edificio m 81, 83
building blocks cubos de construcción m/pl 128
bulb foco m [bombilla f] 28, 75, 119
bullfight corrida f 90
burn quemadura f 139
burn out, to *(bulb)* fundir 28
bus autobús m 18, 19, 65, 72, 73, 80
business negocios m/pl 16, 131
business district barrio comercial m 81
business trip viaje de negocios m 93
bus stop parada de autobús f 72, 73
busy ocupado(a) 96
but pero 15
butane gas gas butano m 32, 106
butcher's carnicería f 98
butter mantequilla f 36, 38, 64
button botón m 29, 117
buy, to comprar 68, 82, 104

C

cabana cabina f 91
cabbage col f [repollo m] 50
cabin *(ship)* camarote m 74
cable telegrama m 133
cable car funicular m 74
cable release cable de disparador m 125
café café m 33
cake pastel m 37, 55, 64
cake shop pastelería f 98
calculator calculadora f 105
calendar calendario m 104
call *(phone)* llamada f 135, 136
call, to llamar 11, 78, 136, 156

cambric batista f 114
camel-hair pelo de camello m 114
camera cámara f 124, 125
camera case funda f 125
camera shop tienda de fotografía f 98
camp, to acampar 32
campbed cama de campaña f 106
camping camping m 32
camping equipment equipo de camping m 106
camp site terreno de camping m 32
can *(of peaches)* lata f 120
can *(to be able)* poder 12, 163
Canada Canadá m 146
Canadian canadiense 93
cancel, to anular 65
candle vela f 106
candy caramelo m 64
can opener abrelatas m 106
cap gorra f 116
caper alcaparra f 50
capital *(finance)* capital m 131
car automóvil [carro] m 19, 20, 75, 76, 78
carafe jarra f 58
carat quilate m 121
caravan caravana f 32
caraway comino m 52
carbon paper papel carbón m 104
carbonated con gas 60
carburettor carburador m 78
card tarjeta f 131; *(game)* carta f 93
card game juego de cartas m 128
car hire alquiler de automóviles m 20
cardigan chaqueta de punto f 116
car park estacionamiento m 77
carpet tapete m [alfombra f] 127
car rental alquiler de automóviles m 20
carrot zanahoria f 50
carry, to llevar 21
cart carrito m 18
carton *(of cigarettes)* cartón (de cigarrillos) m 17, 126
cartridge *(camera)* cartucho m 124
case *(glasses)* estuche m 123
cash, to cobrar 129, 130; hacer efectivo 133
cash desk caja f 103, 155
cassette cassette f 119, 127
castle castillo m 85
catalogue catálogo m 82
cathedral catedral f 81
Catholic católico(a) 84

cauliflower coliflor f 50
caution cuidado m 79, 155
cave cueva f 81
celery apio m 50
cemetery cementerio m 81
centimetre centímetro m 112
centre centro m 19, 21, 76, 81
century siglo m 149
ceramics cerámica f 83
cereal cereales m/pl 38
certificate certificado m 144
chain (jewellery) cadena f 121
chain bracelet pulsera de cadena f 121
chair silla f 106
change (money) vuelto m 62; suelto m 77, 130
change, to cambiar 18, 61, 65, 68, 73, 75, 123, 130; (train) transbordar 68, 69
chapel capilla f 81
charcoal carbón m 106
charge precio m 32; tarifa f 136
charge, to cobrar 20; (commission) cargar 130
charm (trinket) amuleto m 121
charm bracelet pulsera con amuletos f 121
cheap barato(a) 14, 24, 101
check cheque m 130; (restaurant) cuenta f 62
check, to controlar, revisar 75; (luggage) facturar 71
check book chequera f 131
check in, to (airport) presentarse 65
check out, to irse 31
checkup (medical) reconocimiento m 142
cheers! ¡salud! 59
cheese queso m 53, 64, 120
chemist's farmacia [droguería] f 98, 108
cheque cheque m 130
cheque book chequera f 131
cherry cereza f 54
chess ajedrez m 93, 128
chest pecho m 138, 141
chestnut castaña f 53
chewing gum chicle m 126
chewing tobacco tabaco para mascar m 126
chicken pollo m 49, 63
chicken breast pechuga de pollo f 49
chicory (Am.) achicoria f, escarola f 50

chiffon gasa f [soplillo m] 114
child niño(a) m/f 24, 61, 82, 91, 150; hijo(a) m/f 93, 139
children's doctor pediatra m/f 137
Chile Chile m 146
chilli chile m 50, 52
China China f 146
chips papas fritas f/pl 51, 63; (Am.) papas fritas f/pl [chips m/pl] 64
chives cebolleta f 50, 52
chocolate chocolate m 38, 60, 64, 120
chocolate bar tableta de chocolate f 64
choice elección f 40
chop chuleta f 46
Christmas Navidad f 152
chromium cromo m 122
church iglesia f 81, 84
cigar puro m 126
cigarette cigarrillo m 17, 95, 126
cigarette case pitillera f 121, 126
cigarette holder boquilla f 126
cigarette lighter encendedor m 121, 126
cine camera cámara de filmar f 124
cinema cine m 86, 96
cinnamon canela f 52
circle (theatre) galería f [balcón m] 87
city ciudad f 81
city terminal terminal de la ciudad f 65
clam almeja f 41, 44
classical clásico(a) 128
clean limpio(a) 61
clean, to limpiar 29, 76
cleansing cream crema limpiadora f 110
cliff acantilado m 85
clip clip m 121
cloakroom guardarropa m 87
clock reloj m 121, 153
clock-radio radio-despertador m 119
close (near) cercano(a) 78, 98
close, to cerrar 11, 82, 108, 132
closed cerrado(a) 155
cloth tela f 118
clothes ropa f 29, 116
clothes peg pinza f 106
clothing prendas de vestir f/pl 112
cloud nube f 94
clove clavo m 52
coach (bus) autocar m 72
coat abrigo m 116

coconut coco m 54
cod bacalao m 44
coffee café m 38, 60, 64
coin moneda f 83
cold frío(a) 14, 25, 61, 94
cold (illness) resfriado m 141; catarro m 108
cold cuts fiambres m/pl 64
collar cuello m 117
collect call cobro revertido m 135
Colombia Colombia f 146
colour color m 103, 112, 124, 125
colour chart muestrario m 30
colourfast de color permanente 112
colour rinse enjuague de color m 30
colour shampoo champú colorante m 111
colour slide diapositiva f 124
comb peine m 111
come, to venir 36, 92, 95, 137, 146
comedy comedia f 86
commission comisión f 130
common (frequent) corriente 154
compact disc disco compacto m 127
compartment compartimiento m 70
compass brújula f 106
complaint reclamación f 61
concert concierto m 88
concert hall sala de conciertos f 81, 88
confectioner's confitería f 98
confirm, to confirmar 65
confirmation confirmación f 23
congratulation enhorabuena f 152
connection (plane) conexión f 65; (train) empalme m 68
constipated estreñido(a) 140
consulate consulado m 156
contact lens lente de contacto m 123
contagious contagioso(a) 142
contain, to contener 37
contraceptive anticonceptivo m 109
contract contrato m 131
control control m 16
convent convento m 81
cookie galleta f 64
cool box nevera portátil f 106
copper cobre m 127
copperware cobres m/pl 127
coral coral m 122
corduroy pana f 114
cork corcho m 61
corkscrew sacacorchos m 106

corn (Am.) maíz m 50; (foot) callo m 109
corner rincón m 36; (street) esquina f 21, 77
corn plaster callicida m 109
cosmetic cosmético m 110
cost precio m 131
cost, to costar 11, 80, 133, 136
cot catre m 24
cotton algodón m 114
cotton wool algodón m 109
cough tos f 108, 141
cough, to toser 142
cough drops pastillas para la tos f/pl 109
counter ventanilla f 133
country país m 92
countryside campo m 85
court house palacio de justicia m 81
cousin primo(a) m/f 93
cover charge cubierto m 62
crab cangrejo m 41, 44
cracker galleta salada f 64
cramp calambre m 141
crayon lápiz de color m 104
cream crema f 55, 60; (toiletry) crema f 110
credit crédito m 130
credit, to depositar 131
credit card tarjeta [carta] de crédito f 20, 31, 62, 102, 130
crepe crespón m 114
crisps papas fritas f/pl [chips m/pl] 64
crockery vajilla f 107
cross cruz f 121
crossing (by sea) travesía f 74
crossroads cruce m 77
cruise crucero m 74
crystal cristal m 122
Cuba Cuba f 146
cucumber pepino m 50, 64
cuff link gemelo m 121
cuisine cocina f 35
cup taza f 36, 107
curler tubo [rulero] m 111
currency moneda f 129
currency exchange office oficina de cambio f 18, 67, 129
current corriente f 91
curtain cortina f 28
curve (road) curva f, viraje m 79
customs aduana f 16, 102
cut (wound) cortadura f 139
cut, to cortar 30, 135

cut glass cristal tallado *m* 122
cuticle remover quita-cutículas *m* 110
cutlery cubiertos *m/pl* 107, 121
cutlet costilla *f* 46
cystitis cistitis *f* 142

D

dairy lechería *f* 98
dance, to bailar 88, 96
danger peligro *m* 79, 155, 156
dangerous peligroso(a) 79, 91
dark oscuro(a) 25, 101, 112, 113
date *(day)* fecha *f* 25, 151; *(appointment)* cita *f* 95; *(fruit)* dátil *m* 54
daughter hija *f* 93
day día *m* 16, 20, 24, 32, 80, 143, 151
daylight luz del día *f* 124
day off día libre *m* 151
death muerte *f* 155
decade década *f* 149
decaffeinated descafeinado 38, 60
December diciembre *m* 150
decision decisión *f* 25, 102
deck *(ship)* cubierta *f* 74
deck chair silla de lona *f* 91, 106
declare, to declarar 17
deep hondo(a) 142
degree *(temperature)* grado *m* 140
delay retraso *m* 69
delicatessen tienda de especialidades *f* 98
delicious excelente 62
deliver, to entregar 102
delivery entrega *f* 102
denim dril de algodón *m* 114
dentist dentista *m/f* 98, 145
denture dentadura *f* 145
deodorant desodorante *m* 110
department departamento *m* 83, 100
department store grandes almacenes *m/pl* 98
departure salida *f* 65, 80
deposit depósito *m* 20, 130
deposit, to *(bank)* depositar 131
dessert postre *m* 37, 55
detour *(traffic)* desviación *f* 79
develop, to *(photos)* revelar 124
diabetic diabético(a) *m/f* 37, 141
dialling code indicativo *m* 134
diamond diamante *m* 122
diaper pañal *m* 111
diarrhoea diarrea *f* 140

dictionary diccionario *m* 104
diesel diesel *m* 75
diet régimen *m* 37
difficult difícil 14
difficulty dificultad *f* 28, 102
digital digital 122
dill eneldo *m* 52
dine, to cenar 94
dining car coche comedor *m* 66, 68, 71
dining room comedor *m* 27
dinner cena *f* 34
direct directo(a) 65
direct to, to indicar 13
direction dirección *f* 76
directory *(phone)* guía telefónica *f* 134
disabled incapacitado(a) 82
discotheque discoteca *f* 88, 96
discount descuento *m* 131
disease enfermedad *f* 142
dish plato *m* 37, 47
dishwashing detergent detergente para la vajilla *m* 106
disinfectant desinfectante *m* 109
dislocate, to dislocar 140
display case vitrina *f* 100
dissatisfied descontento(a) 103
district *(town)* barrio *m* 81
disturb, to molestar 155
diversion *(traffic)* desviación *f* 79
dizzy mareado(a) 140
doctor médico(a) *m/f* 79, 137, 144; doctor(a) *m/f* 145
doctor's office consultorio *m* 137
dog perro *m* 155
doll muñeca *f* 128
dollar dólar *m* 18, 102, 130
door puerta *f* 155
double doble 74
double bed cama matrimonial *f* 23
double room habitación doble *f* 19, 23
down abajo 15
downstairs abajo 15
downtown centro *m* 81
dozen docena *f* 149
drawing paper papel de dibujo *m* 104
drawing pin chincheta *f* [chinche *m*] 104
dress vestido *m* 116
dressing gown bata *f* 116
drink bebida *f* 40, 56, 60, 61; copa *f* 95

DICTIONARY

drink, to beber 35, 36
drinking water agua potable *f* 32
drip, to *(tap)* gotear 28
drive, to conducir 21, 76
driving licence licencia de manejar *f* 20, 79
drop *(liquid)* gota *f* 109
drugstore farmacia *f* 98, 108
dry seco(a) 30, 58, 111
dry cleaner's tintorería *f* 29, 98
duck pato *m* 49
dummy chupete [chupón] *m* 111
during durante 15, 150, 151
duty *(customs)* impuestos *m/pl* 17
duty-free shop tienda libre de impuestos *f* 19
dye tinte [teñido] *m* 30

E

each cada 143, 149
ear oreja *f* 138
earache dolor de oídos *m* 141
ear drops gotas para los oídos *f/pl* 109
early temprano 14, 31
earring arete *m* 121
earthquake terremoto *m* 94
east este *m* 77
Easter Pascuas *f/pl* 152
easy fácil 14
eat, to comer 36, 37, 144
Ecuador Ecuador *m* 146
eel anguila *f* 41, 44
egg huevo *m* 38, 64
eggplant berenjena *f* 50
eight ocho 147
eighteen dieciocho 147
eighth octavo(a) 149
eighties años ochenta *m/pl* 149
eighty ochenta 148
elastic elástico(a) 109
elastic bandage venda elástica *f* 109
Elastoplast esparadrapo *m* 109
electric(al) eléctrico(a) 119
electrical appliance aparato eléctrico *m* 119
electrician electricista *m* 98
electricity electricidad *f* 32
electronic electrónico(a) 125, 128
elevator elevador [ascensor] *m* 27, 100, 155
eleven once 147
El Salvador El Salvador *m* 146
embarkation embarco *m* 74
embassy embajada *f* 156

emerald esmeralda *f* 122
emergency urgencia *f* 156
emergency exit salida de emergencia *f* 27, 99, 155
emery board lima de cartón *f* 110
empty vacío(a) 14
enamel esmalte *m* 122
end final *m* 150
endive *(Br.)* achicoria *f*, escarola *f* 50
engagement ring anillo de compromiso *m* 122
engine *(car)* motor *m* 78
England Inglaterra *f* 146
English inglés(esa) 12, 16, 80, 82, 84, 93, 104, 126
enjoy, to gustar 62, 92
enjoyable agradable 31
enjoy oneself, to divertirse 96
enlarge, to ampliar 125
enough bastante 15
enquiry información *f* 68
entrance entrada *f* 67, 99, 155
entrance fee entrada *f* 82
envelope sobre *m* 27, 104
equipment equipo *m* 91, 106
eraser borrador *m* [goma *f*] 104
escalator escalera mecánica *f* 100
estimate estimación *f* 131
Europe Europa *f* 146
evening tarde *f* 10, 151, 153; noche *f* 87, 95, 96; *(party)* velada *f* 95, 96
evening dress traje de noche *m* 88; *(woman)* vestido de noche *m* 116
everything todo 31, 62
examine, to examinar 139
excellent excelente 62
exchange, to cambiar 103
exchange rate cambio *m* 18, 130
excursion excursión *f* 80
excuse, to perdonar 11
exercise book cuaderno *m* 104
exhaust pipe tubo de escape *m* 78
exhibition exhibición *f* 81
exit salida *f* 67, 79, 99, 155
expect, to esperar 130
expenses gastos *m/pl* 131
expensive caro(a) 14, 19, 24, 101
exposure *(photography)* exposición *f* 124
exposure counter escala de exposición *f* 125
express urgente 132
expression expresión *f* 10, 100
expressway autopista *f* 76

Diccionario

extension cord/lead extensión f 119
external externo(a) 109
extra otro(a) 27
extract, to (tooth) sacar 145
eye ojo m 138, 139
eyebrow pencil lápiz de ojos m 110
eye drops gotas para los ojos f/pl 109
eye liner perfilador de ojos m 110
eye shadow sombras f/pl 110
eyesight vista f 123
eye specialist oculista m/f 137

F

fabric tejido m 113
face cara f 138
face pack máscara f 30
face powder polvos (para la cara) m/pl 110
factory fábrica f 81
fair feria f 81
fall (autumn) otoño m 150
fall, to caer 139
family familia f 93, 144
fan ventilador m 28
fan belt correa del ventilador f 75
far lejos 14, 100
fare tarifa f 21, 67; precio m 68, 73
farm estuario m 85
fat grasa f 37
father padre m 93
faucet llave f [grifo m] 28
February febrero m 150
fee (doctor) honorarios m/pl 144
feeding bottle biberón m 111
feel, to (physical state) sentirse 140, 142
felt fieltro m 114
felt-tip pen rotulador m 104
ferry transbordador m 74
fever fiebre f 140
few pocos(as) 14; (a) (alg)unos(as) 14
field campo m 85
fifteen quince 147
fifth quinto(a) 149
fifty cincuenta 147
fig higo m 54
file (tool) lima f 110
fill in, to llenar 26, 144
filling (tooth) empaste m 145
filling station gasolinera [estación de servicio] f 75
film (photography) rollo m 124, 125; (cinema) película f 86

film winder enrollador m 125
filter filtro m 125, 126
filter-tipped con filtro 126
find, to encontrar 11, 12, 76, 84, 100
fine (OK) bien 25, 92
fine arts bellas artes f/pl 83
finger dedo m 138
fire fuego m 156
first primero(a) 68, 73, 149
first-aid kit botiquín m 106
first class primera clase f 69
first course entrada f 40
first name nombre m 25
fish pescado m 44
fish, to pescar 90
fishing tackle equipo de pesca m 106
fishmonger's pescadería f 98
fit, to quedar 115
fitting room probador m 115
five cinco 147
fix, to arreglar 75, 145
fizzy (mineral water) con gas 60
flannel franela f 114
flash (photography) flash m 125
flash attachment zapata para el flash f 125
flashlight linterna f 106
flat plano(a) 118
flat (apartment) apartamento m 22
flat tyre llanta desinflada f 75, 78
flea market mercado de ocasiones m 81
flight vuelo m 65
flippers aletas para nadar f/pl 128
floor piso m 27, 154
florist's florería f 98
flour harina f 37
flower flor f 85
flu gripe f 142
fluid líquido m 75
fog niebla f 94
folding chair silla plegable f 106
folding table mesa plegable f 107
folk music música folklórica f 128
follow, to seguir 77
food alimento m 37, 111; comida f 61
food box fiambrera f 106
food poisoning intoxicación por alimentos f 142
foot pie m 138
football fútbol m 90
foot cream crema para los pies f 110

footpath sendero *m* 85
for por, para 15; durante 143
forbidden prohibido(a) 155
foreign extranjero(a) 58
forest bosque *m* 85
forget, to olvidar 71
fork tenedor *m* 36, 61, 107
form *(document)* forma *f* 25, 26; formulario *m* 133
fortnight quince días *m/pl* 151
fortress fortaleza *f* 81
forty cuarenta 147
foundation cream crema de maquillaje *f* 110
fountain fuente *f* 81
fountain pen pluma fuente *f* 105
four cuatro 147
fourteen catorce 147
fourth cuarto(a) 149
France Francia *f* 146
free libre 14, 70, 80, 82, 96, 155
French bean ejote *m* 50
french fries papas fritas *f/pl* 51, 63
fresh fresco(a) 53, 61
Friday viernes *m* 151
fried frito(a) 45, 47
fried egg huevo frito *m* 38
friend amigo(a) *m/f* 93, 95
fringe flequillo *m* 30
from de, desde 15
front delantero(a) 75
front frente *m* 69
frost helada *f* 94
fruit fruta *f* 53
fruit cocktail ensalada de fruta *f* 53
fruit juice jugo de fruta *m* 37, 38, 60
frying pan sartén *f* 106
full lleno(a) 14; completo(a) 72, 155
full board pensión completa *f* 24
full insurance seguro contra todo riesgo *m* 20
furniture muebles *m/pl* 83
furrier's peletería *f* 98

G

gabardine gabardina *f* 114
gallery galería *f* 98
game juego *m* 128; *(food)* caza *f* 48
garage garaje *m* 26; *(repairs)* taller de reparaciones *m* 78
garden jardín *m* 85
gardens jardines públicos *m/pl* 81
garlic ajo *m* 52
gas gas *m* 156

gasoline gasolina *f* 75, 78
gastritis gastritis *f* 142
gauze gasa *f* 109
general general 27, 100
general delivery lista de correos *f* 133
general practitioner generalista *m/f* 137
gentleman caballero *m* 155
genuine verdadero(a) 118
geology geología *f* 83
Germany Alemania *f* 146
get, to *(find)* conseguir 11, 19, 21, 31, 32, 134; *(fetch)* buscar 21, 156; *(go)* llegar 100
get off, to bajarse 73
get to, to ir a 19; llegar a 70
get up, to levantarse 144
gherkin pepinillo *m* 50, 64
gift regalo *m* 17
gin ginebra *f* [gin *m*] 59
gin and tonic tónica con ginebra *f* 59
girdle faja *f* 116
girl niña *f* 112, 128
girlfriend amiga *f* 93, 95
give, to dar 13, 75, 123, 126, 135
give way, to *(traffic)* cedar el paso 79
gland glándula *f* 138
glass vaso *m* [copa *f*] 36, 59, 61, 143; *(material)* vidrio *m* 127
glasses anteojos *m/pl* 123
gloomy lúgubre 84
glove guante *m* 116
glue cola de pegar *f* 105
go, to ir 96, 163
go away, to irse 156
gold oro *m* 121, 122
golden dorado(a) 113
gold plate oro chapado *m* 122
golf golf *m* 90
golf course campo de golf *m* 90
good bueno(a) 14, 101
good-bye adiós 10
Good Friday Viernes Santo *m* 152
goods artículos *m/pl* 16
goose ganso *m* 48
go out, to salir 96
gram gramo *m* 120
grammar book libro de gramática *m* 105
grape uva *f* 54, 64
grapefruit toronja *f* [pomelo *m*] 54, 64

grapefruit juice jugo de toronja *m* 38, 60
gray gris 113
graze arañazo *m* 139
greasy grasoso(a) 30, 111
great *(excellent)* estupendo(a) 95
Great Britain Gran Bretaña *f* 146
green verde 113
green bean ejote *m* 50
greengrocer's verdulería *f* 98
green salad ensalada de lechuga *f* 42
greeting saludo *m* 10, 152
grey gris 113
grilled a la parrilla 45, 47
grocery tienda de abarrotes *f* 98, 120
groundsheet alfombra (de hule) *f* 106
group grupo *m* 82
Guatemala Guatemala *f* 146
guide guía *m/f* 80
guidebook guía (de viaje) *f* 82, 104, 105
gum *(teeth)* encías *f/pl* 145
Guyana Guyana *f* 146
gynaecologist ginecólogo *m/f* 137

H

habit costumbre *f* 34
haddock róbalo *m* 44
hair pelo *m* 30, 111
hairbrush cepillo para el pelo *m* 111
haircut corte de pelo *m* 30
hairdresser's peluquería *f* 27, 30, 98
hair dryer secador de pelo *m* 119
hairgrip pasador *m* 111
hair lotion loción capilar *f* 111
hair slide pasador *m* 111
hairspray laca *f* 30, 111
hake merluza *f* 44
half medio(a) 149
half mitad *f* 149
half an hour media hora *f* 153
half board media pensión *f* 24
half price *(ticket)* media tarifa *f* 69
hall *(large room)* sala *f* 81, 88
hall porter conserje *m* 26
ham jamón *m* 38, 41, 46, 64
ham and eggs huevos con jamón *m/pl* 38
hammer martillo *m* 106
hammock hamaca *f* 106
hand mano *f* 138
handbag bolso *m* 116

hand cream crema para las manos *f* 110
handicrafts artesanía *f* 83
handkerchief pañuelo *m* 116
handmade hecho(a) a mano 113
hanger gancho *m* 27
happy feliz 152
harbour puerto *m* 74, 81
hard duro(a) 123
hare liebre *f* 49
hardware store ferretería *f* 98
hare liebre *f* 49
hat sombrero *m* 116, 127
have, to tener 163; haber 162
haversack morral *m* 106
hay fever fiebre del heno *f* 108
hazelnut avellana *f* 53
he él 161
head cabeza *f* 138, 139
headache dolor de cabeza *m* 141
headlight faro *m* 79
headphones casco con auriculares *m* 119
health salud *f* 59
health food shop tienda de alimentos dietéticos *f* 98
health insurance seguro *m* 144
health insurance form hoja de seguro *f* 144
heart corazón *m* 138
heart attack ataque al corazón *m* 141
heat calor *m* 94
heating calefacción *f* 23, 28
heavy pesado(a) 14, 101
heel tacón *m* 118
height altura *f* 85
helicopter helicóptero *m* 74
hello *(phone)* hola 135
help ayuda *f* 156
help! ¡socorro! 156
help, to ayudar 13, 21, 71, 134; atender 100; *(oneself)* servirse 120
her su 160
herbs condimentos *m/pl* 52
here aquí 14
herring arenque *m* 44
high alto(a) 91, 141
high season alta estación *f* 149
high tide marea alta *f* 91
hill colina *f* 85
hire alquiler *m* 20
hire, to alquilar 19, 20, 90, 91, 155
his su 160
history historia *f* 83

hitchhike, to hacer auto-stop 74
hole hoyo *m* 29
holiday día feriado *m* 151
holidays vacaciones *f/pl* 16, 151
home address domicilio *m* 25
Honduras Honduras *m* 146
honey miel *f* 38
hope, to esperar 96
horseback riding equitación *f* 90
hospital hospital *m* 99, 144
hot caliente 14, 25, 38, 60
hotel hotel *m* 19, 21, 22, 80, 96
hotel guide guía de hoteles *f* 19
hotel reservation reservación de hotel *f* 19
hot water agua caliente *f* 23, 28, 38
hot-water bottle bolsa de agua caliente *f* 27
hour hora *f* 80, 143, 153
house casa *f* 83, 85
how cómo 11
how far a qué distancia 11, 76, 85
how long cuánto tiempo 11, 24
how many cuántos(as) 11
how much cuánto 11, 24
hundred cien(to) 148
hungry *(to be)* tener hambre 13, 35
hurricane huracán *m* 94
hurry *(to be in a)* tener prisa 21
hurry up! ¡dése prisa! 13
hurt, to doler 139, 140, 145; *(oneself)* herirse 139
husband marido *m* 93
hydrofoil hidroplano *m* 74

I

I yo 161
ice hielo *m* 106
ice-cream helado *m* 55, 64
ice cube cubito de hielo *m* 59
ice pack saco para hielo *m* 106
ill enfermo(a) 140, 156
illness enfermedad *f* 140
important importante 13
imported importado(a) 113
in en 15
include, to incluir 20, 24, 31, 32, 62
included incluido(a) 20, 80
India India *f* 146
indigestion indigestión *f* 141
inexpensive barato(a) 35, 124
infect, to infectar 140
infection infección *f* 141
inflammation inflamación *f* 142
inflation inflación *f* 131

inflation rate índice de inflación *m* 131
influenza gripe *f* 142
information información *f* 68
injection inyección *f* 142, 143, 144
injure, to herir 139
injured herido(a) 79, 139
injury herida *f* 139
ink tinta *f* 105
inn fonda *f* 33; posada *f* 34
inquiry información *f* 68
insect bite picadura de insecto *f* 108, 139
insect repellent repelente para insectos *m* 109
insect spray spray para insectos *m* 109
inside dentro 15
instead en lugar de 37
insurance seguro *m* 20, 79, 144
insurance company compañía de seguros *f* 79
interest interés *m* 80, 131
interested, to be interesar 83, 96
interesting interesante 84
international internacional 133, 134
interpreter intérprete *m/f* 131
intersection cruce *m* 77
introduce, to presentar 92
introduction *(social)* presentación *f* 92; *(letter)* carta de recomendación *f* 130
investment inversión *f* 131
invitation invitación *f* 94
invite, to invitar 94
invoice factura *f* 131
iodine yodo *m* 109
Ireland Irlanda *f* 146
Irish irlandés(esa) 93
iron *(laundry)* plancha *f* 119
iron, to planchar 29
ironmonger's ferretería *f* 99
its su 160
ivory marfil *m* 122

J

jacket saco *m* 116
jam mermelada *f* 38, 120
jam, to atrancar 28; atorar 125
January enero *m* 150
Japan Japón *m* 146
jar tarro *m* 120
jaundice ictericia *f* 142
jaw mandíbula *f* 138
jazz música de jazz *f* 128

jeans blue jeans *m/pl* 116
jersey jersey *m* 116
jewel joya *f* 121
jewel box joyero *m* 121
jeweller's joyería *f* 99, 121
jewellery joyas *f/pl* 127
joint articulación *f* 138
journey trayecto *m* 72
juice jugo *m* 38, 41, 60
July julio *m* 150
jumper *(sweater)* suéter *m* 116
June junio *m* 150
just *(only)* sólo 16, 100

K

kerosene petróleo *m* 106
key llave *f* 27
kidney riñón *m* 138
kilo(gram) kilo(grama) *m* 120
kilometre kilómetro *m* 20, 78
kind amable 95
kind *(type)* tipo *m* 44; clase *f* 140
knee rodilla *f* 138
knife cuchillo *m* 36, 61, 107
know, to saber 16, 24; conocer 96, 114

L

label etiqueta *f* 105
lace encaje *m* 114
lady señora *f* 155
lake lago *m* 85, 90
lamb cordero *m* 46
lamp lámpara *f* 29, 106, 119
landscape paisaje *m* 92
lane *(traffic)* fila *f* 79
lantern linterna *f* 106
large grande 20, 101, 118, 130
last último(a) 14, 68, 73; pasado(a) 92, 149, 151
last name apellido *m* 25
late tarde 13
later más tarde 135
Latin-American latinoamericano(a) 35
laugh, to reír(se) 95, 162
launderette lavandería *f* 99
laundry *(place)* lavandería *f* 29, 99; *(clothes)* ropa *f* 29
laundry service servicio de lavandería *m* 23
laxative laxante *m* 109
lead *(metal)* plomo *m* 75
leap year año bisiesto *m* 149
leather cuero *m* 114, 118

leave, to irse 31, 95; salir 68, 69, 74; dejar 71, 96; *(deposit)* depositar 26
leek puerro *m* 50
left izquierdo(a) 21, 63, 69, 77
left-luggage office depósito de equipajes *m* 67, 71
leg pierna *f* 138
lemon limón *m* 37, 38, 54, 60, 64
lemonade limonada *f* 60
lens *(glasses)* lente *f* 123; *(camera)* objetivo *m* 125
lentil lenteja *f* 50
less menos 15
let, to *(hire out)* alquilar 155
letter carta *f* 132
letterbox buzón *m* 132
letter of credit carta de crédito *f* 130
lettuce lechuga *f* 50
library biblioteca *f* 99
licence *(permit)* licencia *f* 20, 79
lie down, to acostarse 142
life belt cinturón salvavidas *m* 74
life boat bote salvavidas *m* 74
lifeguard vigilante *m* 91
lift elevador [ascensor] *m* 27, 100, 155
light ligero(a) 14, 55, 58, 101; *(colour)* claro(a) 101, 112, 113
light luz *f* 28, 124; *(cigarette)* fuego *m* [lumbre *f*] 95
lighter encendedor *m* 126
lighter fluid gasolina para encendedor *f* 126
lighter gas gas para encendedor *m* 126
light meter exposímetro *m* 125
lightning relámpago [rayo] *m* 94
like como 112
like, to *(want)* querer 13, 20, 23, 96, 103; *(take pleasure)* gustar 25, 61, 92, 96, 102, 112
line línea *f* 73, 136
linen *(cloth)* lino *m* 114
lip labio *m* 138
lipsalve cacao para labios *m* 110
lipstick lápiz de labios *m* 110
liquid líquido *m* 123
listen, to escuchar 127
litre litro *m* 58, 75, 120
litter basura *f* 155
little *(a)* un poco 14
live, to vivir 83
liver hígado *m* 46, 138

lobster *(spiny)* langosta f 44
local local 36
local train tren local m 69
long largo(a) 116, 117
long-sighted présbite 123
look, to mirar 100, 123
look for, to buscar 13
look out! ¡cuidado! 156
loose *(clothes)* ancho(a) 116
lorry camión m 79
lose, to perder 123, 145, 156
loss pérdida f 131
lost perdido(a) 13, 156
lost and found office oficina de objetos perdidos f 67, 156
lost property office oficina de objetos perdidos f 67, 156
lot *(a)* mucho 14
lotion loción f 110, 111
loud *(voice)* fuerte 135
lovely hermoso(a) 94
low bajo(a) 91, 141
lower inferior 69, 71
low season baja estación f 150
low tide marea baja f 91
luck suerte f 135, 152
luggage equipaje m 17, 18, 26, 31, 71
luggage locker consigna automática f 18, 67, 71
luggage trolley carrito de equipaje m 18, 71
lump *(bump)* bulto m 139
lunch comida f 34, 80
lung pulmón m 138

M

machine máquina f 114
magazine revista f 105
magnificent magnífico(a) 84
maid muchacha de servicio f 26
mail correo m 28, 133
mail, to mandar por correo 28
mailbox buzón m 132
main principal 80
make, to hacer 131
make-up remover pad toallita de maquillaje f 110
man caballero m 115, 155
manager gerente m 26
manicure manicura f 30
many muchos(as) 15
map mapa m 76, 105; plano m 105
March marzo m 150
marinated en escabeche 45

market mercado m 81, 99
marmalade mermelada de naranjas f 38
married casado(a) 93
mass *(church)* misa f 84
match cerillo [fósforo] m 106, 126; *(sport)* partido m 90
match, to *(colour)* hacer juego 112
matinée función de tarde f 87
mattress colchón m 106
mauve malva 113
May mayo m 150
may *(can)* poder 12, 163
meadow prado m 85
meal comida f 24, 34, 62, 143
mean, to querer decir 11; significar 25
means medio m 74
measles sarampión m 142
measure, to medir 114
meat carne f 46, 47, 61
mechanic mecánico m 78
mechanical pencil portaminas m 121
medical médico(a) 144
medical certificate certificado médico m 144
medicine medicina f 83, 143
medium *(meat)* término medio [regular] 47
meet, to citarse 96
melon melón m 54
memorial monumento m 81
mend, to arreglar 75; *(clothes)* zurcir 29
menthol *(cigarettes)* mentolado(a) 126
menu menú m 37; *(printed)* carta f 36, 39, 40
message recado m 28, 136
methylated spirits alcohol de quemar m 106
metre metro m 112
Mexico México m 146
mezzanine *(theatre)* galería f [balcón m] 87
middle medio m 30, 69, 87
midnight medianoche m 153
mild suave 126
mileage kilometraje m 20
milk leche f 38, 60, 64
milkshake batido m 60
milliard mil millones m/pl 148
million millón m 148
mineral water agua mineral f 60, 64

minister *(religion)* ministro [pastor] *m* 84
mint menta *f* 52
minute minuto *m* 21, 69, 153
mirror espejo *m* 115, 123
miscellaneous diverso(a) 127
Miss Señorita *f* 10
miss, to faltar 18, 29, 61
mistake error *m* 62
moccasin mocasín *m* 118
modified American plan media pensión *f* 24
moisturizing cream crema hidratante *f* 110
moment momento *m* 12, 136
monastery monasterio *m* 81
Monday lunes *m* 151
money dinero *m* 129, 130
money order giro postal *m* 133
month mes *m* 16, 150
monument monumento *m* 81
moon luna *f* 94
moped velomotor *m* 74
more más 15
morning mañana *f* 151, 153
mortgage hipoteca *f* 131
mosquito net red para mosquitos *f* 106
mother madre *f* 93
motorbike motocicleta *f* 74
motorboat lancha *f* 91
motorway autopista *f* 76
mountain montaña *f* 85, 91
moustache bigote *m* 31
mouth boca *f* 138, 142
mouthwash gargarismo *m* 109
move, to mover 139
movie película *f* 86
movie camera cámara de filmar *f* 124
movies cine *m* 86, 96
Mr. Señor *m* 10
Mrs. Señora *f* 10
much mucho 14
mug tazón con asa *m* 107
muscle músculo *m* 138
museum museo *m* 81
mushroom champiñón *m* 41, 50; hongo *m* 41
music música *f* 83, 128
musical comedia musical *f* 86
mussel mejillón *m* 42
must, to tenir que 31, 95
mustard mostaza *f* 52, 64
my mi 160

N
nail *(human)* uña *f* 110
nail brush cepillo de uñas *m* 110
nail clippers cortador de uñas *m* 110
nail file lima de uñas *f* 110
nail polish esmalte de uñas *m* 110
nail polish remover quita-esmalte *m* 110
nail scissors tijeras de uñas *f/pl* 110
name nombre *m* 23, 25, 79
napkin servilleta *f* 36, 105, 106
nappy pañal *m* 111
narrow estrecho(a) 79, 118
nationality nacionalidad *f* 25, 92
natural natural 83
natural history historia natural *f* 83
nausea nausea *f* 140
near cerca (de) 14, 15
nearest el (la) más cercano(a) 73, 75, 78, 98
neck cuello *m* 30, 138
necklace collar *m* 121
need, to necesitar 29, 118, 137
needle aguja *f* 27
negative negativo *m* 124, 125
nephew sobrino *m* 93
nerve nervio *m* 138
nervous nervioso(a) 138
nervous system sistema nervioso *m* 138
never nunca 15
new nuevo(a) 14
newspaper periódico *m* 104, 105
newsstand quiosco [puesto] de periódicos *m* 19, 67, 99, 104
New Year Año Nuevo *m* 152
New Zealand Nueva Zelandia *f* 146
next próximo(a) 14, 65, 68, 73, 74, 76, 149, 151
next to junto a 15, 77
nice *(pretty)* bonito(a) 84
niece sobrina *f* 93
night noche *f* 10, 24, 151
nightclub centro nocturno *m* 88
night cream crema de noche *f* 110
nightdress camisón *m* 116
nine nueve 147
nineteen diecinueve 147
ninety noventa 148
ninth noveno(a) 149
no no 10
noisy ruidoso(a) 25
nonalcoholic sin alcohol 60

none ninguno(a) 15
nonsmoker no fumador *m* 36, 70
noon mediodía *m* 31, 153
normal normal 30
north norte *m* 77
North America América del Norte *f* 146
nose nariz *f* 138
nosebleed hemorragia nasal *f* 141
nose drops gotas nasales *f/pl* 109
not no 15, 163
note *(banknote)* billete *m* 130
notebook cuaderno *m* 105
note paper papel de cartas *m* 105
nothing nada 15, 17
notice *(sign)* indicación *f* 155
notify, to avisar 144
November noviembre *m* 150
now ahora 15
number número *m* 26, 65, 135, 136, 147
nurse enfermera *f* 144
nutmeg nuez moscada *f* 52

O

occupation *(job)* ocupación *f* 93
occupied ocupado(a) 14, 155
October octubre *m* 150
octopus pulpo *m* 44
office oficina *f* 19, 67, 99, 132, 156
oil aceite *m* 37, 75, 111
oily *(greasy)* grasoso(a) 30, 111
old viejo(a) 14
old town ciudad vieja *f* 81
olive aceituna *f* 41
omelet tortilla [de huevo] *f* 49
on sobre, en 15
once una vez 149
one uno(a) 147
one-way *(ticket)* ida 65, 69; *(traffic)* en un solo sentido 79
onion cebolla *f* 50
only sólo 15, 24, 80, 109
on time puntualmente 68
onyx ónix *m* 127
open abierto(a) 14, 82, 155
open, to abrir 11, 17, 82, 108, 130, 132, 142
opening hours horas de apertura *f/pl* 82
opera ópera *f* 88
opera house teatro de la ópera *m* 81, 88
operation operación *f* 144
operator telefonista *m/f* 134

operetta opereta *f* 88
opposite frente a 77
optician óptico *m* 99, 123
or o 15
orange naranja 113
orange naranja *f* 54, 64
orange juice jugo de naranja *m* 38, 60
orchestra orquesta *f* 88; *(seats)* luneta [platea] *f* 87
order *(goods)* encargo *m* 102
order, to *(meal)* pedir 36, 61; *(goods)* encargar 102, 103
oregano orégano *m* 52
ornithology ornitología *f* 83
other otro(a) 58, 74
our nuestro(a) 160
out of order averiado(a) 155
out of stock agotado(a) 103
outlet *(electric)* enchufe *m* 27
outside (a)fuera 15, 36
oval oval 101
overalls guardapolvo *m* 116
overdone demasiado hecho(a) 61
overtake, to adelantar 79
owe, to deber 144
oyster ostra *f*, ostión *m* 44

P

pacifier chupete [chupón] *m* 111
packet paquete *m* 120; *(cigarettes)* cajetilla *f* 126
page *(hotel)* botones *m* 26
pail cubo [balde] *m* 106, 128
pain dolor *m* 140, 141
painkiller analgésico *m* 140
paint pintura *f* 155
paint, to pintar 83
paintbox caja de pinturas *f* 105
painter pintor *m* 83
painting pintura *f* 83
pair par *m* 116, 118, 149
pajamas piyama *m* 117
palace palacio *m* 81
palpitation palpitación *f* 141
Panama Panamá *m* 146
panties pantaletas [bragas] *f/pl* 116
pants *(trousers)* pantalones *m/pl* 116
panty girdle faja truga *f* 116
panty hose leotardos *m/pl* 116
paper papel *m* 105
paperback libro de bolsillo *m* 105
paperclip sujetapapeles *m* 105

paper napkin servilleta de papel f 106

paraffin *(fuel)* petróleo m 106

Paraguay Paraguay m 146

parcel paquete m 133

parents padres m/pl 93

park parque m 81

park, to estacionar(se) 26, 77, 79

parking estacionamiento m 77, 79

parking meter parquímetro m 77

parliament parlamento m 82

parsley perejil m 52

part parte f 138; *(hair)* raya [partida] f 30

parting *(part)* raya [partida] f 30

partridge perdiz f 49

party *(social gathering)* fiesta f 95

pass *(permit)* pase m 72; *(mountain)* puerto m 85

pass, to *(car)* adelantar 79

passport pasaporte m 16, 17, 25, 26, 156

passport photo foto para pasaporte f 124

pass through, to estar de paso 16

paste *(glue)* pasta para pegar f 105

pastry pastel m 55, 64

pastry shop pastelería f 99

patch, to *(clothes)* remendar 29

path camino m 85; sendero m 155

patient paciente m/f 144

pay, to pagar 31, 62, 102, 136

payment pago m 131

pea guisante m 50

peach durazno m 54

peak pico m 85

peanut cacahuate m 53; maní m 54

pear pera f 54

pearl perla f 122

pedestrian peatón m 79

pen pluma f 105

pencil lápiz m 105

pencil sharpener sacapuntas m 105

pendant colgante m 121

penicilline penicilina f 143

penknife navaja f 106

pensioner jubilado(a) m/f 82

people gente f 79, 93

pepper pimienta f 37, 38, 52, 64

per cent por ciento 149

percentage porcentaje m 131

perch perca f 44

per day por día 20, 32

perfume perfume m 110

perfume shop perfumería f 108

perhaps quizá, tal vez 15

per hour por hora 77

period *(monthly)* reglas f/pl 141

period pains dolores menstruales m/pl 141

permanent wave permanente f 30

permit permiso m 90

per night por noche 24

person persona f 32

personal personal 17

personal call llamada personal f 134

person-to-person call llamada personal f 134

Peru Perú m 146

per week por semana 20, 24

petrol gasolina f 75, 78

pewter peltre m 122

pheasant faisán m 48

photo foto(grafía) f 82, 124, 125

photocopy fotocopia f 131

photograph, to fotografiar, tomar fotografías 82

photographer fotógrafo m 99

photography fotografía f 124

phrase expresión f 12

pick up, to *(person)* recoger 80, 96

picnic picnic m 63

picnic basket bolsa para merienda [picnic] f 106

picture cuadro m 83; *(photo)* fotografía f 82

piece trozo m 120

pig cerdo m 46

pigeon pichón m 49

pill píldora f 141, 143

pillow almohada f 27

pin alfiler m 121

pineapple ananá [piña] f 53, 54

pink rosa 113

pipe pipa f 126

pipe cleaner limpiapipas m 126

pipe tobacco tabaco de pipa m 126

place lugar m 25

place of birth lugar de nacimiento m 25

plane avión m 65

planetarium planetario m 81

plaster *(cast)* yeso m 140

plastic plástico m 107

plastic bag bolsa de plástico f 106

plate plato m 36, 61, 107

platform *(station)* andén m 67, 68, 69, 70

platinum platino m 122

play *(theatre)* pieza f 86

play, to jugar 90, 93; *(music)* tocar 88
playground campo de juego *m* 32
playing card naipe *m* 105
please por favor 10
plimsolls zapatos de lona *m/pl* 118
plug *(electric)* clavija de enchufe *f* 29
plum ciruela *f* 54
pneumonia neumonía *f* 142
pocket bolsillo *m* 121
pocket calculator calculadora de bolsillo *f* 105
pocket watch reloj de bolsillo *m* 121
point punto *m* 80
point, to *(show)* señalar 12
poison veneno *m* 109, 156
poisoning intoxicación *f* 142
police policía *f* 78, 156
police station comisaría *f* 99, 156
polish *(nails)* esmalte *m* 110
poncho jorongo [poncho] *m* 127
pond estanque *m* 85
pop music música pop *f* 128
poplin popelina *f* 114
pork cerdo *m* 46
port puerto *m* 74; *(wine)* oporto *m* 59
portable portátil 119
porter cargador [maletero] *m* 18, 71; *(hotel)* mozo *m* 26
portion porción *f* 37, 55, 61
possible posible 145
post *(letters)* correo *m* 28, 133
post, to mandar por correo 28
postage franqueo *m* 132
postage stamp estampilla *f* 28, 126, 132
postcard tarjeta postal *f* 105, 126, 132
poste restante lista de correos *f* 133
post office oficina de correos *f* 99, 132
potato papa [patata] *f* 51
pottery cerámica *f* 83, 127
poultry aves *f/pl* 48
pound *(money)* libra (esterlina) *f* 18, 102, 130; *(weight)* libra *f* 120
powder polvos *m/pl* 110
powder compact polvera *f* 121
powder puff borla *f* 110
prawn camarón grande *m* 44
preference preferencia *f* 101
pregnant embarazada 141
premium *(gasoline)* super 75

prescribe, to recetar 143
prescription receta *f*, 108, 143; prescripción *f* 143
present *(gift)* regalo *m* 17
press, to *(iron)* planchar 29
press stud broche de presión *m* 117
pressure presión *f* 75, 141
pretty lindo(a) 84
price precio *m* 24
priest sacerdote *m* 84
print *(photo)* copia *f* 125
private privado(a) 155; particular 23, 80, 155
processing *(photo)* revelado *m* 124
profession profesión *f* 25
profit ganancia *f* 131
programme programa *m* 87
prohibit, to prohibir 79, 155
pronunciation pronunciación *f* 6
propelling pencil portaminas *m* 121
Protestant protestante 84
public holiday día festivo *m* 152
pull, to tirar 155
pullover pullover *m* 117
pumpkin zapallo *m* 50
puncture llanta desinflada *f* 75
purchase compra *f* 131
pure puro(a) 114
purple purpúreo 113
push, to empujar 155
put, to poner 24
pyjamas piyama *f* 117

Q

quail codorníz *m* 48
quality calidad *f* 103, 113
quantity cantidad *f* 14, 103
quarter cuarto *m* 149; *(part of town)* barrio *m* 81
quarter of an hour cuarto de hora *m* 153
quartz cuarzo *m* 122
question pregunta *f* 11
quick rápido(a) 14, 156
quickly rápidamente 79, 137
quiet tranquilo(a) 25

R

rabbi rabino *m* 84
rabbit conejo *m* 48
racket *(sport)* raqueta *f* 90
radiator radiador *m* 78
radio *(set)* radio *f* 23, 28, 119
radish rábano *m* 50
railroad crossing paso a nivel *m* 79

railway ferrocarril *m* 154
railway station estación de ferrocarril *f* 19, 21, 67
rain lluvia *f* 94
rain, to llover 94
raincoat impermeable *m* 117
raisin pasa *f* 53
rangefinder telémetro *m* 125
rare *(meat)* poco hecho(a) 47
rash salpullido *m* 139
raspberry frambuesa *f* 54
rate *(price)* tarifa *f* 20; *(inflation)* índice *m* 131
raw crudo(a) 45
razor máquina de afeitar *f* 110
razor blade hoja de afeitar *f* 110
read, to leer 40
reading lamp lámpara de mesa *f* 27
ready listo(a) 29, 118, 123, 125, 145
real verdadero(a) 121
rear trasero(a) 75
receipt recibo *m* 103, 144
reception recepción *f* 23
receptionist recepcionista *m/f* 26
recommend, to recomendar 22, 35, 80, 88, 137, 145
record *(disc)* disco *m* 127, 128
record player tocadiscos *m* 119
rectangular rectangular 101
red rojo(a) 105, 113; *(wine)* tinto 58
redcurrant grosella *f* 54
reduction reducción *f* 24, 82
refill *(pen)* carga *f* 105
refund, to devolver el dinero 103
regards recuerdos *m/pl* 152
region región *f* 92
register, to *(luggage)* facturar 71
registered mail certificado(a) 133
registration inscripción *f* 25
registration form forma de registro *f* 25
regular *(petrol)* normal 75
religion religión *f* 83
religious service servicio religioso *m* 84
rent, to alquilar 19, 20, 90, 91, 119, 155
rental alquiler *m* 19, 20
repair reparación *f* 79, 125
repair, to arreglar 29, 119, 121, 123, 145; reparar 118, 125
repeat, to repetir 12
report, to *(a theft)* denunciar 156
require, to necesitar(se) 88

reservation reservación *f* 19, 23, 65, 69
reservations office oficina de reservaciones *f* 19, 67
reserve, to reservar 19, 23, 36, 69, 87, 155
restaurant restaurante *m* 19, 32, 34, 35, 67
return *(ticket)* ida y vuelta 65, 69
return, to *(give back)* devolver 103
reversed charge call llamada por cobro revertido *f* 135
rheumatism reumatismo *m* 141
rib costilla *f* 138
ribbon cinta *f* 105
rice arroz *m* 51
right derecho(a) 21, 63, 69, 77; *(correct)* correcto(a) 14
ring *(on finger)* anillo *m* [sortija *f*] 122
ring, to *(doorbell)* tocar el timbre 155; *(phone)* telefonear 134
river río *m* 85, 90
road carretera *f* 76, 77, 85
road assistance auxilio en carretera *f* 78
road map mapa de carreteras *m* 105
road sign señal de circulación *f* 79
roast asado *m* 46
roll *(bread)* bollito *m* 38; panecillo *m* 64
roller skate patín de ruedas *m* 128
roll film carrete *m*, rollo *m* 124
roll-neck cuello vuelto *m* 117
room habitación *f* 19, 23, 24, 25, 28; *(space)* sitio *m* 32
room service servicio de habitación *m* 23
rope cuerda *f* [soga *f*/lazo *m*] 107
rosary rosario *m* 122
rosé rosado 58
rosemary romero *m* 52
rouge colorete *m* 110
round redondo(a) 101
round-neck cuello redondo *m* 117
roundtrip *(ticket)* ida y vuelta 65, 69
rowing boat barca de remos *f* 91
rubber *(material)* goma *f* 118; *(eraser)* borrador *m* [goma *f*] 105
ruby rubí *m* 122
rucksack mochila *f* 107
ruin ruina *f* 81
ruler *(for measuring)* regla *f* 105
rum ron *m* 59
running water agua corriente *f* 23

S

safe *(not dangerous)* seguro(a), sin peligro 91
safe caja fuerte *f* 26
safety pin imperdible [traba] *f* 110
saffron azafrán *m* 52
sailing boat velero *m* 91
salad ensalada *f* 42, 63
sale venta *f* 131; *(bargains)* rebajas *f/pl* 101, 155
sales tax IVA *m* 102
salmon salmón *m* 44
salt sal *f* 37, 38, 52, 64
salty salado(a) 61
same mismo(a) 118
sand arena *f* 91
sandal sandalia *f* 118
sandwich torta *f* [sandwich *m*] 64
sanitary towel/napkin paño higiénico *m* 109
sapphire zafiro *m* 122
sardine sardina *f* 44
satin raso *m* 114
Saturday sábado *m* 151
sauce salsa *f* 48
saucepan cacerola *f* 107
saucer platillo *m* 107
sausage salchicha *f* 46, 64
scarf bufanda *f* 117
scarlet escarlata 113
scenic route carretera panorámica *f* 85
school escuela *f* 79
scissors tijeras *f/pl* 107, 110
scooter escúter *m* 74
Scotland Escocia *f* 146
scrambled egg huevos revueltos *m/pl* 38
screwdriver destornillador *m* 107
sculptor escultor *m* 83
sculpture escultura *f* 83
sea mar *m* 23, 85
sea bass mero *m* 44
sea bream besugo *m* 44
seafood mariscos *m/pl* 44
season estación *f* 150
seasoning condimentos *m/pl* 37, 52
seat asiento *m* 69, 70, 87
second segundo(a) 149
second segundo *m* 153
second class segunda clase *f* 69
second hand segundero *m* 122
second-hand de segunda mano 104
secretary secretario(a) *m/f* 27, 131
see, to ver 12, 163

sell, to vender 100
send, to mandar 78, 102, 103, 132
sentence frase *f* 12
separately por separado 62
September septiembre *m* 150
service servicio *m* 24, 62, 98, 100; *(religion)* oficio *m* 84
serviette servilleta *f* 36
set menu comida corrida *f* 36, 39, 40
setting lotion fijador *m* 30, 111
seven siete 147
seventeen diecisiete 147
seventh séptimo(a) 149
seventy setenta 148
sew, to coser 29
shade *(colour)* tono *m* 112
shampoo champú *m* 30, 111
shampoo and set lavado y marcado *m* 30
shape forma *f* 103
share *(finance)* acción *f* 131
shave, to afeitar 30
shaver máquina de afeitar *f* 27
shaving brush brocha *f* 111
shaving cream crema de afeitar *f* 111
she ella 161
shelf estante *m* 120
sherry jerez *m* 59
ship embarcación *f* 74
shirt camisa *f* 117
shivers escalofríos *m/pl* 140
shoe zapato *m* 118
shoelace cordón *m* [cinta *f*] 118
shoemaker's zapatero *m* 99
shoe polish crema para zapatos *f* 118
shoe shop zapatería *f* 99
shop tienda *f* 98, 99; comercio *m* 98
shopping compras *f/pl* 97
shopping area zona de tiendas *f* 82, 100
shopping centre centro comercial *m* 99
shop window aparador *m* 100, 112
short corto(a) 116, 117
shorts shorts *m/pl* 117
short-sighted miope 123
shoulder espalda *f* 138
shovel pala *f* 128
show *(theatre)* espectáculo *m* 86, 88; *(performance)* función *f* 87
show, to enseñar 12, 13, 76, 100, 101, 103, 119, 124

shower ducha f 23, 32
shrimp camarón m [gamba f] 41, 44
shrink, to encoger(se) 114
shut cerrado(a) 14
shutter *(window)* postigo m 29;
   (camera) obturador m 125
sick *(ill)* enfermo(a) 140, 156
sickness *(illness)* enfermedad f 140
side lado m 30
sideboards/burns patillas f/pl 31
sightseeing visita turística f 80
sightseeing tour recorrido
   turístico 80
sign *(notice)* letrero m 155; *(road)*
   señal f 79
sign, to firmar 26, 130
signature firma f 25
signet ring anillo de sello m 122
silk seda f 114
silver *(colour)* plateado(a) 113
silver plata f 121, 122
silver plate plata chapada f 122
silverware objetos de plata m/pl 122
simple sencillo(a) 124
since desde 15, 150
sing, to cantar 88
single *(not married)* soltero(a) 93;
   (ticket) ida 65, 69
single room habitación sencilla f
   19, 23
sister hermana f 93
six seis 147
sixteen dieciséis 147
sixth sexto(a) 149
sixty sesenta 147
size *(format)* tamaño m 124;
   (clothes) talla f 114, 115; *(shoes)*
   número m 118
ski esquí m 91
ski, to esquiar 91
skiing esquí m 90, 91
ski lift telesquí m 91
skin piel f 138
skin-diving buceo m 91
skirt falda f 117
sky cielo m 94
sleep, to dormir 144
sleeping bag saco de dormir m 107
sleeping-car coche cama m 66, 68,
   69, 70
sleeping pill somnífero m 109, 143
sleeve manga m 117
slice *(meat)* lonja f 120
slide *(photo)* diapositivo m 124
slip combinación f 117

slipper zapatilla f 118
slow lento(a) 14
slowly despacio 12, 21, 79, 135
small pequeño(a) 14, 20, 25, 101,
   118, 130
smoke, to fumar 95, 155
smoked ahumado(a) 44
smoker fumador m 70
snack merienda f 63
snack bar snack bar m 34, 67
snail caracol m 41
snap fastener broche de presión m
   117
sneakers zapatos de lona m/pl 118
snorkel tubo respiratorio m 128
snow nieve f 94
snow, to nevar 94
snuff rapé m 126
soap jabón m 27, 111
soccer fútbol m 90
sock calcetín m 117
socket *(outlet)* enchufe m 27
soft blando(a) 123; *(drink)* sin
   alcohol 64
soft-boiled *(egg)* blando 38
sold out *(theatre)* completo 87
sole suela f 118; *(fish)* lenguado m
   44
soloist solista m/f 88
some unos(as) 15
someone alguien 31, 95
something algo 29,36, 55, 108,
   112, 113, 125, 139
somewhere en algún lugar 87
son hijo m 93
song canción f 127
soon pronto 15
sore throat garganta irritada f 141
sorry *(I'm)* lo siento 11, 16
sort *(kind)* clase f 86, 120
soup sopa f 42
south sur m 77
South Africa África del Sur f 146
South America América del Sur f
   146
souvenir recuerdo m 127
souvenir shop tienda de regalos f 99
Soviet Union Unión Soviética f 146
spade pala f 128
Spain España f 146
Spanish español(a) 11, 95, 104
spare tyre llanta de repuesto f 75
sparking plug bujía f 75
sparkling *(wine)* espumoso(a) 58
spark plug bujía f 75

speak, to hablar 12, 135, 163
speaker *(loudspeaker)* altavoz *m* 119
special especial 20, 37
special delivery urgente 132
specialist especialista *m/f* 142
speciality especialidad *f* 40
specimen *(medical)* muestra *f* 142
spectacle case estuche para anteojos *m* 123
spell, to deletrear 12
spend, to gastar 101
spice especia *f* 52
spinach espinaca *f* 50
spine columna *f* 138
spiny lobster langosta *f* 44
sponge esponja *f* 111
spoon cuchara *f* 36, 61, 107
sport deporte *m* 89
sporting goods shop tienda de artículos deportivos *f* 99
sprain, to torcer 140
spring *(season)* primavera *f* 150; *(water)* manantial *m* 85
square cuadrado(a) 101
square plaza *f* 82
squid calamar *m* 44
stadium estadio *m* 82
staff personal *m* 26
stain mancha *f* 29
stainless steel acero inoxidable *m* 122
stalls *(theatre)* luneta [platea] *f* 87
stamp *(postage)* estampilla *f* 28, 132
staple grapa *f* 105
star estrella *f* 94
start, to empezar 80, 87, 88; *(car)* arrancar 78
starter *(appetizer)* entrada *f* 41
station estación *f* 19, 21, 67, 70, 73
stationer's papelería *f* 99, 104
statue estatua *f* 82
stay estancia *f* 31
stay, to quedarse 16, 24, 26; *(reside)* hospedarse 93
steak filete [lomo] *m* 46
steal, to robar 156
steamed cocido(a) al vapor 44
stew guisado *m* 43
stewed estofado(a) 47
stiff neck tortícolis *m* 141
still *(mineral water)* sin gas 60

sting picadura *f* 139
stitch, to coser 29, 118
stock exchange bolsa *f* 82
stocking media *f* 117
stomach estómago *m* 138
stomach ache dolores de estómago *m/pl* 141
stools heces *f/pl* 142
stop *(bus)* parada *f* 72, 73
stop! ¡deténgase! 156
stop, to parar 21, 68, 70; detenerse 72, 74
stop thief! ¡al ladrón! 156
store *(shop)* tienda *f* 98, 99; comercio *m* 98
straight ahead derecho 21, 77
strange extraño(a) 84
strawberry fresa *f* 53
street calle *f* 25
street map plano de la ciudad *m* 19, 105
string cordón *m* [cuerda *f*] 105
strong fuerte 126, 143
student estudiante *m/f* 82, 93
study, to estudiar 93
sturdy resistente 101
subway *(railway)* metro *m* 73
suede ante *m* [gamuza *f*] 114, 118
sufficient suficiente 68
sugar azúcar *m* 37, 64
suit *(man)* traje [terno] *m* 117; *(woman)* traje sastre *m* 117
suitcase maleta *f* 18
summer verano *m* 149
sun sol *m* 94
sunburn quemadura del sol *f* 108
Sunday domingo *m* 150
sunglasses anteojos de sol *m/pl* 123
sunshade *(beach)* sombrilla *f* 91
sunstroke insolación *f* 141
sun-tan cream crema bronceadora *f* 111
sun-tan oil aceite bronceador *m* 111
super *(petrol)* super 75
superb soberbio(a) 84
supermarket supermercado *m* 99
suppository supositorio *m* 109
surfboard tabla de surf *f* 91
surgeon cirujano *m* 137
surgery *(consulting room)* consultorio *m* 137
surname apellido *m* 25
suspenders *(Am.)* tirantes *m/pl* 117
swallow, to tragar 143
sweater suéter *m* 117

sweatshirt suéter de tela de punto *m* 117

sweet dulce 58, 61

sweet *(candy)* caramelo *m* 64

sweet corn maíz *m* 50

sweetener edulcorante *m* 37, 51

swell, to hinchar 139

swelling hinchazón *f* 139

swim, to nadar 90; bañarse 91

swimming natación *f* 90

swimming pool piscina [alberca] *f* 32, 90

swimming trunks bañador *m* 117

swimsuit traje de baño *m* 117

switch interruptor *m* 29

switchboard operator telefonista *m/f* 26

swollen hinchado(a) 139

synagogue sinagoga *f* 84

synthetic sintético(a) 114

system sistema *m* 138

T

table mesa *f* 36, 107

tablet tableta *f* 109

tailor's sastrería *f* 99

take, to tomar 25, 72, 73; *(time)* durar 72, 74; tardar 61, 76, 102; *(bring)* llevar 18, 67

take away, to *(carry)* llevar 63, 102

talcum powder talco *m* 111

tampon Tampax *m* 109

tangerine mandarina *f* 54

tap *(water)* llave *f* [grifo *m*] 28

tape recorder grabadora *f* 119

tart tarta *f* 55

tax impuesto *m* 24, 32; IVA *m* 24, 102

taxi taxi *m* 19, 21, 31, 67

tea té *m* 38, 60, 64

team equipo *m* 90

tear, to desgarrar 140

tearoom salón de té *m* 34

teaspoon cucharilla *f* 107

telegram telegrama *m* 133

telegraph office oficina de telégrafos *f* 99

telephone teléfono *m* 28, 78, 79, 134

telephone, to telefonear 133

telephone booth cabina telefónica *f* 134

telephone call llamada *f* 135, 136

telephone directory guía telefónica *f* 134

telephone number número de teléfono *m* 135, 136

telephone office oficina de teléfonos *f* 99

telephoto lens teleobjetivo *m* 125

television *(set)* televisor *m* 23, 28, 119

telex télex *m* 133

telex, to mandar un télex 130

tell, to decir 13, 73, 76, 136, 153

temperature temperatura *f* 91, 142; *(fever)* calentura *f* 140

temporary temporal 145

ten diez 147

tendon tendón *m* 138

tennis tenis *m* 90

tennis court pista de tenis *f* 90

tennis racket raqueta de tenis *f* 90

tent tienda (de campaña) *f* 32, 107

tenth décimo(a) 149

tent peg estaca de tienda *f* 107

tent pole mástil de tienda *m* 107

term *(word)* expresión *f* 131

terrace terraza *f* 36

terrifying aterrador 84

terrycloth albornoz *m* 114

tetanus tétano *m* 140

than que 15

thank you gracias 10

that ése(a), aquél(la) 161

the el, la *(pl* los, las) 159

theatre teatro *m* 82, 86

theft robo *m* 156

their su 160

then entonces 15

there ahí, allí 14

thermometer termómetro *m* 109, 144

these éstos(as) 161

they ellos(as) 161

thief ladrón *m* 156

thigh muslo *m* 138

thin *(fabric)* ligero(a) 113

think, to *(believe)* creer 31, 70, 94; opinar 92

third tercero(a) 149

third tercio *m* 149

thirsty, to be tener sed 13, 35

thirteen trece 147

thirty treinta 147

this éste(a) 161

those ésos(as), aquéllos(as) 161

thousand mil 148

thread hilo *m* 27

three tres 147

throat garganta f 138, 141
throat lozenge pastilla para la garganta f 109
through por, a través de 15
through train tren directo m 68, 69
thumb pulgar m 138
thumbtack chincheta f [chinche m] 105
thunder trueno m 94
thunderstorm tormenta f 94
Thursday jueves m 151
thyme tomillo m 51
ticket billete m 65, 69, 72; (theatre) entrada f 87
ticket office boletería f 67
tide marea f 91
tie corbata f 117
tie clip pisacorbata m 122
tie pin alfiler de corbata m 122
tight (clothes) ajustado(a) 116
tights leotardos m/pl 117
time tiempo m 80; (clock) hora f 137, 153; (occasion) vez f 143
timetable horario m 68
tin (can) lata f 120
tinfoil papel de estaño m 107
tin opener abrelatas m 107
tint coloración f 11
tinted ahumado(a) 123
tire llanta [goma] f 75, 76
tired cansado(a) 13
tissue (handkerchief) pañuelo de papel m 111
to a, para 15
toast pan tostado m 38
tobacco tabaco m 126
tobacconist's tabaquería f [estanquillo m] 99, 126
today hoy 29, 151
toe dedo del pie m 138
toilet (lavatory) servicios m/pl 27, 32, 37, 67
toilet paper papel higiénico m 111
toiletry artículos de tocador m/pl 110
toilet water agua de olor f 111
toll cuota f 75, 79
tomato tomate m 50
tomato juice jugo de tomate m 61
tomb tumba f 82
tomorrow mañana 29, 151
tongs tenazas f/pl 107
tongue lengua f 138
tonic water agua tónica f 60
tonight esta noche 29, 86, 87, 96

tonsil amígdala f 138
too demasiado 15; (also) también 15
tooth diente m 145
toothache dolor de muelas m 145
toothbrush cepillo de dientes m 111, 119
toothpaste pasta de dientes f 111
topaz topacio m 122
torch (flashlight) linterna f 107
torn desgarrado(a) 140
touch, to tocar 155
tough (meat) duro(a) 61
tour recorrido m 80; vuelta f 74
tourist card tarjeta de turista f 16
tourist office oficina de turismo f 80
tourist tax impuesto para turista m 32
towards hacia 15
towel toalla f 27, 111
tower torre f 82
town ciudad f 76, 81, 88, 105
town hall ayuntamiento [palacio de gobierno] m 82
tow truck grúa f 78
toy juguete m 128
toy shop juguetería f 99
tracksuit chandal de entrenamiento m 117
traffic tráfico m 76, 79
traffic light semáforo m 77
trailer caravana f 32
train tren m 66, 68, 69, 70, 73
tranquillizer tranquilizante m 143
transfer (bank) transferencia f 131
transformer transformador m 119
translate, to traducir 12
transport transporte m 74
travel, to viajar 93
travel agency agencia de viajes f 99
travel guide guía de viaje f 104, 105
traveller's cheque cheque de viajero m 18, 62, 102, 130
travel sickness mareo m 108
treatment tratamiento m 143
tree árbol m 85
tremendous tremendo(a) 84
trim, to (beard) recortar 31
trip viaje m 93, 152; trayecto m 72
trolley carrito m 18, 71
trousers pantalones m/pl 117
trout trucha f 44
truck camión m 79
try, to probar 115

T-shirt camiseta *f* 117
tube tubo *m* 120
Tuesday martes *m* 150
tumbler vaso *m* 107
tuna atún *m* 45
tunny atún *m* 45
turkey pavo *m* 49
turn, to *(change direction)* girar 21, 77
turquoise turquesa 113
turquoise turquesa *f* 122
turtleneck cuello vuelto *m* 117
tweezers pinzas *f/pl* 111
twelve doce 147
twenty veinte 147
twice dos veces 149
twin beds dos camas *f/pl* 23
two dos 147
type tipo *m* 124
typewriter máquina de escribir *f* 27, 105
typing paper papel de máquina *m* 105
tyre llanta [goma] *f* 75, 76

U

ugly feo(a) 14, 84
umbrella paraguas *m* 117; *(beach)* sombrilla *f* 91
uncle tío *m* 93
unconscious inconsciente 139
under debajo 15
underdone *(meat)* poco hecho(a) 47, 61
underground *(railway)* metro *m* 73
underpants calzoncillos *m/pl* 117
undershirt camiseta *f* 117
understand, to comprender 12, 16; entender 12
undress, to desvestirse 142
United States Estados Unidos *m/pl* 146
university universidad *f* 82
unleaded sin plomo 75
until hasta 15
up arriba 15
upper superior 69
upset stomach molestias de estómago *f/pl* 108
upstairs arriba 15
urgent urgente 13, 145
urine orina *f* 142
use uso *m* 17, 109
use, to usar 78, 134
useful útil 15

V

vacancy habitación libre *f* 23
vacant libre 14, 22, 155
vacation vacaciones *f/pl* 151
vaccinate, to vacunar 140
vacuum flask termo *m* 107
vaginal infection infección vaginal *f* 141
valley valle *m* 85
value valor *m* 131
value-added tax IVA *m* 24, 102
vanilla vainilla *f* 55
VAT *(sales tax)* IVA *m* 24, 102
veal ternera *f* 46
vegetable verdura *f* 50
vegetable store verdulería *f* 99
vegetarian vegetariano(a) 37
vein vena *f* 138
velvet terciopelo *m* 114
velveteen terciopelo de algodón *m* 114
venereal disease enfermedad venérea *f* 142
Venezuela Venezuela *f* 146
venison venado *m* 49
very muy 15
vest camiseta *f* 117; *(Am.)* chaleco *m* 117
veterinarian veterinario *m* 99
video cassette video-cassette *f* 124
video-recorder video-grabadora *f* 119
view vista *f* 23, 25
village pueblo *m* 76, 85
vinegar vinagre *m* 37, 52
vineyard viñedo *m* 85
visit visita *f* 144
visit, to visitar 84
visiting hours horas de visita *f/pl* 144
vitamin pills vitaminas *f/pl* 109
volleyball balonvolea *m* 90
voltage voltaje *m* 27, 119
vomit, to vomitar 140

W

waistcoat chaleco *m* 117
wait, to esperar 21, 95, 108
waiter mesero *m* 26, 36
waiting room sala de espera *f* 67
waitress mesera *f* 26, 36
wake, to despertar 27, 71
Wales Gales *m* 146
walk, to caminar 74; ir a pie 85
wall muro *m* 82

wallet cartera f 156
walnut nuez f 54
want, to *(wish)* desear, querer 13
wash, to lavar 29, 114
wash-basin lavabo m 28
washing powder jabón en polvo m 107
washing-up liquid detergente para la vajilla m 107
watch reloj m 121, 122
watchband correa de reloj f 122
watchmaker's relojería f 99, 121
watchstrap correa de reloj f 122
water agua f 23, 28, 32, 38, 75, 91
waterfall cascada f 85
water flask cantimplora f 107
watermelon sandía f 54
waterproof impermeable 122
water ski esquí acuático m 91
wave ola f 91
way camino m 76
we nosotros(as) 161
weather tiempo m 94
weather forecast boletín meteorológico m 94
wedding ring anillo de boda m 122
Wednesday miércoles m 151
week semana f 16, 20, 24, 80, 151
weekend fin de semana m 20, 151
well bien 10, 140
well-done *(meat)* bien hecho(a) 47
west oeste m 77
what qué, cómo 11
wheel rueda f 78
when cuándo 11
where dónde 11
which cuál 11
white blanco(a) 58, 113
who quién 11
whole entero(a) 143
why porqué 11
wick mecha f 126
wide ancho(a) 118
wide-angle lens objetivo granangular m 125
wife mujer f 93
wig peluca f 111
wind viento m 94
window ventana f 28, 36, 69; *(shop)* aparador m [vitrina f] 100, 112
windscreen/shield parabrisas m 76
windsurfer patín de vela m 91
wine vino m 17, 57, 58, 61
wine list carta de vinos f 57

wine merchant's tienda de vinos f 99
winter invierno m 150
wiper limpiaparabrisas m 76
wish deseo m 152
with con 15
withdraw, to *(bank)* retirar 130
withdrawal retiro m 130
without sin 15
woman mujer f 141; señora f 115
wonderful maravilloso(a) 96
wood *(forest)* bosque m 85
wood alcohol alcohol de quemar m 107
wool lana f 114
word palabra f 12, 15, 133
work, to *(function)* funcionar 28, 119
work *(construction)* obra f 79
working day día laborable m 151
worse peor 14
worsted estambre m 114
wound herida f 139
wrap, to envolver 103
wrinkle resistant inarrugable 114
wristwatch reloj m 122
write, to escribir 12, 101
writing pad bloc de papel m 105
writing paper papel de cartas m 27
wrong incorrecto(a) 135; equivocado(a) 14

X

X-ray *(photo)* radiografía f 140

Y

year año m 149
yellow amarillo(a) 113
yes sí 10
yesterday ayer 151
yet todavía 15, 16
yield, to *(traffic)* ceder el paso 79
yoghurt yogur m 38
you tú, usted 161
young joven 14
your tu(s), su(s) 160
youth hostel albergue de juventud m 22, 32

Z

zero cero m 147
zip(per) cierre [zipper] m 117
zoo zoológico m 82
zoology zoología f 83

Índice en español

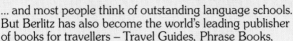

BERLITZ® Books
for travellers

TRAVEL GUIDES

They fit your pocket in both size and price. Modern, up-to-date, Berlitz gets all the information you need into 128 lively pages with colour maps and photos throughout. What to see and do, where to shop, what to eat and drink, how to save.

ASIA, MIDDLE EAST	China (256 pages)
	Hong Kong
	India (256 pages)
	Japan (256 pages)
	Singapore
	Sri Lanka
	Thailand
	Egypt
	Jerusalem and the Holy Land
	Saudi Arabia
AUSTRAL-ASIA	Australia (256 pages)*
	New Zealand
BRITISH ISLES	Channel Islands
	London
	Ireland
	Oxford and Stratford
	Scotland
BELGIUM	Brussels

AFRICA — Kenya, Morocco, South Africa, Tunisia

*in preparation

PHRASE BOOKS

World's bestselling phrase books feature all the expressions and vocabulary you'll need, and pronunciation throughout. 192 pages, 2 colours.

Arabic	Hebrew	Serbo-Croatian
Chinese	Hungarian	Spanish (Castilian)
Danish	Italian	Spanish (Lat. Am.)
Dutch	Japanese	Swahili
Finnish	Norwegian	Swedish
French	Polish	Turkish
German	Portuguese	European Phrase Book
Greek	Russian	European Menu Reader

FRANCE	Brittany		Costa Blanca
	France (256 pages)		Costa Brava
	French Riviera		Costa del Sol and Andalusia
	Loire Valley		Ibiza and Formentera
	Normandy*		Madrid
	Paris		Majorca and Minorca
GERMANY	Berlin	**EASTERN**	Budapest
	Munich	**EUROPE**	Dubrovnik and Southern
	The Rhine Valley		Dalmatia
AUSTRIA	Tyrol		Hungary (192 pages)
and	Vienna		Istria and Croatian Coast
SWITZER-	Switzerland (192 pages)		Moscow & Leningrad
LAND			Split and Dalmatia
GREECE,	Athens	**NORTH**	U.S.A. (256 pages)
CYPRUS &	Corfu	**AMERICA**	California
TURKEY	Crete		Florida
	Rhodes		Hawaii
	Greek Islands of the Aegean		New York
	Peloponnese		Toronto
	Salonica and Northern Greece		Montreal
	Cyprus		
	Istanbul/Aegean Coast	**CARIBBEAN,**	Puerto Rico
ITALY and	Florence	**LATIN**	Virgin Islands
MALTA	Italian Adriatic	**AMERICA**	Bahamas
	Italian Riviera		Bermuda
	Italy (256 pages)*		French West Indies
	Rome		Jamaica
	Sicily		Southern Caribbean
	Venice		Mexico City
	Malta		Rio de Janeiro
NETHER-	Amsterdam	**EUROPE**	Business Travel Guide –
LANDS and	Copenhagen		Europe (368 pages)
SCANDI-	Helsinki		Pocket guide to Europe
NAVIA	Oslo and Bergen		(480 pages)
	Stockholm		Cities of Europe (504 pages)
PORTUGAL	Algarve	**CRUISE**	Caribbean cruise guide
	Lisbon	**GUIDES**	(368 pages)
	Madeira		Alaska cruise guide
SPAIN	Barcelona and Costa Dorada		(168 pages)
	Canary Islands		Handbook to Cruising
			(240 pages)

*in preparation   **Most titles with British and U.S. destinations are available
in French, German, Spanish and as many as 7 other languages.**

DICTIONARIES

Bilingual with 12,500 concepts each way. Highly practical for travellers,
with pronunciation shown plus menu reader, basic expressions and useful
information. Over 330 pages.

| Danish | Finnish | German | Norwegian | Spanish |
| Dutch | French | Italian | Portuguese | Swedish |

**Berlitz Books, a world of information in your pocket!
At all leading bookshops and airport newsstands.**

Imagine, in a short time from now, being able to speak an entirely new language. French, perhaps. Or Spanish. German. Or Italian.

Berlitz, the world-renowned language instruction institution, has developed these self-study programs *expressly* for those people who want to learn to speak a foreign language *fast.* And without going through the tedious, repetitive drills and grammar rule memorization that are featured in other courses.

Instead, with the Berlitz Express programs, you learn to speak *naturally,* by listening to—and then joining in on—"real-life" dialogue on cassette tapes. This helps you *absorb* correct grammar and vocabulary almost unconsciously. And because the tapes use *sound effects* to convey meaning, you can learn your new language while you're driving, biking, walking, or doing just about anything.

Each Express Program Contains:

- TWO CASSETTES TOTALLING 100 minutes of instruction and using lively *sound effects* to identify objects, actions, and situations in your new language.

- LESSON TEXT explains new words and grammar variations as you encounter them.

- BERLITZ ROTARY VERB FINDER. How do you change the expression "I go" to "I will go" or "I went" in the language you're learning? Just spin the dial and you'll have your answer for a wide variety of common verbs.

- CONVENIENT STORAGE ALBUM protects tapes, book, and Verb Finder from damage.

Dial (no charge, USA)
24 hours, 7 days a week.

In the U.S.A. **In Great Britain**

1-800-431-9003 **0323-638221**

Refer to Dept. No. 11604. Why not give us a ring – right now!